University of London Legal Series

under the auspices of
The Institute of Advanced Legal Studies

XI

LAW REFORM
IN THE MUSLIM WORLD

This volume is published with the help of
a grant from
The Iranian Oil Participants Ltd

Law Reform in the Muslim World

by

NORMAN ANDERSON

UNIVERSITY OF LONDON
THE ATHLONE PRESS
1976

Published by
THE ATHLONE PRESS
4 *Gower Street, London* WC 1
UNIVERSITY OF LONDON
Distributed by Tiptree Book Services Ltd
Tiptree, Essex

U.S.A. and Canada
Humanities Press Inc
New Jersey

ISBN 0 485 13411 X

Printed in Great Britain at
THE UNIVERSITY PRINTING HOUSE, CAMBRIDGE
(EUAN PHILLIPS, UNIVERSITY PRINTER)

PREFACE

It is some seventeen years since I gave a series of lectures in the Law School of New York University which were subsequently published by the New York University Press, in 1959, under the title *Islamic Law in the Modern World.* This book (which was also published in London by Stevens) has now for long been out of print, and for some years I intermittently considered an invitation to prepare a new edition. But I continually rejected the idea, chiefly because I thought it would be premature to bring out a new edition of a book on this subject at a time when the United Arab Republic appeared to be on the verge of enacting a comprehensive Law of Personal Status.

With the passage of time, however, it seems less and less likely that the proposed Law will be promulgated, even in an amended form, in the foreseeable future. Meanwhile, a very great deal has happened in many other countries which needs to be brought together and assessed as part of a movement which now embraces almost the whole Muslim world. And while it would, no doubt, have been possible to fit most of these legal developments into the structure of a revised edition of *Islamic Law in the Modern World*, with successive chapters devoted to 'Conceptions of Law: Islamic and Western', 'The Islamic Law of Marriage and Divorce', 'The Islamic Law of Inheritance', etc., it seemed preferable to write a new book, in an entirely different form, concentrating exclusively on the reform movement as such: its background and pressures, its philosophy and methods, its achievements and results, and—finally—its problems and prospects.

This arrangement, it seems to me, has considerable advantages, for it makes the whole movement for reform, which has spread from one country to another in recent years, much more intelligible to those with little previous knowledge of the subject. How and why did this movement begin? In what ways and by what means has it been carried on? What has it in fact accomplished? What problems still remain, in one type of country or another; what chance is there that these different problems will be solved; and what predictions can be made about the way things will go? But this arrangement has one corresponding disadvantage which cannot, I think, be wholly avoided; for it inevitably involves a certain overlap, and near repetition, from one chapter to another. It is impossible, for example, to describe the methods adopted by the reformers in any intelligible way without giving concrete examples of why they felt compelled to resort sometimes to one expedient and sometimes to another, and the jurisprudential considerations which made this necessary. But when one comes, in a later chapter, to review what has been achieved and how the law now stands, one can scarcely omit these same points—previously selected as examples—from a reasonably comprehensive survey of the legislation which has in fact been promulgated. The approach and treatment will, of course, differ from chapter to chapter; for in one the purpose will be to illustrate and discuss the problems which had to be faced, how they were tackled and the jurisprudential arguments involved, while in another the primary emphasis will be on the content, form and effect of the legislation, the administrative action or the judicial decisions concerned, and how the relevant reforms have taken their place in the overall structure of the law which currently prevails. Even in a final consideration of present problems and future prospects, moreover, one cannot but revert, to some degree, to the same basic subjects. All the same, it seems to me that the advantages of this method far outweigh its disadvantages, and I have decided to proceed accordingly.

A note should be added about the policy I have adopted in regard to the transliteration of Arabic words and names. I have tried to be consistent in using what I consider to be the most appropriate transliteration in technical terms, names, etc., when writing about Arab countries – except, first, for a very few place names, where the reader who does not know Arabic might not recognize Oman, or even Jeddah, if written as ʻUmān and Jidda; secondly, that I have sometimes put an 's' on the end of an Arabic term such as *waqf* rather than using the Arabic plural *awqāf*; and thirdly, that although I have normally put such words as *qāḍī* and *sunna* in italics, I have often written Qāḍī or Sunnah in a quotation from legislation (even translated) where this seems more appropriate. When writing about countries such as India or Afghanistan, however, where names of Arabic origin are not normally written in this way, I have in most cases adopted the form more commonly in use. But it is exceedingly difficult to be consistent.

NORMAN ANDERSON

CONTENTS

CHAPTER I

The Background and Pressures for Reform

I. INTRODUCTORY

IT has been pertinently remarked that law is the distilled essence of the civilization of a people[1] and that it reflects that people's soul more clearly and truly than any other organism.[2] But if these observations are true of peoples and civilizations in general, they certainly have a particular relevance to the Muslim world and to the religion and civilization of Islam; for Joseph Schacht has insisted that 'Islamic law is the epitome of Islamic thought, the most typical manifestation of the Islamic way of life, the core and kernel of Islam itself',[3] while Hamilton Gibb has affirmed that it is the Sharī'a[4] which, all down the centuries, has not only represented the master science in the Muslim world but the most effective agent in moulding the social order and community life of Muslim peoples and in holding the social fabric of Islam compact and secure through all the fluctuations of political fortune.[5]

As a broad generalization, the Sharī'a law—which is divinely incumbent on every Muslim—reigned supreme, nominally at least, throughout the vastly greater part of the Muslim world until little more than a century ago. But this is no longer true, for Islamic law, together with the system of *qāḍīs'* courts which used to apply it, has now been substantially displaced, in one Muslim country after another, by statutory laws of largely Western inspiration and by a system of secular courts set up to apply these

1 Cf. A. S. Diamond, *Evolution of Law and Order* (Watts & Co, 1951), p. 303.

2 D. Hughes Parry, *Haldane Memorial Lecture*, 1951 (Birkbeck College), p. 3.

3 *An Introduction to Islamic Law* (O.U.P., 1964), p. 1.

4 The technical term for Islamic law: see section 2.

5 *Mohammedanism* (O.U.P., 2nd edn, London, 1953), pp. 9–11.

new codes. Even in those spheres of life where the Sharīʿa officially prevails, moreover—and is, indeed, frequently still applied in special courts—a vast number of modifications and reforms have been introduced, during the last 125 years, in most of the countries concerned.

The purpose of this book is to provide a conspectus of these reforms in a way which gives a coherent and comparatively comprehensive picture of a phenomenon of outstanding significance, interest and importance which is sweeping through the Muslim world. Its significance lies in the light it sheds on the sociological amalgam of the medieval and the modern, the indigenous and the alien, which characterizes so many of these countries today; its interest in the insight it provides into the traumatic tension between orthodoxy and modernism which racks contemporary Islamic thought, where theology and law always go hand in hand; and its importance in the impact it has had—and will increasingly have—on the way of life of hundreds of millions of contemporary Muslims.

But it is impossible to appreciate the significance of these reforms, the theological and practical problems which confronted the reformers, what has already been achieved and what hopes there are for future progress, without some understanding of the situation which previously prevailed. In particular, we need to know how the Sharīʿa in fact originated and developed, the way in which Muslims have habitually regarded it, and the extent to which it was applied in practice in different parts of the Muslim world. It is only against this essential background that we can assess the changes which have been made in the way in which this law is now applied by the courts and how these changes have been effected. It should then be possible, when we come to describe what has in fact been achieved, to refer to the relevant legislation or judicial decisions, together with their sociological significance and juridical basis, without the need for anything in the nature of a full exposition of the substantive provisions of the Sharīʿa as these had developed in the different schools of law and had been applied in the various countries which make up the Muslim world. For this, reference may be made to a number of standard works,[6] although there is no one book which can be said to cover the whole field.

2. THE SHARĪʿA

Traditionally, the life of a Muslim has been largely dominated by the twin sciences of theology and the sacred law. If the former taught him what he should believe, it was the latter which prescribed the way in which he should behave and all that he should do or abstain from doing. The technical term for this 'system of duties', as it has aptly been described, is the Sharīʿa: a word which originally signified the way to a watering place, and then came to mean the path of God's commandments. As such it covers every aspect of law as this is classified today (national and international, public and private, criminal and civil), together with a vast amount which would not be regarded as law at all in contemporary Western thought (religious and social duties, matters of ritual and devotion, and rules for seemly conduct). According to a common classification, all human behaviour was thus subsumed under one of five categories: what God has commanded, what he has recommended, what he has left legally indifferent, what he has reprobated and what he has positively forbidden.

Inevitably, then, the whole system rests on the foundation of what is regarded as divine revelation, for how else can man know the mind of God about difficult points of conduct? According to the strictest school of Muslim orthodoxy, indeed, man is not only totally incapable of discerning moral values without the aid of revelation, but such values would not in fact exist at all unless the Almighty had commanded this and forbidden that. He does not command the good because it is inherently good or forbid the evil because it is intrinsically evil, but good is good solely because he has commanded it, and evil evil exclusively because he has

[6] E.g. A. A. A. Fyzee, *Outlines of Muhammadan Law* (O.U.P., 3rd edn., 1964) for Islamic law in India; or J. Schacht, *An Introduction to Islamic Law* (O.U.P., 1964) for a more general treatment.

forbidden it. Such is the view of the Ashʿariyya. But other Muslims, such as the Māturīdīs, the Shīʿīs and many Ḥanafī jurists, were far less extreme, for they not only taught that God commands the good because it is good and forbids the evil because it is evil, but also that man can frequently discern for himself the difference between virtue and vice (and in such cases revelation serves chiefly to confirm what he could in fact have known without it), while in other cases he stands in stark need of revelation to make clear what he could not otherwise discern.

With such an all-inclusive scope, it is obvious that there is a vast amount of the Sharīʿa which could never be enforced or applied by any human court. It would be anomalous to try to enforce behaviour which God has recommended but not positively enjoined, or to punish acts which he has reprobated but not actually forbidden, for to attempt to do this would be for the courts to intrude into the sphere of private morality and personal piety. Even in regard to those things which are regarded as positively commanded or forbidden, moreover, it is clear that there is much which could scarcely be enforced by human sanctions but must be left to the bar of eternity. And it is equally obvious that it is only within the category of what is classified as legally indifferent that there is any proper scope for human legislation, since human enactments about matters concerning which the mind of the Almighty has been made plain might well be regarded as bordering on blasphemy—for Islam is far more stringent about the evil of throwing the slightest doubt on the authority of divine revelation than about the comparatively venial sin of failing to observe its precepts. But to this very important question of the scope, standing and permissibility of human legislation we must return later.

How, then, was the mind of God discerned in such matters; or, in other words, from what sources was the Sharīʿa in fact derived? No Muslim, however orthodox he may be, believes for a moment that it dropped down complete from heaven in any way analogous to that in which the Goddess Athene is depicted, in Greek mythology, as having sprung fully armed from the mind of Zeus.

Instead, the Sharīʿa would be described by Muslims as both a divine law (as they always affirm) and also a lawyers' law (as most would readily admit), since it is regarded as firmly based on divine revelation, on the one hand, and as having been worked out by a series of great jurisconsults, on the other. But at this point a distinction must be made between the traditional teaching of Muslim jurisprudence and the recent attempts of Orientalists to reconstruct what actually happened.

The orthodox Muslim view is commonly based on a tradition about a conversation between the Prophet of Islam and a man named Muʿādh, whom he is alleged to have sent as a judge to the Yemen. When asked on what he would base his judgments, Muʿādh is said first to have replied 'On the book of God' (that is, the Qur'ān). Next, when asked what he would do if he could find nothing there to help him, he is reported to have replied that he would turn to the 'practice (*sunna*) of the Prophet of God'. Finally, when asked what he would do if this, too, failed to give him any adequate guidance, he is said to have answered that he would exercise his own judgment or opinion (*ra'y*); and Muḥammad is depicted as having given thanks to God for so right-minded an emissary. It was not very long, however, before Muslims became distinctly uneasy about the idea of a divine law based, in numerous respects, on anything as subjective and as fallible as the opinion of a mere human being. So, in place of the essentially subjective nature of what some individual Muslim believed to be in accordance with the divine will, there came to be substituted the somewhat more objective standard of the science of analogy (*qiyās*), by means of which some precept of the Qur'ān, or of those traditions (*aḥādīth*) which were accepted as enshrining the practice (*sunna*) of Muḥammad, was extended, on the basis of the reason (*ʿilla*) which underlay it, to cover some similar, but not strictly identical, situation or problem. Even so, the conclusion of an individual jurist about the cardinal point in the original text, or the method of its extension and application to another situation, could never be regarded as wholly authoritative, so it was not long before recourse was had to a tradition that

Muḥammad had once declared that 'My community will never agree in error'; and on this basis it came to be accepted that when the 'Companions' of the Prophet, on one view, or the great jurisconsults of any age, in the commonly accepted doctrine, were in agreement (*ijmāʿ*) about some conclusion, this was an authoritative indication of the divine will. In course of time, moreover, the scope of *ijmāʿ* became virtually all-pervasive. It is true that Muslim scholars rightly insist that it seldom, if ever, stands alone, for it was almost always based on some verse in the Qur'ān or some tradition of the Prophet. But the fact remains that it was the consensus which came to decree which verses of the Qur'ān were applicable to a particular point and how they were to be interpreted; which traditions were to be accepted as authentic and how they were to be applied; and which views were authoritative, permissible or heretical. It has even been argued—with considerable cogency—that in the final analysis it is an informal consensus which guarantees the accepted text of the Qur'ān and the basic authority of traditions from the Prophet.

In course of time, then, all orthodox (Sunnī) Muslims came to regard the Qur'ān, the *sunna* of the Prophet, the *ijmāʿ* or consensus of the great jurisconsults, and analogical deductions from these primary sources, as the four major roots of the Sharīʿa. The first three of these were accepted as wholly authoritative (*qaṭʿī*),[7] the fourth as only presumptively so (*ẓannī*); and some of the schools of law accepted certain subsidiary roots as well. But those Muslims regarded as 'heterodox' by the Sunnīs did not altogether agree; for the Shīʿīs, while they accepted the Qur'ān, would not accept any tradition which had not been recorded by one of their own Imāms, whom they regarded as inerrant teachers of the divine will, while the Ibāḍīs, too, ignored the consensus of Sunnī jurists and substituted a system of their own. In practice,

[7] But here a curious paradox must be noted; for while it is only the text of the Qur'ān and the authenticity of Traditions guaranteed by *ijmāʿ* which can be said to be *qaṭʿī*, yet it is the Qur'ān and Traditions which give authority to *ijmāʿ*. There is really no escape from this circular reasoning; but the fact remains that where Orientalists are inclined to regard *ijmāʿ* as fundamental, Muslims habitually refer primarily to the Qur'ān and *sunna*.

however, the body of substantive law elaborated by the Ibāḍīs does not differ very greatly from that of the Sunnī schools, and even that of the various sub-sects of the Shīʿa has a vast amount in common with (as well as notable differences from) the great body of Sunnī doctrine.

But we must return to the Sunnīs, who constitute some ninety per cent of the five hundred million (or more) persons who make up the Muslim world. In the earliest days it is clear that any adequately qualified jurist was regarded as having the right to go back to the primary sources of the law and make his own deductions. Such persons were called *mujtahids*, and the process of deduction in which they indulged was termed *ijtihād*. With the passage of time, however, different 'schools' of law were formed in various areas or under the aegis of certain outstanding jurists; and with the crystallization of these schools the right of independent deduction came to be progressively restricted until, about the end of the third century of the Muslim era, it was commonly accepted that the 'door of *ijtihād*' had become closed, and that all later jurists were mere *muqallids*, who had the duty of accepting the conclusions reached by previous generations of scholars as authoritative (that is, the duty of *taqlīd*). It is true that the Sunnīs never denied that, in theory at least, another jurist might one day arise who could exercise the faculty of *ijtihād* (and a number of scholars did in fact make this claim), while the Shīʿīs, on their part, never regarded the door of *ijtihād* as entirely closed; but the fact remains that the development of the law became progressively more and more moribund. There was always, it is true, a certain measure of progress or evolution, since new situations and problems arose which had to be solved by the *fatāwī*, or reasoned opinions, of some leading jurist; but, in the main, the continual sequence of accepted textbooks took the form of commentaries and digests based, century after century, on the commentaries and digests of the past. It was against this almost immovable background that the reformers had to fight.[8]

[8] Cf. my article 'Law as a Social Force in Islamic Culture and History', in *Bulletin of the School of Oriental & African Studies*, Vol. xx (1957), pp. 13 f.

What, then, have the researches of Orientalists done to challenge or correct this traditional view of Islamic jurisprudence? First, they have shown that the picture which Muslim writers are apt to draw of the scholar-jurists of early Islam, congregated in Mecca or Madina and building up the vast structure of the Sharīʿa direct from the Qur'ān and the traditions of what the Prophet had said or done, is both idealized and over-simplified. The earliest centres of active jurisprudence were in Iraq rather than Arabia; and the law was derived primarily from the raw material of the existing customary law and administrative practice, which was worked through and systematized by the scholar-jurists in the light of such Islamic teaching as was already current—with the result that some of this raw material was retained, some modified and some rejected.[9] Secondly, it is clear that in the earliest days the term *sunna* was not confined to the practice of Muḥammad himself, and certainly was not based on precise accounts of what he had said or done—authenticated by a chain of narrators reaching right back to those who first reported this. Instead, the terms *sunna* and *ijmāʿ* were both used of the commonly accepted doctrine of the ancient schools of law. It was only from the time of al-Shāfiʿī,[10] who has aptly been called the father of Islamic jurisprudence, that the term *sunna* came to be used exclusively of the practice of the Prophet; that traditions which could, allegedly, be traced back to Muḥammad himself came to be accepted as of binding authority; and that the chain of narrators came to be scrutinized and criticized—and, indeed, often invented. Thirdly, even Shāfiʿī himself seems to have had no knowledge of the famous tradition that the community of the Prophet would never agree in error; and he appears to have limited the scope of *ijmāʿ* to the agreement of the whole Muslim community (about such matters as the five obligatory prayers) rather than the consensus of the jurists on those points of law about which they alone were competent to speak. Fourthly, it seems clear that the differences in the law which was

[9] For a detailed discussion of this subject, reference may most conveniently be made to Joseph Schacht's *Origins of Muhammadan Jurisprudence* (O.U.P., 1950).

[10] Born in 150 A.H. (A.D. 767).

accepted by the various schools—and among the Sunnīs it was only those of the Ḥanafīs, Mālikīs, Shāfiʿīs and Ḥanbalīs which ultimately survived—was the result less of questions of jurisprudential principle than of the conditions of life and society in the communities in which these schools grew up. It is true, of course, that the Ḥanbalīs were more inclined than the other schools to accept a tradition, however weakly attested, rather than an inference of logic; but it is equally true that the differences between the Ḥanafīs and Malikīs were far less due to questions of this sort than to the fact that the Ḥanafī doctrine was developed in the cosmopolitan atmosphere of Kūfa and Baṣra, while the Mālikī law grew up in the very milieu in which Muḥammad himself had lived and taught.

Be that as it may, the fact remains that there are wide differences between the schools. They differ about the meaning and application of a number of Qur'anic verses, and whether some of these were, or were not, 'abrogated' by others. They differ, too, in what traditions they accept as authentic, and how they apply them. And they differ yet again in what points they regard as covered by consensus. There were also numerous minor differences between individual scholars in each of the schools, particularly in the early days—although with the passage of the years one particular opinion, about this point or that, usually came to prevail. In addition, it must also be remembered that there were a number of other schools which flourished for a time and then ceased to exist, but whose views have in some cases been preserved. Yet, for all their differences, the Sunnī schools that survived came to accept each other as mutually orthodox, and there is a sense in which their alternative, and even conflicting, doctrines and conclusions were regarded as all authenticated by a form of consensus. The result was that the dead hand of tradition came very near to ossifying the Sharīʿa, for any innovation was alleged to be contrary to *ijmāʿ*. The law, moreover, was regarded as a divinely given blue-print to which society—ruler and subject alike—must always do their utmost to approximate. An early suggestion that it should be officially codified was successfully resisted; so it remained an amorphous volume of partly contradictory doctrine, to which lip-service, at least, was invariably given and which came to stand, like a sentinel, to bar the path of progress.

3. CUSTOMARY AND ADMINISTRATIVE LAW

We have seen that recent scholarly research has shown that the Sharīʿa was originally fashioned from the raw material of local customary law and administrative practice, systematized and islamicized by the work of early scholar-jurists. Yet the fact remains that no place whatever is expressly given, in the traditional doctrine, to customary law as such. It is true that one of the major differences between the Sunnīs and the Shīʿīs is that the former tacitly regarded the teaching of the Qur'ān and *sunna* as modifying, rather than abolishing, the pre-Islamic customary law, while the latter sought to build up a wholly new system of law on the basis of the Islamic texts alone.[11] But even in the Sunnī view it is only in so far as the customary law can be regarded as incorporated in Islamic doctrine through the Qur'ān, the Traditions or the consensus that it is recognized as authoritative.

Naturally enough, therefore, no custom which runs counter to Islamic law is accorded the official recognition of the jurists. It is true that in areas where, for example, there is a general custom that a certain proportion of the dower due to a wife is paid on the conclusion of the contract of marriage and the remainder at a later date, this may be regarded as implicit in a contract where the contrary has not been expressly stipulated. But the scope of customary law is, in practice, much more extensive than this. Throughout the whole Muslim world, for example, merchants have found the complete prohibition of fixed rates of interest or of speculative contracts, as prescribed by a rigid interpretation of the classical doctrine, an intolerable restriction on trade; so they have continued to follow customary practices in their commercial transactions—sometimes in frank disregard of the Sharīʿa, and sometimes after these practices have been brought into outward

[11] See pp. 147, 149–50 etc. below.

conformity with it by means of a number of stratagems invented by the jurists themselves.

This is true even in the most orthodox parts of the Muslim world. But elsewhere, and particularly in those countries in which Islam has been introduced at a comparatively late date or has had to compete with well-established local customs—whether in regard to marriage, divorce, inheritance or rights of property—things have gone much further than this. Even in the most orthodox areas of Northern Nigeria, for example, customary law has continued to prevail over the pure Mālikī doctrine in a number of different points.[12]

But this is as nothing to the situation in parts of North Africa, where Berber customary law reigns supreme. Among the Kabyles of Algeria, for example, marriage still approximates to a form of purchase in which the dower is paid to the bride's father by the husband, and is largely recovered by him, should the marriage be terminated by divorce (which is always irrevocable), either from her father or from the next husband to whom she is given in marriage. In Morocco, moreover, the lives of almost half the population are governed by a patriarchal customary law, administered by special tribunals, under which women are denied any right to inherit.[13] In Indonesia and much of Malaysia, again, there are many spheres of life in which the *adat* or customary law alone holds sway; and here the structure of society is largely matriarchal—especially, for example, in the Minangkabou region of Sumatra.[14] Much the same is true in many parts of Africa, where a large number of tribes, such as the Ashantis of Ghana and the Wa Digo of Kenya, follow a matriarchal customary law—although this is frequently adapted, to some extent, by those who embrace Islam, or even wholly abandoned by such of the Wa Digo or Wa Giriama as become absorbed in the Swahili culture

[12] Cf. my *Islamic Law in Africa* (H.M.S.O., 1954), pp. 171 ff.

[13] Cf. G.-H. Bousquet, *Du droit musulman et de son application effective dans le monde* (Algiers, 1949), pp. 91 f., and *Justice française et coutumes kabyles* (Algiers, 1950), pp. 48 f.

[14] Cf. B. ter Haar, *Adat Law in Indonesia* (translated from the Dutch, Institute of Pacific Relations, New York, 1948).

of the East African coast. In other tribes—as, for instance, the Yao of Malawi and the Yoruba of Nigeria—Islamic family law has virtually no influence. The Yao as a whole profess Islam as a religion, but know and care little about the Sharīʿa; while among the Yoruba it is not at all uncommon to find Muslims, Christians and even pagans living, amicably enough, in one family—divided, indeed, in their religious allegiance, but united in the customary law which governs their family life.[15] Even in the Indian sub-continent it was only in 1937, while still under British rule, that the customary law of such communities as the Ismāʿīlī Khojas, the Bohoras, the Cutchī Memons and others was severely limited in its scope, by the Shariat Act and other legislation, in favour of the dictates of orthodox doctrine.[16]

Very much the same situation, *mutatis mutandis*, applies to what may be termed administrative law. The requirements of the Sharīʿa in regard to procedure, evidence and proof were so rigid and exacting[17] that few, if any, Muslim rulers were willing to leave the maintenance of law and order, and the prevention of crime, exclusively to those courts which were, by their very nature, officially bound to observe them. Instead, other courts were set up which, however much they may have paid lip-service to the Sharīʿa, felt free largely to follow the dictates and directions of the executive authority. Sometimes, as in the case of customary law, this was frowned upon by the jurist-theologians; but the need to avoid anarchy soon led them to recognize a lawful use of executive discretion, commonly called *siyāsa sharʿiyya*, which allowed the ruler to go well beyond the strict dictates of the prescribed doctrine in what he regarded as the public interest. There were also, of course, innumerable examples of rulers who habitually flouted the law in practice, however much they may have paid homage to it in theory. But the fact remains that, right up till the

[15] Cf. Anderson, op. cit., pp. 270 ff., 108 ff., 166 ff., and 222 ff., and 'Customary Law & Islamic Law in British African Territories', in *The Future of Customary Law in Africa* (University of Leyden Press, 1955), pp. 70 ff.

[16] Cf. A. A. A. Fyzee, *Outlines of Muhammadan Law* (O.U.P., 3rd edn, 1964), pp. 53 ff.

[17] Cf. pp. 15, 34 ff., 66 ff., 87 f., 100 etc. below.

era of recent reforms, it was the Sharī'a alone which was regarded as law in the fullest sense of that term.

4. THE COURTS

Reference has already been made to different varieties of courts which have existed, all down the centuries, in most parts of the Muslim world. But from a comparatively early date in the history of Islam it was the jurisdiction of the *qāḍīs*, or specialists in the Sharī'a, which came to be regarded as the basic courts of general jurisdiction. These *qāḍīs* were in practice not only appointed by the ruler (whether the Caliph or local Governor) but dependent on him for the execution of their decrees; yet in theory at least they were bound strictly to apply the Sharī'a even if the ruler himself were a litigant. The practice was for a single *qāḍī* to preside in each court, although he sometimes had a jurisconsult (*muftī*) or two to advise him on points of law. His sphere of jurisdiction was commonly prescribed on his appointment, whether in terms of geographical area or even, occasionally, the type of cases in which he was empowered to adjudicate. There was no hierarchy of courts or regular system of appeal; but a litigant might always request the *qāḍī* who gave a judgment with which he disagreed to reconsider it. At various times it was common practice, moreover, for the ruler to appoint *qāḍīs* from different schools—even, indeed, from all four of the Sunnī schools—to exercise concurrent jurisdiction in some of the major cities of the Muslim world. Each would follow the authoritative doctrine of his own school in the judgments he gave; so it was the plaintiff who could, in most cases, determine which doctrine should govern the case in hand by the simple expedient of choosing which *qāḍī* he would approach. Commonly, moreover, a *qāḍī* of a different school would not upset a judgment which had already been given in accordance with the doctrine of another Sunnī school, however much he would himself have applied different principles; for the acknowledgement of the basic orthodoxy of all the Sunnī schools meant that a judgment given according to any one of them was regarded as a legitimate exercise of judicial discretion.

But the *qāḍīs'* courts, as we have seen, were seldom, if ever, the only courts. From a very early date the local governor (*wāli*) habitually exercised a certain jurisdiction, as did also the police (*shurṭa*). There was also the court of the *muḥtasib*, or inspector of markets, whose jurisdiction was not confined to such matters as false weights and measures but also extended to matters of morality—as an extension, and personification, of that general moral oversight (*ḥisba*) which the law accorded to every Muslim. More important still, there was the Court of Complaints (that of the *ṣāḥib al-maẓālim*), which represented a survival of the personal jurisdiction of the Persian rulers. This was sometimes presided over by the Caliph himself, and sometimes by a powerful official appointed by him as his deputy; and it had a multiple function. Primarily it was designed as an informal court of appeal, in the sense that anyone who felt outraged by the judgment of another court, whether that of a *qāḍī* or anyone else, could appeal to the Caliph for justice. But it also served as a court of first instance, in modern parlance, in cases in which one of the litigants was so powerful that it might be feared that no ordinary court could be trusted to do justice. In addition, of course, it was the obvious court to deal with cases under that *siyāsa shar'iyya* to which reference has already been made.

5. THE MOTIVES BEHIND THE REFORM MOVEMENT: THE OTTOMAN EMPIRE

No discussion of the background to the reforms which have changed the face of the law in recent years in the great majority of countries that make up the Muslim world would be meaningful or complete without a consideration of the motives and impulses which gave rise to this movement. And these, in their turn, were not only varied and complex, but fall into two distinct categories —which correspond, naturally enough, to the two main stages into which the movement for reform can itself be divided and the dual form it has almost everywhere taken.

In the early days, dating from about the middle of the last century, the impulse for reform came not from below but from above. It was not that ordinary Muslims, generally speaking, were dissatisfied with the law to which they were subject and began to demand its reform, but that these reforms were imposed on them by the Government. In the case of the Ottoman Empire, this was primarily in the interests of bureaucratic efficiency and military strength, in order to enable 'the sick man of Europe' to keep up with the challenge, and resist the encroachments, of the Western powers. But some of the Tanẓīmāt reforms[18] were also designed to disarm European criticisms of those aspects of the Sharīʿa which were considered savage or crude, and thus to avert the danger of further interference. This is why the earliest reforms in the sphere of personal law were the introduction of a Commercial Code, a Penal Code,[19] a Code of Commercial Procedure and a Code of Maritime Commerce, for we have already seen that the rigid rules of the Sharīʿa had always been far too restrictive either for the life of the markets or for the maintenance of criminal justice. In more recent years, moreover, the situation had been considerably complicated by the encroachments of foreigners and the system of Capitulations—although this was, in part, a revival of the ancient principle of the personality, or personal nature, of the law—which had been known in the Middle East from antiquity, was revived in the Mediterranean basin on the break-up of the Roman Empire, was recognized in early Islam, and was current practice in Venice and other city states.[20] Unless and until Muslim merchants could be provided with a code of law more suited to the conditions of commerce in the nineteenth century, there was, indeed, a grave danger that the economic development of the Empire would be left very largely in the hands of foreigners.

[18] The Arabic word *tanẓīm* basically means to organize or put in order; and Tanẓīmāt was the term used of a whole succession of reforms in the Ottoman Empire starting in 1839.

[19] There had, in fact, been a few rather half-hearted attempts, at a slightly earlier date, to introduce legislation on this subject which kept considerably closer to the Sharīʿa; but these soon gave place to codes of frankly Western inspiration.

[20] See Herbert J. Liebesny, 'The development of western judicial privileges', in Majid Khadduri and Herbert J. Liebesny (eds.), *Law in the Middle East* (Washington, D.C., 1955), pp. 309–33.

The Islamic criminal law, moreover, was largely made up of a very limited number of offences for which specific—and, generally speaking, extremely severe—penalties were expressly prescribed, and a broad principle that all other offences should be subject to such discretionary punishment (*taʿzīr*) as seemed suitable to the court. But this comparatively simple (if not altogether satisfactory) classification was complicated by the fact that certain crimes were regarded as 'offences against God' and others primarily as 'offences against man' (a classification which roughly corresponds to the modern distinction between crimes and civil wrongs), with the result that the latter, alone, could be compounded or pardoned by the victim. It was further complicated by the fact that the prescribed penalties (*ḥudūd*) were applicable only where the offence could be proved by evidence so exacting in its nature as to be almost impossible to obtain, and where the accused could not, or did not, avail himself of any one of a number of possible defences. The necessary evidence, moreover, consisted almost exclusively of oral testimony, and there were elaborate rules (which were designed to make the whole system largely self-operative, and to leave as little as possible to the discretion of the court) about the number of witnesses required, and what factors would, or would not, make their testimony eligible or even binding.

The effect of these Ottoman reforms was to put the Sharīʿa entirely on one side in regard to such matters as commercial and criminal law and procedure, to substitute in its place codes of quite alien inspiration, and to establish a whole system of secular (*niẓāmiyya*) courts, operating under modern rules of procedure and evidence, to apply them. In the light of the attitude habitually taken by Muslims to their sacred law, this might well seem to be the most drastic expedient to which a Muslim government could possibly resort; but we must reserve any detailed consideration of this phenomenon to the next chapter, when we shall discuss the methods adopted by the reformers. Two points, however, call for immediate comment. First, that when the Ottoman reformers turned their attention to the compilation of a Code of Obligations (contract, tort and certain principles of procedure), a controversy arose as to whether they should again resort to French models or should produce a code based on principles derived from the Sharīʿa; and, in the event, it was those who advocated the latter course whose view prevailed. So, for the first time in the history of Islam, principles derived from the Sharīʿa were enacted as law by the authority of the State. This represented a complete reversal of the position previously occupied by the Sharīʿa—as an uncodified, divine law which had an authority, inherent in itself, over every Muslim, from Caliph to slave. Not only so, but the Law in question, commonly known as the Majalla, did not take the form of a straightforward codification of those opinions which had come to prevail, on this matter or that, in the school of law which was accepted as official in the Ottoman Empire (that is, the Ḥanafī school), but represented an eclectic choice from among the wide range of opinions which had at any time been advocated by a Ḥanafī jurist (even though some of these opinions had been adopted only quite recently by certain Ḥanafīs, and had in fact originated in other schools of law), selected on the basis of their apparent suitability to the exigencies of modern life.

But it is important to note that the Ottoman reformers, throughout the entire period of these Tanẓīmāt reforms, did not venture in any way to touch the personal or family law of Muslims—which continued to be applied in the traditional way, in specifically Sharīʿa courts, by personnel trained after the age-old pattern, under the system of procedure and evidence which they had habitually followed. It was not until 1915, in point of fact, that any reform whatever was effected in this sacrosanct preserve; for although every part of the Sharīʿa is regarded as based on divine revelation, there can be no doubt that it is in the field of family law (and especially in such matters as marriage, divorce and inheritance) that the Qur'ān itself is most explicit, that the sacred law has been most meticulously followed and that Muslims have regarded that law as partaking most closely of the very warp and woof of their religion. Naturally enough, moreover, in this case the motive and impulse were very different, and emanated from the public opinion of better educated Muslims rather than the dictates of a governmental bureaucracy—for it was the miserable plight of many Turkish wives, under the dominant opinion of the Ḥanafī school, which made a change imperative. But in this sphere Ottoman Muslims were not at that time prepared to abandon the Sharīʿa for a code of alien inspiration; so they were forced to face up to the agonizing problem of how a law which was regarded as having divine authority could possibly be changed. This, too, will form an essential part of our next chapter.

Much the same sort of thing happened in Egypt, which had attained its juridical independence within the Ottoman Empire in 1874 under the Khedive Ismāʿīl. Here, too, the system of Capitulations prevailed, and was extensively abused; and here, again, tentative legislation which ran mildly counter to the principles of the Sharīʿa was progressively replaced by codes of frankly Western inspiration.[21] Almost the only reminder of the Sharīʿa in the Egyptian Criminal Code, for example, was a provision that no Muslim should be executed unless the Muftī of Egypt confirmed that the death penalty might properly be imposed, in the relevant circumstances, according to Ḥanafī principles; and two Civil Codes, one promulgated for the Mixed Courts in 1875 and one promulgated for the National Courts in 1883, differed sharply from the Majalla in the fact that the Egyptian codes basically represented a wholesale adoption of the Code Napoleon, although a small minority of their provisions was derived from the Sharīʿa. As in the Ottoman Empire as a whole, moreover, it was only in such matters as family law, testate and intestate succession, gifts and *waqf* endowments that the Ḥanafī law was still applied by specifically Sharīʿa courts, manned by personnel trained in the traditional way, uncodified and unreformed—although it is interesting to note that an unofficial codification of the dominant opinions in the Ḥanafī school was, in fact, compiled in Egypt by Qadrī Pasha. But this had no binding force, and the Sharīʿa courts

[21] For a bird's-eye view of the course of law reform in Egypt, see my chapter on 'Law Reform in Egypt: 1850–1950', in *Political and Social Change in Modern Egypt* (edited by P. M. Holt, O.U.P., 1968), pp. 209–30.

continued—officially, at least—to rely on their own selection of the appropriate Ḥanafī doctrine, on any point at issue, from the classical compendia. But perhaps the most significant factor of all in preparing the way for a new day in Egypt was the standing and repute of the Mixed Courts (which were set up to determine cases in which the litigants were either foreigners of different nationalities or foreigners and Egyptians). Staffed by a distinguished cadre of judges from a wide variety of nationalities, and served by a very competent bar, these courts not only set an exceedingly high standard of impartial justice and judicial independence, but also fostered a new concept of the Rule of Law—not in terms of the ultimate spiritual authority of the Sharīʿa (liable as this was, in practice, to be flouted by those in power), but in terms of the inviolability of statute law, and the courts that administered it, from executive interference or legal chicanery. Nor was the influence of these courts by any means confined to the judicial process. On the contrary, it is noteworthy that it was a new generation of Egyptian lawyers, trained and equipped in these courts, who took the lead in the formation of political parties, in social, political and economic reform, and in the on-going struggle for national independence.[22]

6. INDIA

Another most illuminating example of law reform in the Muslim world can be found in the Indian sub-continent, for the situation there differed from that in the Ottoman Empire in a number of important respects. To begin with, the great majority of the population were Hindus rather than Muslims; but there was a substantial minority of Muslims, and the greater part of the peninsula had been under Muslim rule for some centuries before the advent of the East India Company. As a consequence, it was the Islamic criminal law which almost everywhere prevailed, although the Mogul rulers had left their Hindu subjects, for the

[22] Cf. a paper on 'The Case of Lawyers in Egypt' contributed by F. J. Ziadeh to a Conference on 'Enterprise in the Emerging Socialist Societies of the Near East' in Princeton University in 1964.

most part, to administer their own religious law and settle their own civil disputes before Brahmin judges, with the threat of excommunication as a sufficient sanction. As for disputes between Hindus and Muslims, these were sometimes taken before a Muslim *qāḍī* under the Sharīʿa, and sometimes before a lay official who applied customary law (*ʿurf*).

Even after the advent of the East India Company, moreover, no responsibility was assumed for the administration of law in India, up till the year 1765, outside the three 'Presidency towns' of Madras, Bombay and Calcutta, where the Company's 'factories' had been established and where the Company had come to exercise authority from 1639, 1668 and 1698, respectively—although it was not until 1726 that 'Mayors' Courts' were set up in these centres. These were not courts of the Company but of the English Crown, so the law they applied was, by implication, that of England. But it was provided, under a Charter of 1753, that they were not to try cases between Indians except by consent of both parties; and this, no doubt, represented existing practice. It was not until Clive received the grant of the Dīwān, or fiscal administration and civil justice, in Bengal in 1765 from the puppet Mogul Emperor in Delhi that the Company's sway began to extend outside the Presidency towns. And at much the same time, but by a more dubious title, the Company received the grant of the Niẓāmāt, or criminal jurisdiction. But this was exercised, at first, under very indirect control. Under Warren Hastings, moreover, civil jurisdiction came to be exercised under Regulation II of 1772, Article 27, which expressly provided that Hindus and Muslims were to be governed by their own laws in 'suits regarding inheritance, marriage and caste and other religious usages and institutions'. No specific directions were given regarding the law applicable to them in other matters; but in 1781 Sir Elijah Impey declared that, where no other law was expressly applicable, the courts should act 'according to justice, equity and good conscience'. It is clear, then, that these provisions as a whole reflect the second fundamental difference between the Indian and the Ottoman Empires: that, whereas the Ottoman Empire remained independent under a Muslim government, India had come under an alien and non-Muslim rule, but one that went to great lengths to avoid any interference in matters of religious law and practice.

Three further points about the system of civil justice instituted in India under the British should be emphasized. First, that English law as such was not made applicable to the Indian provinces (by contrast with the Presidency towns). Secondly, that in personal and family matters Hindus and Muslims were put on an entirely equal footing and left to follow their own laws. Thirdly, that no law at all was prescribed, in general terms, for other civil litigation, and the judges were not professional lawyers; so cases of contract and debt were largely handled by arbitration, while in cases under Islamic or Hindu law the advice of 'Law Officers' (*mawlawīs* and *pandits*) was called in aid. This last principle received legislative authority by an Act of Parliament, in 1781, which gave civil jurisdiction even over Indian inhabitants in the Presidency town of Calcutta to the Supreme Court, with the proviso that 'their inheritance and succession to lands, rents and goods and all matters of contract and dealing between party and party' should be determined, in the case of Muslims and Hindus, by their respective laws—and, where the parties differed in religion, 'by the laws and usages of the defendant'. Similar provisions were soon extended to Madras and Bombay, with the result that the broad distinction between the law applicable in the Presidency towns, on the one hand, and the Provinces, on the other, was that the *residual* law in the former was that of England, and in the latter 'justice, equity and good conscience'.

How, then, did English law come to assume the place it occupies in the Indian sub-continent today? This was largely because the formula 'justice, equity and good conscience' was so imprecise; because no provision had been made for the personal laws of others than Muslims and Hindus; and because there was a manifest need for greater uniformity and certainty. So, after much argument and debate, recourse was had to codification. In this the influence of Bentham and Fitzjames Stephen was certainly not far to seek; but the attitude which prevailed can best, perhaps, be summarized in words used by Lord Macaulay in the second reading of the Charter Act of 1833:

We do not mean that all the people of India should live under the same law; far from it, . . . we know how desirable that object is but we also know that it is unobtainable . . . Our principle is simply this—uniformity where you can have it; diversity where you must have it—but in all cases certainty . . . A code is almost the only blessing—perhaps it is the only blessing—which absolute governments are better fitted to confer on a nation than popular governments.

But the need for such action was even more obvious in regard to criminal law, for here it was almost exclusively Islamic law which was applied, and under Warren Hastings even impalement had been permitted. But in 1790, when criminal jurisdiction was taken over by the Company, it became the practice for a Muslim 'Law Officer' to write a *fatwā*, or legal opinion on the case, at the bottom of the record, and for the Company's judge to consider this carefully and then, provided it seemed to him consonant with both Islamic law and natural justice, to pass judgment accordingly. If, on the other hand, the *fatwā* seemed to be contrary either to natural justice or Islamic law, it had to be transmitted to the Court of Appeal, together with the judge's objections; and if the court of appeal considered the *fatwā* to be in accordance with Islamic law but contrary to natural justice, it would accept it if it was in favour of the accused but recommend pardon or mitigation of sentence if it was against him.

Next, progressive modifications were introduced in the Sharīʿa, as this was administered in the courts. Even in 1790, for example, the right of the heirs of blood[23] to pardon one found guilty of deliberate homicide was abolished, and the criterion as to whether a homicide was to be regarded as 'deliberate' was changed from the simple test of the weapon that had been used to a more

[23] I.e. the close relatives of the victim, who could (in suitable circumstances) demand talion (or retaliation), accept blood-money, or even pardon those who had killed him.

subjective consideration of whether the accused had, or had not, actually intended to kill. In 1791, again, the mutilation of one hand for theft or of two limbs for highway robbery was abolished, and a sentence of imprisonment for seven or fourteen years, respectively, imposed instead. Then, from 1792 onwards, reform was achieved, and the consciences of the Muslim Law Officers relieved, by the ingenious expedient of asking them to give their *fatāwī* on certain assumptions. Where, for example, the heirs of blood had refused to prosecute a murderer, or had either pardoned or commuted the offence, they were asked to certify whether the death penalty would have been applicable on the assumption that the heirs of blood had in fact demanded it. Where, again, talion was not applicable under the Sharīʿa because of the relationship of the murderer to his victim,[24] or because one of several accomplices was for some reason exempt,[25] they were asked whether the death penalty would have been appropriate on the assumption that the relevant circumstances had been different. Where a case against a Muslim rested on the evidence of non-Muslims (which, under the pure Sharīʿa, is not eligible testimony in such circumstances), they were asked to give their *fatwā* on the assumption that the witnesses had been Muslims. And where the available evidence did not fulfil the exacting criteria for the imposition of one of the prescribed penalties (*ḥudūd*), they were asked to give it, again, on the assumption that the evidence had been somewhat different.

But this was, at best, an awkward expedient. In the years that followed, moreover, further encroachments were made upon the Sharīʿa. In 1811, for example, the sale of slaves was made a criminal offence, and in 1843 slavery itself made illegal, while in 1832 non-Muslims were granted the right to claim exemption from being tried under the Islamic criminal law—although no other law was in fact provided to take its place. So it is scarcely surprising that a draft 'Indian Penal Code', first submitted by

[24] E.g. a father could not be put to death for killing his own son or daughter.

[25] Where one of those involved in a deliberate homicide was exempt from talion under the Sharīʿa, the others too were exempt.

Lord Macaulay in 1837, was eventually promulgated in 1860. With this the period of codification—closely parallel to the Tanẓīmāt reforms in the Ottoman Empire—was inaugurated, and the Indian Penal Code was soon followed by the Code of Criminal Procedure, the Indian Succession Act, the Indian Evidence Act, the Indian Contract Act, the Indian Majority Act, the Transfer of Property Act, and similar legislative enactments.

In the preceding period two principles had prevailed: that existing law should be changed as little as possible and that, where this seemed essential, the changes should be confined to what justice and equity appeared to demand. The first of these principles was persuasively stated by Sir William Jones in 1788, when he affirmed that nothing could be wiser than 'to assure the Hindu and Mussulman subjects of Great Britain that the private laws, which they severally hold sacred, and violation of which they would have thought the most grievous oppression, should not be suppressed by a new system, of which they could have no knowledge, and which they must have considered as imposed on them by a spirit of rigor and intolerance'. And the way in which the second of these principles was applied seems to have aroused little opposition—partly, no doubt, because the family law was left very largely inviolate,[26] and partly, it would seem, because many Muslims were themselves conscious of the need for certain reforms. It is perhaps significant in this context that the Muslim Law Officers would frequently add, at the end of their *fatāwī*, a reference to the fact that punishments could be altered by the will and fiat of the Ruler. But the position just before the promulgation of the Penal Code was summarized by Sir George Campbell in these words:

> The foundation of our criminal law is still the Mahomedan Code (*sic*!); but so altered and added to by our regulations that it is hardly to be recognised; and there has, in fact, by practice and continual emendative enactments, grown up a system of our own, well understood by those whose profession it is, and towards which the original Mahomedan law and Mahomedan lawyers are really little consulted. Still the hidden

[26] See under India in Index, and particularly pp. 211 ff.

sub-structure on which the whole building rests is this Mahomedan law, take away which and we should have no definition of or authority for punishing many of the most common crimes.[27]

A number of references to the methods by which reforms in the law have been introduced in the Indian sub-continent, to the results that have been achieved and to the need that still remains for further action, will be made in subsequent chapters of this book. Two points, however, should be emphasized at this point. First, that in the Indian peninsula, unlike most of the Muslim world, there has been no dichotomy between the courts which deal with family matters under the relevant personal or religious law, on the one hand, and those which administer the common law of the land, on the other. On the contrary, the same courts apply the general law to all and sundry, and a whole plethora of special systems of law to different religious communities where this is applicable. In all cases, moreover, the common law principle of *stare decisis* prevails; and this has opened the door to the possibility of law reform by means of judicial decision as well as legislation. Secondly, it seems clear that there is a very real sense in which a non-Muslim government hesitates even more than most Muslim governments before it introduces legislation which may be regarded by Muslims as contrary to their sacred law.[28]

7. IRAN, ARABIA, MALAYSIA AND THE SUDAN

Many other examples could be given of the situation which existed, only a few decades ago, in one predominantly Muslim country after another. The degree to which the Sharīʿa prevailed in the community, governed the lives of individual Muslims, and was applied by the courts, differed very considerably from country to country; but it is this composite picture which alone can provide the background against which the positive spate of recent

[27] *Modern India* (1853), p. 464.

[28] For a somewhat fuller treatment of this whole subject, in its Indian setting, cf. my article 'The Impact of Islamic Law on Commonwealth Legal Systems', in *International and Comparative Law of the Commonwealth* (ed. Robert R. Wilson, Duke University Press, Durham, N.C., 1968), pp. 63 ff.

reforms which have transformed the face of the Muslim world can be seen and evaluated.

Iran, for instance, provides a good example of an independent Muslim country in which much the same pressures as we have noted in regard to the Ottoman Empire led first to the promulgation of a Civil Code, and then, more recently, to some fascinating further reforms in the sphere of family law. These will engage our attention in subsequent chapters; but it is significant at this point that the Iranian Civil Code of 1937 is considerably more comprehensive than the very varied enactments which make up the Tanẓīmāt reforms in the Ottoman Empire, and that it represents a substantial retention of Islamic principles (as developed, in this case, by Shīʿī jurists), combined with a not inconsiderable admixture of French law. Saʿūdī Arabia and North Yemen, on the other hand, provide the outstanding examples of independent Muslim countries which, in different degrees, have virtually retained the Sharīʿa as a whole, with only minimal modifications in its scope and method of administration. Again, those countries in North Africa which were until recently under French or Italian rule have all adopted a codified criminal and civil law,[29] but differ very considerably among themselves in the degree to which these codes are based on material of indigenous and Islamic, or foreign and secular, inspiration; and they also differ in what reforms, if any, they have introduced in regard to family law. To these, too, we must return later; but it is clear that the background to all these different reforms, whether in regard to criminal, civil or family law, is closely parallel to what has already been noted in regard to the Ottoman Empire, Egypt, India and Iran.

In Indonesia and Malaysia, as we have noted in passing, the background was (and still is) a compound of Islamic and customary law, although there have been a number of interesting reforms in Singapore and in some of the Malay States to which reference must be made in due course. In the Sudan, under the virtually British rule of the former Anglo-Egyptian Condominium, the Ottoman law, in so far as this was previously in

[29] Cf. pp. 34, 86–8 below.

force, was ousted in favour of that principle of 'justice, equity and good conscience' which at one time prevailed in the Indian provinces; and with the passage of time this came to be more and more identified—although not in any very rigid way—with the general principles of English law.[30] Just recently, an attempt was made to change this radically in favour of a widespread adoption of Egyptian law; but this movement has now, it seems, been put into reverse. In matters of family law, on the other hand, a whole series of reforms have been effected in the Sudan in recent years much along the lines of those adopted in Egypt, although not infrequently action was taken in the Sudan even before the corresponding Egyptian reforms had been promulgated. And in what was formerly British Somaliland, again, the law represented, in the main, a fascinating amalgam of the Sharīʿa with Somali customary law, together with a limited number of legislative reforms.[31]

8. AFRICA SOUTH OF THE SAHARA

In most of the African countries south of the Sahara Muslims represent a minority (in some comparatively small, in others very substantial) of the total population; but there have been few recent reforms, except in Tanzania, Northern Nigeria and Somalia—although very interesting suggestions have been under consideration in both Ghana and Kenya. Until recently the case of Northern Nigeria was, indeed, almost unique, for up till less than twenty years ago this was the only place outside the Arabian peninsula[32] in which the Islamic law, both substantive and procedural, was applied in criminal litigation—sometimes even in regard to capital offences. The situation was greatly complicated, moreover, by a number of unusual factors. First, there was also a Nigerian Criminal Code—corresponding, in general terms, to English criminal law—which was administered in the magistrates'

30 Cf. Zaki Mustapha, *Common Law in the Sudan, an Account of the 'Justice, Equity and Good Conscience Provision'* (Clarendon Press, Oxford, 1971).

31 Cf. *Islamic Law in Africa*, pp. 40 ff.

32 Except, to some extent, in Afghanistan.

courts and in the High Court, although in point of fact more than ninety per cent of all criminal cases were tried in the indigenous or 'native' courts. Secondly, there were fundamental differences between the Mālikī form of the Sharīʿa, as applied in the native courts—particularly in regard to homicide cases—and the relevant sections of the Nigerian Criminal Code; with the result that an accused person might well be condemned to death in one of the Emirs' courts in circumstances in which that penalty would not have been applicable in the High Court—although various attempts were made to mitigate this manifest injustice, sometimes by transferring a case from one court to another, and sometimes on appeal. Thirdly, where anyone had been convicted of the deliberate homicide of a Muslim, the heirs of blood could always claim talion under Mālikī law; but, where a Muslim had been convicted of the deliberate homicide of a Christian or pagan, talion could never be demanded, and the death penalty was applicable only in cases which involved highway robbery or other special circumstances. Instead, where the victim was a Christian, only one-third of the blood-money which would have been due in the case of a Muslim victim could be demanded and, where the victim was a pagan, a mere fifteenth of that sum was payable—together, in both cases, with a prescribed penalty of one year's imprisonment. The reason for this blatant discrimination on grounds of religion can be explained, of course, only by the fact that the blood of a Muslim is regarded, in Mālikī law, as vastly more valuable than that of a non-Muslim. So it is scarcely surprising that the Christians and pagans of the then Northern Region, who represented about one-third of the total population, were exceedingly apprehensive, when Nigeria was on the threshold of independence, that the withdrawal of the colonial administration would leave them without those safeguards which had previously existed, or even exposed to a radical extension of the scope of the Sharīʿa. This, then, was the background to recent reforms in that country—the essential element in which consisted in the introduction of a new Criminal Code and Code of Criminal Procedure, based substantially on those of the Sudan (which were themselves inspired by the corresponding Indian Codes) and the elimination of Islamic law in all criminal cases.[33]

One more example of the situation that prevailed in a basically Muslim country previously governed by a colonial regime may be of interest: namely, that of Zanzibar. The unique feature in this case was the 'dual jurisdiction' exercised by the British and the Zanzibar courts, respectively. In brief summary, the 'British Court' had jurisdiction in all cases in which any plaintiff or defendant, accused person or complainant, was a British subject, a British 'Protected person', a subject of any of the foreign powers which had agreed to this arrangement, a subject of any other Christian power not represented by a consul in Zanzibar, or someone in the regular service of any of the above mentioned persons. In addition, the British Court alone had jurisdiction under certain Decrees regarding which the Sultan had made a complete surrender of jurisdiction. The 'Zanzibar Court' of the Sultan, on the other hand, had jurisdiction in all other cases. But both the organization and personnel of the courts which exercised the jurisdiction of the British Crown and the Sultan of Zanzibar were completely assimilated by the British Subordinate Courts Order of 1923 and the Zanzibar Courts Decree of the same date (as repeatedly amended); and appeals from both courts went to the Court of Appeal for Eastern Africa and thence to the Privy Council in London. As a consequence, the same judge would sit, sometimes as the British Court and sometimes as the Zanzibar Court. This must at times have been distinctly confusing, but an effective safeguard against any mistake was provided in the Jurisdiction Decree, 1934, Section 5 of which enacted, in effect, that should the British Court inadvertently exercise jurisdiction in a case which properly belonged to the Zanzibar Court, the relevant judgment would not be liable to appeal or revision on that account.

Clearly, then, Zanzibar represents an outstanding example of the principle of 'indirect rule' exercised in such a way as to leave all

[33] Cf. my article 'The Impact of Islamic Law on Commonwealth Legal Systems'.

real authority in the hands of the colonial Power. And this is still more evident when we consider the law which the British and the Zanzibar courts administered, respectively. There were, it is true, certain differences; but the vast majority of the law applied by both systems of courts consisted in the Sultan's Decrees which, when countersigned by the British Resident, were binding on all and sundry—together with any legislation of the British Parliament which was applicable in Zanzibar. Thus the Penal Decree (taken together with two or three other Decrees) prescribed the whole of the criminal law, while the Criminal Procedure Decree, the Evidence Decree, the Rules of Court, the Civil Procedure Decree and Rules, and the Litigation Decree covered virtually all matters of procedure and evidence. It is significant, moreover, that section 2 of the Evidence Decree expressly prohibited the application of the Islamic law of evidence in any court in Zanzibar —a provision which seems a trifle anomalous in a legislative enactment which commences with the phrase 'In the name of God, the Compassionate and Merciful'. Section 7 of the Courts Decree, it is true, explicitly provided that 'in civil matters the Law of Islam is and is hereby declared to be the fundamental law of the Protectorate'; but this 'fundamental law' had in fact been ousted to a very great extent, even in civil matters, by a whole series of Decrees, while nothing whatever of the Islamic criminal law or law of evidence remained—except, perhaps, such shreds of the latter as were preserved under the Oaths Decree of 1917. But this does not mean that the Qāḍīs in Zanzibar did not, in fact, follow the basic rules of evidence and procedure laid down in the Sharīʿa, as a matter both of conscience and training; and in practice their judgments were quashed or varied on this account on appeal only where some miscarriage of justice or flagrant breach of the relevant statute law seemed to have resulted.

Again, the Contract Decree and the Transfer of Property Decree, both of 1917 and countersigned, largely covered matters of contract and commerce, although Section 1 (2) of the former provided that 'nothing herein contained shall effect . . . any usage or custom of trade, nor any incident of any contract, not inconsistent with the provisions of this Decree', while Sections 2 and 116 of the latter enacted that nothing in certain specified parts of the Decree 'shall be deemed to affect any rule of Hindu, Muhammadan or Buddhist law'. Even in theory, therefore, cases might still come before the courts regarding contracts made under the Sharīʿa, although such cases, except those in regard to gifts, seem to have been increasingly rare and unimportant. In addition, cases properly covered by these Decrees were, no doubt, sometimes decided by the Qāḍīs without reference to the relevant legislation. But in general the application of 'the law of Islam' seems largely to have been limited, before Independence, to actions in tort before the Zanzibar Court and to questions of family law, succession, gifts, *awqāf*[34] and certain cases concerning real property under the jurisdiction of both systems of courts—and it is significant that no reform of importance had been introduced in any of these matters, with the solitary exception of the Waqf Validating Decree, 1946. For the rest, the position in Zanzibar was that the application of Islamic law by the courts had been progressively excluded, rather than modernized and reformed.

The immediate effect of Independence on all this was, of course, the abolition of the British courts and the concentration of all jurisdiction in those of the Sultan. A unique feature of these, moreover, had been the fact that two Qāḍīs, one a Shāfiʿī and one an Ibāḍī, had sat in adjoining rooms and had each administered the law of his own school; but this, too, was brought to an end after the Revolution, when the Sultanate was abolished and most of those Ibāḍī Arabs who survived left the country. It is difficult to be sure what, precisely, the legal position is today; but it seems most unlikely that the application of Islamic law has been in any way extended.

It was largely (but by no means exclusively) from Zanzibar that Islam had, down the centuries, penetrated into the mainland

[34] The plural of *waqf*, which is the technical term for a pious or 'charitable' endowment in Islamic law—with an exceedingly wide meaning given to the concept of what is charitable.

of East Africa. As a result, Islamic law is applied, to a very considerable extent, in the coastal parts of what was formerly Tanganyika Territory, and also in a few inland centres; in the 'Protectorate', or coastal area, of Kenya; and even, to a very limited extent, in Uganda. But in all these countries it is found in close juxtaposition with the indigenous customary law—although it is interesting to observe that whereas, in West Africa, Islamic and customary law have largely fused into a single system, in East Africa they remain predominantly separate and distinct. There is also a whole series of legislative enactments—instances of which can be found in almost all those countries in both East and West Africa previously under British rule—which are either specifically applicable to Asiatic Muslim immigrants or also, in some circumstances, to indigenous Muslims as well, in regard to marriage, divorce, succession or even, in East Africa, *waqf* endowments.[35]

9. CONCLUSION

Such, then, is the general background to those reforms in the law which have swept through the greater part of the Muslim world in recent years and which form the subject of this book. In most Muslim countries which had retained their independence, and in almost all those countries under colonial rule[36] in which Muslims constitute a majority, or a significant minority, of the population, the political, economic and ideological stresses of modern life were exerting an ever-increasing pressure on the age-old rigidity of the Sharīʿa, as traditionally interpreted and applied. The precise position previously occupied by the canon law of Islam differed considerably from one country to another, as did the nature of the

[35] For a detailed study, in this context, of the law in Zanzibar, Tanganyika, Kenya and Uganda—and, indeed, in the former Nyasaland and the Commonwealth countries in West Africa—reference may be made to my *Islamic Law in Africa*. Cf. my article on 'Customary Law and Islamic Law in British African Territories'.

[36] The examples of such countries given in this chapter are all taken from those previously under British rule, since these are known to me personally. In countries previously under French rule the same problems occurred, but the solution, though somewhat similar, was (generally speaking) more uniform.

Government and the detailed form of the action that was taken. Yet the general pattern of the reforms with which we are primarily concerned manifests a singular uniformity, for almost everywhere they took two main forms: first, that the Sharīʿa was more and more widely displaced in practice—in such matters as commercial law, criminal law, and much else—in favour of codes of largely alien origin, applied by a system of secular courts; and, secondly, that even in the sacred sphere of family law (administered as this still was, in most of the countries concerned, in specifically Sharīʿa courts) a number of most significant changes were made in the way in which it was interpreted and applied. In our next chapter, therefore, we must consider the rationale which underlay each of these two main ways in which law reform was effected, and the philosophy and precise methods of the reformers.

CHAPTER II

The Philosophy and Methods of Reform

I. COMMERCIAL AND CRIMINAL LAW

BRIEF references have already been made, in the course of our consideration of the pressures which gave rise to those reforms in the law and its administration which have swept through most of the Muslim world in recent years, to two fundamentally different forms which this movement has almost everywhere taken, and to the chronological sequence in which—initially at least—this dual phenomenon has occurred. In the Ottoman Empire, for example, the first stage—after a few tentative attempts to combine the old and the new in a somewhat uneasy union—was to put the Sharīʿa almost completely on one side in the sphere of commercial and criminal law, from about the middle of the nineteenth century, in favour of legislation of a basically alien inspiration. And what happened in the Ottoman Empire also happened, as we have seen, in a number of other predominantly Muslim countries, whether independent or under 'colonial' rule, in which the Sharīʿa had previously been widely applied. Much the same is broadly true, although to a lesser degree, of the law of contract and tort; although here an attempt was made, in some of the countries concerned, to retain—whether in whole or in part—principles derived from the Sharīʿa but embodied in a codified law which was imposed by the executive or enacted by the legislature.[1] It was only into the sphere of family law, in the widest connotation of

[1] In addition to the Majalla, in the Ottoman Empire, and the Egyptian Civil Code (cf. pp. 18–19 above), part of the 'Code Santillana' was enacted in Tunisia as the Tunisian Code of Obligations and Contracts. And in Algeria a Draft Code of Algerian Muslim Law (the 'Code Morand') was published in 1916, had much influence, but was never in fact enacted.

that term, that the reformers did not venture to intrude until a considerably later date. As a result, a clear-cut dichotomy emerged not only in the law but also, in most of the countries concerned, in the courts which applied it. On the one side there was statute law, in the form of codes of largely secular origin, applied by a new set of 'national' courts in which lawyers, trained in modern law schools, followed contemporary principles of evidence and procedure; and on the other side the family law of Islam, uncodified and unchanged, administered by courts of the classical pattern in which lawyers, trained in the traditional way, applied the time-honoured system of evidence and procedure.

Now at first sight, as has already been remarked, it might seem the most radical expedient possible, in a Muslim country, virtually to eliminate—from *any* sphere of life—a law regarded by all Muslims as having divine authority. Such action might be natural enough, however hazardous, in the case of a colonial regime, but almost beyond belief in the case of an independent Muslim government such as that of the Ottoman Empire. However great the pressure for modernization and reform may have been, could not the necessary changes have been effected, it may be asked, in some way less alien to Ottoman sentiment and less offensive to Muslim orthodoxy? But the fact is that this was not, apparently, the way in which Muslims themselves thought in the middle of the last century. At that time it seemed to them preferable to keep the Sharīʿa intact and inviolable (as the perfect law which had at one time, they believed, held absolute sway and which would no doubt come into its own again in the golden age which would eventually dawn), even if this meant excluding vast sections of it from the hurly-burly of everyday life in favour of legislation of wholly different origins—forced upon them, as they felt, by the exigencies of the modern world—rather than to submit the sacred law to any profane meddling with its immutable provisions. In other words it was better to keep it in its pristine purity, as the eternal law which challenged the consciences of all Muslims, even if this meant putting it (as it were) under a glass case, for reverent contemplation rather than practical application. This seems, no doubt, very strange to the Western mind; but it must again be remembered that, to a Muslim, it has always been a far more heinous sin to deny or question the divine revelation than to fail to obey it. So it seemed preferable to continue to pay lip-service to an inviolate Sharīʿa, as the only law of fundamental authority, and to excuse a departure from much of it in practice by appealing to the doctrine of necessity (*ḍarūra*), rather than to make any attempt to adapt that law to the circumstances and needs of contemporary life.

It must be realized, moreover, that this was not quite so unprecedented a step as might at first sight appear to be the case. We saw in the last chapter that, from a very early date in the history of Islam, other courts had been set up alongside those of the *qāḍīs*—courts of provincial governors, police, inspectors of markets and, above all, the Caliph's 'Court of Complaints'—to administer a law which departed, in many respects, from the pure Sharīʿa, and made concessions to the exigencies of daily life either in the form of compromises with the customary law of the markets or the administrative orders of the executive. It might well be argued, then, that this first stage in the great movement for reform which started around the middle of the last century—in the Ottoman Empire, in India, and elsewhere—represented no more than a further development of a principle which had been operative for centuries. In a sense this would be true; but in another sense it must be recognized that the reformers did in fact inaugurate a new departure.

For, however true it may be that other courts had in practice existed for centuries alongside the specifically Sharīʿa courts, yet the fact remains that these other courts were always regarded as in some sense exceptional. It was the Sharīʿa courts alone which were recognized as the normal, regular courts—the courts of basic, residual jurisdiction. And precisely the same principle applied, even more strongly, to the law which these courts applied; for concessions to customary law and administrative regulations were regarded as necessary, indeed, yet of somewhat questionable authority. The Sharīʿa was the only basic, written law; the only law to which lip-service, at least, was always paid; and the only law accepted as having universal validity. With the advent of this first stage in the reform movement, however, all this was changed; for now it was the national courts which came to be regarded, in the Ottoman Empire and elsewhere, as the basic courts of general or residual jurisdiction, and the Sharīʿa courts which were accorded a special, and clearly defined, competence. Again, no one could deny that the new codes represented a written law of over-riding authority, however deeply the Sharīʿa remained enshrined in the hearts of loyal Muslims and was still applied in those matters of family law and inheritance which touched their lives most closely.

It must, of course, be recognized that the Islamic criminal law, in particular, had in some degree left the door open to reform. As we have seen, it included a limited number of offences (five or six, according to the doctrine of different schools of law) for which certain very severe penalties were regarded as divinely prescribed; but the standard of proof which was required before these penalties became incumbent, or even permissible, was so stringent that they could very seldom be lawfully imposed. In default of this standard of proof, or where there was some factor which mitigated the offence, it was for the judge to decide whether a discretionary penalty of some sort was to be exacted; and those duly convicted of any other wrong-doing, whatever it might be, were similarly subject to a discretionary sanction. But this clearly left almost the whole criminal law to the arbitrary decision of individual judges—a fact which might be thought to make it highly desirable for a tariff of suitable penalties to be introduced (or, in other words, a penal code which prescribed maximum, and perhaps minimum, sentences for specific offences). In criminal law, therefore, the real problem for the orthodox Muslim was not so much practical as theoretical: namely, whether it could ever be right to exclude the divinely prescribed penalties—barbarous though such punishments as stoning and mutilation had come to be considered in the modern world—in those very rare cases in which the circumstances were such that their applicability could not be denied.

But however easy it was, comparatively speaking, to introduce a criminal code, and however possible it was, in commercial law, to point to the innovations of modern life—and, indeed, to the age-old customs of Muslim merchants—it remains true that a fundamental change of attitude was inescapably inherent even in this stage of the reform movement. As we have seen, the orthodox position was that the Sharīʿa provided the blueprint to which society and all its members were bound always to attempt to approximate; that this blueprint had been divinely given and had an inherent authority of its own; and that the only scope for human legislation was in that intermediate category of behaviour left legally indifferent by the divine Lawgiver. It was God himself and his law which were sovereign, not the Government or people; and even a code of law such as the Majalla, the provisions of which were derived from the Sharīʿa, should not properly be promulgated by the authority of a human executive or legislature, for it was essentially inappropriate for man to determine or decree what parts of the divine law were to be enforced by the courts, and in what circumstances.

2. FAMILY LAW

But no such reforms were regarded as appropriate, at this time at least, to the family law of Islam. For, however true it may be that the whole of the Sharīʿa is regarded as based on divine revelation, this is particularly true, as we have seen, of all that pertains to family relations. It was in this sphere that the provisions of the Qur'ān itself were most explicit and abundant; that the practice of the courts had always been most meticulous; and that the connection between law and doctrine, between daily life and the very structure of Islam itself, was most clearly perceived. As a consequence, Muslim governments have never been willing—except only in Turkey since Ataturk and in Albania under Communist rule—to put the Sharīʿa on one side in this sphere in favour of a law of alien origin and inspiration. On the contrary, Muslims in general feel strongly that their family law must somehow remain essentially Islamic.

This was why it was not until 1915 that any attempt whatever was made, in the Ottoman Empire, to reform the family law. Yet the need for some changes, at least in the way in which that law was administered, became more and more apparent; and this time the pressure came from below, from the needs of society, rather than from above, from administrative convenience and national interest. So now the reformers were faced, fairly and squarely, with the problem of whether the Sharīʿa, as interpreted and applied by the courts, could itself be reformed—and how this could conceivably be done. Clearly, this presented them with an agonizing problem, and it is fascinating to see how they found at least a partial solution.

In point of fact it was the unhappy lot of certain Muslim wives under the dominant doctrine of the Ḥanafī school which, as we have seen, sparked off the initial reform; for it had become distressingly common for Muslims from all parts of the Islamic world to visit Istanbul, marry local wives, live with them for the duration of their visit, and then return home without so much as troubling to divorce them. The result was that the women concerned were left stranded: unable to obtain support, companionship or any other benefit from their husbands, yet precluded from any hope of judicial release from the bonds of these profitless marriages, or the possibility of marrying anyone else. This was an intolerable situation. Somewhat similarly, a woman was sometimes contracted in marriage to a man who, unknown to her, was afflicted with some disease of body or mind which made married life positively dangerous; but here, again, she could obtain no relief. Yet solutions to both these problems lay close at hand in some of the other schools of Sunnī law; for in the first case both the Ḥanbalī and Mālikī doctrine provided for a judicial dissolution of the marriage, and in the second even a variant view in the Ḥanafī school—to say nothing of the other Sunnī schools—did the same. So in 1915 the Ottoman Sultan issued two imperial decrees providing for the courts to act accordingly. Once the dike had been breached, moreover, the tide came in very fast indeed, and in 1917 the Ottoman Law of Family Rights was promulgated. This represented a fairly comprehensive code of the law of marriage and divorce (but not testate and intestate succession) which even included sections applicable to non-Muslims. In the event it remained in force only for some two years in the Ottoman Empire, where it was repealed in 1919; but it continued to be applied for many years in Syria and Jordan, and still governs the family relations of Sunnīs in the Lebanon and also—except in so far as it has been abrogated by parts of the 'Fundamental Law'—of Muslims in Israel.

Next, it was Egyptian jurists who took over the vanguard of reform—although it is noteworthy that it was the 'Grand Qāḍī' of the Sudan, at that time an Egyptian jurist, who on occasion tried out, as it were, in the Sudan reforms which had not yet been introduced in Egypt. The earliest Egyptian legislation in the field of family relations, Laws No. 25 of 1920 and 1929 respectively, were much more piecemeal, although considerably more radical, than the Ottoman Law of 1917; and there was also a significant development in Egypt in 1923, to which reference must be made later.[2] It was not until 1943 that any attempt at codification was made, in the 'Law of Inheritance'; and this was followed in 1946 by the 'Law of Testamentary Dispositions' and a rather less comprehensive piece of legislation, rushed through somewhat earlier in the same year, entitled the 'Law of Provisions of the Waqf'.[3]

These reforms all represent legislation promulgated by an executive or legislature which was predominantly Muslim. But it is interesting to note that the problem inherent in a non-Muslim government introducing reforms in the sphere of Islamic law was neatly solved, in the Sudan, by Article 8 of the Sudan Muhammadan Law Courts Organization and Procedure Regu-

[2] For these Egyptian reforms, together with the Ottoman Law, cf. my articles 'Recent Developments in Sharīʿa Law' (I–V), in successive numbers of *The Muslim World* (Oct. 1950–Oct. 1951 inclusive).

[3] For these three Laws, cf. my articles 'Recent Developments in Sharīʿa Law' (VI, VII and IX, respectively), in *The Muslim World* (Jan., April and Oct. 1952).

lations, 1915, which provided that the Sharīʿa Courts should always apply the dominant doctrine of the Ḥanafī school except in those matters in regard to which the Grand Qāḍī (himself, of course, always a Muslim) had issued a Judicial Circular[4] specifying an alternative doctrine, advocated by some reputable Muslim jurist of the past, which was to be applied in its place. In all, more than fifty such circulars have been issued—some of them of little importance, but others introducing reforms of great significance.[5]

Next, in 1951, the Jordanian Law of Family Rights was promulgated, to replace the Ottoman Law which had previously been applied in Jordan.[6] This was followed in 1953 by the Syrian Law of Personal Status, which for the first time included both family relations and succession (testate and intestate) in a single enactment. Whereas, moreover, the Jordanian Law included most of the more radical Egyptian reforms, the Syrian Law went still further.[7] But the most radical piece of legislation of this type hitherto introduced in any Arab country is the Tunisian Law of Personal Status (promulgated in 1956, and brought into effect at the beginning of 1957, with an important addition in 1959).[8] Meanwhile, the Moroccan Code of Personal Status, 1958, appeared in successive stages,[9] to be followed by the Iraqī Law of Personal Status, 1959 (with an important amendment in 1963). This last enactment is noteworthy, *inter alia*, for its combination of Sunnī and Shīʿī principles in a series of provisions, some of which are common to both communities, while others are made up of two

[4] With the consent of the (British) Governor-General.

[5] Cf. my articles 'Recent Developments in Sharīʿa Law in the Sudan', in *Sudan Notes and Records*, Vol. XXXI, Part I (1950), and 'The Modernization of Islamic Law in the Sudan', in *The Sudan Journal and Reports* (University of Khartoum, 1960).

[6] For details, cf. my article 'Recent Developments in the Sharīʿa Law' (VIII), in *The Muslim World* (July, 1952).

[7] Cf. my article 'The Syrian Law of Personal Status', in *The Bulletin of the School of Oriental & African Studies* (1955).

[8] Cf. my articles 'The Tunisian Law of Personal Status', and 'Recent Reforms in the Islamic Law of Inheritance', in *The International and Comparative Law Quarterly* (April 1958 and April 1965, respectively).

[9] For the earlier parts of this Code, cf. my article 'Reforms in Family Law in Morocco', in *Journal of African Law*, Vol. 2, No. 3 (1958).

separate parts, one applicable to Sunnīs and the other to Shīʿīs.[10] The next major reform in regard to family law was the Muslim Family Law Ordinance of 1961 in Pakistan[11]—although it is noteworthy that minor reforms had been introduced previously in what were then the Eastern and Western Aden Protectorates. Comprehensive codes have also been prepared in Egypt (one of them specifically designed as a common code for both Egypt and Syria at a time when the United Arab Republic was more than a name); but these have not yet been promulgated, and their future remains uncertain. Meanwhile, a very interesting—and, in part, exceedingly radical—reform has been effected in Iran by the Family Protection Act, 1967.[12] In addition, minor but significant reforms have also been introduced in Singapore and, to a lesser extent, in some of the Malay States.[13] More recently still, a uniform Law of Marriage Act has been promulgated in Tanzania in 1971, a radical Family Law in South Yemen in 1974, and a somewhat similar Law of the same name in Somalia this year (1975).

3. THE METHODS OF REFORM

But it is time to examine in some detail the methods adopted by the reformers in this second stage of their work. In the first stage, it will be remembered, they virtually refused to interfere in any way with the Sharīʿa itself. Instead, for the most part, they simply put it on one side in favour of legislation of quite different origin. It was only when they found themselves face to face with the need

[10] Cf. my articles 'A Law of Personal Status for Iraq' and 'Changes in the Law of Personal Status in Iraq', in *The International and Comparative Law Quarterly* (Oct. 1960 and July 1963, respectively).

[11] For details, cf. N. J. Coulson, 'Reform of Family Law in Pakistan', in *Studia Islamica*, Vol. vii (1956).

[12] Cf. my article 'Reforms in Islamic Law in Iran', in *Iqbal Review*, Vol. 12, No. 3 (Oct. 1971).

[13] By the Muslims Ordinance, 1957 (now replaced by the Administration of Muslim Law Act, 1968), in Singapore and by a series of enactments in the different States. Cf. Ahmad Ibrahim, 'The Status of Muslim Women in Family Law in Malaysia and Brunei', in *Malaya Law Review* (Dec. 1963, July 1964 and Dec. 1964).

to effect changes in that part of the law in which they felt that the Sharīʿa must, of necessity, be retained that they were confronted by the acute problem of how reforms could possibly be made in the sacred law itself—or, as Muslims would say, in the sacred law as this was applied by the courts. So it is fascinating to observe the methods they used;[14] the legal arguments they adduced to support them; and the circumstances in which one or another of them was employed. Yet the first two expedients were not, in fact, wholly new, for they had already been used, to some extent, in the earlier stage of reform. We must begin, therefore, by discussing these in more detail, and seeing how they were extended and applied in the much more difficult task to which the reformers had now set their hands.

(*a*) *The procedural expedient*

Underlying all the reforms we have outlined in such matters as commercial and criminal law, and particularly in the establishment of a system of courts to administer the new codes, was a principle known in Arabic as *takhṣīṣ al-qaḍā'*, or the right of the Ruler to define and confine the jurisdiction of his courts. This had always been known to some extent in Islam. It had been recognized in a geographical sense, in that an individual judge was given jurisdiction only over a prescribed area. It had been recognized in a chronological sense, in that a judge might be appointed only for a prescribed period. And it had also, in some degree, been recognized in regard to the type of litigation with which a particular court was authorized to deal. With the advent of the reform movement, however, this principle was given a far wider and more significant application; for it was fundamental to the new system that the Sharīʿa courts, for example, were to be restricted to questions of family law, inheritance, gifts and *awqāf*, and that the new secular codes were to be administered by courts staffed by personnel trained in a very different way.

[14] A procedural and an eclectic expedient, and the expedients of re-interpretation and administrative orders—together, in India, with reform by judicial decision.

But this same principle could also be applied, and was in fact applied, as a means of introducing reforms in the way in which the family law was to be applied even by the Sharīʿa courts, although now the principle was given a new, and still more controversial, application. This had, moreover, obvious attractions for all concerned; for instead of venturing to change the substance of the divine law, the reformers could, in this way, achieve their object by the purely procedural device of forbidding the courts to apply that law in specified circumstances. But the controversial element in this new application of the principle was that, in this case, it was not merely a question of deciding whether litigation on some particular subject should go to this court or that, but of giving instructions that no judicial relief whatever should be available, in any court, for certain specified claims. This was naturally denounced by some as a denial of justice; but those who supported this method of reform replied that there was an essential difference between denying a theoretical right, on the one hand, and precluding the enforcement of that right through the machinery of the State courts, on the other. As in almost all these reforms, moreover, the principle was at first applied in a way which was only mildly controversial and then given a more extended application—as a few examples will demonstrate.

Under the Sharīʿa as traditionally applied the primary means of proof was always the oral testimony of eligible witnesses. Their eligibility, moreover, was determined by means of the positive test of *taʿdīl* (that is, testimony to, or evidence of, the fact that they were pious and consistent Muslims) and the absence, or failure, of the negative test of *tajrīḥ* (that is, testimony to some factor which would make their testimony unacceptable). Provided the requisite number of eligible witnesses testified to some relevant fact, the court *must* decide accordingly—however doubtful the judge might be, in some cases, as to whether this testimony was trustworthy. But such a system was clearly liable to abuse, particularly in an age when the number of people prepared to give false testimony had—allegedly, at least—greatly increased, and when the mobility of modern life meant that it was much more difficult for a court to know, or ascertain, the characters of those who presented themselves as witnesses.

One example of the sort of case in which this problem was likely to arise in the Sharīʿa courts (for it was only in them that the specifically Islamic rules of evidence and procedure were still applied) was when someone claimed that a deceased person had made an oral bequest in his favour; for, provided he could produce two 'eligible' witnesses who would support his claim with their testimony, no denial by the heirs of the alleged testator would have any effect. But in such cases a possible method of reform was readily available. It was quite unnecessary to introduce any basic change in the principles of the divine law, or even to deny the theoretical possibility that such a claim might be valid; all that was needed was to prescribe that no claim to a bequest which was denied by the heirs should be upheld by the courts unless the plaintiff could produce documentary evidence—or, in some cases, even notarial evidence—to support it.[15] In point of fact, this expedient had been used long before the period in which reforms in family law became common, for the Egyptian Code of Organization and Procedure for Sharīʿa Courts, 1897, had provided, in Article 31, that 'no claim of marriage, divorce or acknowledgement thereof shall be heard after the death of either party unless it is supported by documents free from suspicion of forgery which indicate the truth of the claim'; and in the Code of 1909–1910, as amended in 1931, Article 101 dealt with this matter in considerably more detail by providing that 'No disputed claim of marriage, divorce or acknowledgement thereof shall be heard after the death of either party in respect of events previous to 1911, whether brought by one of the spouses or by some third party, unless it is supported by documents free from suspicion of forgery which indicate its truth. Provided that it is allowable to hear a claim of marriage or acknowledgement thereof brought by one of the parties, in respect of events previous to 1897 only, on the basis of oral testimony, on condition that the marriage was

[15] Cf. Article 2 of the Egyptian Law of Testamentary Dispositions, 1946, and my article on this subject mentioned above.

known by general repute. But none of the foregoing claims shall be heard, whether brought by one of the spouses or by a third party, in respect of events subsequent to 1911, unless it is established by official documents or ones wholly written in the handwriting of the deceased and bearing his signature '. This provides an example of how this expedient was applied in Egypt with increasing rigour with the passage of the years.

But this same expedient of precluding the courts from entertaining certain claims (known in Arabic as the principle of *ʿadam samāʿ*) could easily be extended to facilitate other reforms. It was used in Egypt, for example, in order to restrict the contraction of child marriages; for the Egyptian reformers hesitated, in view of the fact that the Prophet of Islam had himself married one of his wives at an exceedingly tender age, to go so far as to declare child marriage either illegal or invalid. Instead, legislation introduced in 1931 precluded the courts from entertaining any claim of marriage whatever (except only by command of the King) if the husband had not reached the age of eighteen, and the bride sixteen, at the time of litigation, or from hearing any *disputed* claim of marriage unless the contract had been registered—and by a reform promulgated in 1923 it had been made a criminal offence for a registrar of marriage to register any union in which the parties had not in fact reached these ages. As a result, the contraction of child marriages was strongly discouraged, since the father of a child bride knew that it would be impossible to bring any matrimonial suit whatever[16] in respect of such a marriage, if it were subsequently denied or disputed by the husband, unless it had been registered; and he could secure its premature registration only by some such device as getting a doctor to certify that his daughter was not less than sixteen years of age.

Another example of how this expedient was used by the reformers can be found in regard to claims for maintenance brought by divorced wives and claims of paternity (involving, not infrequently, a right to inherit) brought by a child born to a widow or divorcee. Under the Ḥanafī law a divorced woman was

[16] Except only a claim of paternity on behalf of a child of the union.

entitled to maintenance for the duration of her *ʿidda* (a period, subsequent to divorce, during which she was precluded from re-marriage); and this lasted, in the case of a woman who had reached puberty but not the menopause, until she had completed three menstrual periods; so divorced wives not infrequently made fraudulent claims that their *ʿidda* had not yet ended. Again, the Ḥanafī law prescribed two lunar years as the maximum period of gestation; so a child born to a widow or divorcee[17] not more than two years after her widowhood or divorce was accepted as the legitimate son of her former husband. In the Shāfiʿī law, indeed, the maximum period of gestation was fixed at four years, and in the Mālikī law at five.[18] So the Egyptian reformers solved both these problems by this same expedient—namely, by precluding the courts from hearing any claim to maintenance by a divorced wife in regard to any period longer than a solar year after her divorce, or any claim to paternity brought by a child born more than a solar year after his mother had been widowed or divorced—or, indeed, after her husband had left her.

It should be noted in this context, however, that in a number of other Muslim countries marriage before the bride and bride-groom have reached certain prescribed ages (which differ widely from one country to another) has been directly forbidden under penal sanction, and the maximum period of gestation has, somewhat similarly, been directly prescribed—without any recourse to this procedural device of merely precluding the courts from entertaining litigation in such cases.

(b) *The eclectic expedient*

Another expedient—this time of fundamental importance—was first put to systematic use in the compilation of the Majalla (the Ottoman Law of Obligations, which was completed in 1876). This code, as we have seen, was made up of principles which were derived from the Ḥanafī law but which, unlike the Code of Qadrī Pasha in Egypt, were not always based on the dominant

[17] Unless she had remarried not less than six months before the child was born.
[18] In the majority view.

opinion in that school. Instead, a selection was made of any Ḥanafī opinions, or opinions which had ever been advocated by a Ḥanafī jurist, which seemed most suited and appropriate to the contemporary world. And this same eclectic principle (known in Arabic as *takhayyur*), progressively expanded in its scope, has proved the major expedient in legislation introduced, in one Muslim country after another, to effect reforms in family law.

In the Ottoman Law of Family Rights, for example, the principle adopted was a little wider than in the Majalla, in that a selection was made, in section after section, from different opinions in the Ḥanafī school (whether previously regarded as stronger or weaker), on the one hand, or from the dominant doctrine of any other Sunnī school, on the other. This was comparatively easy to defend; for although it is true that the freedom of choice enjoyed, in theory at least, by an individual Muslim in following the precepts of this school or that—either in general, or in some specific matter—was not normally enjoyed by the *qāḍī* or *muftī* in their public capacity (in which they were commonly regarded as bound to follow the dominant doctrine of their own school in every particular), yet there was authority, in both the Shāfiʿī and Ḥanafī schools, for the proposition that it was within the competence of the Ruler to instruct his judges to apply one particular doctrine, to the exclusion of all others, should the public interest so demand. This was the principle on which a series of Judicial Circulars have been issued in the Sudan, it will be remembered. It attracted, moreover, widespread support from the argument that modern Muslims should regard themselves as bound by the Sharīʿa alone rather than by one particular interpretation of it, so they may justly refuse to be restricted to the doctrine of any one school.

Two examples of the application of this principle have already been given in relation to the imperial decrees promulgated by the Ottoman Sultan in 1915. But the Ottoman Law of Family Rights includes many other instances of the same type of choice. Article 9 adopts the Shāfiʿī view, for example, when it prescribes that insane persons should not be given in marriage by their guardians except in case of need—and, even so, adds that this must be only with consent of court; Article 10 follows the doctrine of Muḥammad al-Shaybānī (which on this point represents a 'weaker' Ḥanafī view) in prescribing that marriage guardianship should be limited to agnates in their own right, in due order of priority; Article 36 chooses the Shāfiʿī opinion in requiring that words used for the declaration and acceptance of a marriage contract must always be ones which expressly refer to marriage as such; and Articles 45 and 47 make a selection between various Ḥanafī doctrines in regard to the rules applicable to 'equality in marriage' (*kafā'ā*) and the right of marriage guardians in this respect. It is also noteworthy that this Law even includes an attempt to restrict polygamy, for Article 38 provides that 'If a woman stipulates in her marriage contract that her husband shall not marry another wife and that, should he do so, then either she herself or this other wife will be divorced, the contract is valid and the stipulation recognized'.[19] This runs directly counter to the accepted doctrine of the Ḥanafīs, Mālikīs and Shāfiʿīs, who all held that the divine Lawgiver had prescribed the legal effects of a contract of marriage and that these were not subject to variation at the whim of the parties. Since, therefore, a Muslim is permitted to have as many as four wives at one and the same time, a stipulation to the contrary would be void, but a marriage concluded on that basis itself valid and binding. The Ḥanbalīs replied, however, that polygamy was indeed permitted to a Muslim, but was certainly not mandatory, so this licence could not be regarded as of the essence of marriage. If, therefore, a Muslim agreed to forgo this right, his stipulation to this effect would be valid on the basis of the principle that 'Muslims are bound by their stipulations'—and his wife would be entitled to claim a judicial divorce should he fail to keep it. But many other examples of the use of this somewhat conservative principle of selection could also be cited.

It is noteworthy, however, that even the Ottoman Law of Family Rights goes beyond this distinctly restricted range of selection when it provides that marriage guardians are *forbidden* to

[19] Cf. pp. 72, 79f., 115–17 etc. below.

conclude a contract of marriage on behalf of wards who have not reached the minimum age of puberty (twelve for a boy and nine for a girl), and that a boy between twelve and eighteen, and a girl between nine and seventeen, may get married only by leave of court (and also, in the case of a girl, with the consent of her guardian). Should a marriage be concluded in defiance of these Articles (Nos. 4, 5 and 6) it would be regarded as irregular (*fāsid*) rather than void (*bāṭil*), but those responsible would be liable to penal sanctions under Article 52 (together with an amendment to the Penal Code). These provisions largely represent the view of three early jurists (Ibn Shubruma, ʿUthmān al-Battī and Abū Bakr al-Aṣamm) that there is no justification for a guardian giving his ward in marriage before he or she has reached the minimum age of puberty (on the ground that there can be no benefit in such a union, so it represents a totally unnecessary restriction of the ward's liberty of choice). But it is significant that the Explanatory Memorandum issued with this Law supports the adoption of this view not only on juristic grounds but by an almost impassioned description of the evils—to husband, wife, children and society—of premature marriage, and by asking the pertinent question whether marriage is not to be accorded an importance at least equal to that of the attainment of financial competence. The requirement that those who are between the minimum and maximum ages of puberty may be married only by leave of court may, moreover, be regarded as an instance of the Ruler imposing a precautionary rule which is in tune both with this social consideration and with the doctrine of the jurists to whom reference has already been made. It should also be noted that Article 33 provides that an intended marriage must be publicized before the contract is concluded, and Article 37 that a contract of marriage must be arranged and registered by a Sharīʿa judge or his authorized deputy, who must actually be present on the occasion of its conclusion; and here the Explanatory Memorandum observes that it has always been meritorious to publicize marriages, and that it is clearly preferable to take precautions before they are concluded rather than to upset married life later, when a child may have been conceived. These provisions were, moreover, expanded in a Code of Administrative Procedure, issued together with the Law of Family Rights, which prescribes detailed regulations for the conclusion of marriage contracts.

When we turn to the Sudanese, the Egyptian and subsequent reforms, moreover, we find that the reformers progressively extended the scope of this principle of *takhayyur*. At first they continued to limit themselves to variant opinions in the Ḥanafī school or to the dominant doctrines of the other Sunnī schools—as in the earliest Judicial Circulars in the Sudan, Law No. 25 of 1920 in Egypt, and the Dissolution of Muslim Marriages Act, 1939, in British India.[20] But soon they extended their field of choice to *any* opinion put forward in one of the Sunnī schools; or even to doctrines advocated by early jurists at a time before the schools became crystallized, by one of the Sunnī schools which previously existed but have now become extinct, or by a later jurist of highly independent views—such as Ibn Taymiyya or Ibn al-Qayyim. Not only so, but on some occasions they ventured to adopt a doctrine which was really of Shīʿī origin, although they seldom, if ever, expressly acknowledged this in regard to legislation promulgated in a predominantly Sunnī country. In addition, they often resorted to an expedient known in Arabic as *talfīq* (literally, 'patching'), by combining part of the doctrine of one school or jurist with part of the doctrine of another school or jurist in a provision which would not have been approved, in its entirety, by any of the schools or jurists of the past, although each of its component parts could claim the most impeccable ancestry. But the term *talfīq* is not reserved exclusively, by any means, for

[20] Although it is noteworthy that this legislation approximates to, rather than accurately embodies, the mainly Mālikī authorities on which it is allegedly based. There is no doubt that it was from the Mālikī doctrine that the Indian reformers derived their major inspiration; but some of the provisions of this law represent considerable modifications of that doctrine, while the article which provides that 'renunciation of Islam by a married Muslim woman . . . shall not by itself operate to dissolve her marriage' is directly contrary to the accepted doctrine of all the schools.

such extreme examples, for it is applied by some critics to any legislative enactment which brings together provisions from a number of different sources—particularly when these provisions were originally based on juristic foundations, or lines of deduction, which were not only heterogeneous but even mutually contradictory. Examples of this can, indeed, be found in most of the codes and enactments with which we are now concerned; for the reformers appear to have made their selection on the sole criterion of which provision, from the vast field of possible alternatives available in the ancient texts, seemed in each case most fitted to the needs of modern life. Fortunately enough, the Prophet of Islam is alleged not only to have said that his community would never agree upon an error but also, on another occasion, that 'The differences of opinion in my community are a mercy from God'. But, however this may be, there can be no doubt that the reformers have exploited this particular mercy to the utmost, and have been happy to take their pick from the varied dicta and conclusions of the great jurists of the past, regardless of the mutual incompatibility of the reasoning on which these dicta were based or these conclusions reached. It might, indeed, be argued that this represents an extreme application of the doctrine of *taqlīd*—that is, that it is not for modern jurists to reason for themselves, but to accept the conclusions of the great masters of the past without any indulgence in independent deduction—were it not that the reformers later had recourse to the directly opposite principle of a new use of the faculty of *ijtihād*. But the fact is that the more extreme examples of *talfīq* represent an intermediate stage in which the naked truth of a contemporary exercise of *ijtihād* is still obscured from view behind the somewhat diaphanous covering of a threadbare *taqlīd*.

A few comparatively random examples of this wider use of the expedient of *takhayyur* must suffice. In the Egyptian Law No. 25 of 1929, for instance, very considerable progress was made in restricting the unconscionable scope previously accorded to formulae of repudiation of their wives pronounced by Muslim husbands. Now it is true that support can readily be found in the dominant doctrine of one or other of the Sunnī schools for the provision that a divorce formula uttered under compulsion or in a state of intoxication should be regarded as invalid (Article 1); that ambiguous expressions, which might or might not imply divorce, should only have the effect which the speaker actually intended (Article 4); and that every divorce is to be regarded as revocable with the exception of a third pronouncement of repudiation, one effected before the marriage concerned has been consummated, one concluded by agreement of the parties for a financial consideration, or one expressly declared by legislation to be final (Article 5). But the same cannot be said for the provision that a pronouncement of 'suspended' or conditional divorce is inoperative if intended only as an inducement that some specific act should be done or should not be done (Article 2)—a wording designed to cover not only its use as a threat to a wife, or as an inducement either to her or to some third party, but also its use as an oath ('by the triple divorce') to reinforce some assertion or promise made by the husband. Such formulae, in other words, are to be regarded as effective only if the husband really desires and intends that his wife should be divorced if the condition attached to the suspended or conditional divorce is fulfilled. Here the authorities cited to support the reform, in so far as the use of formulae of divorce as an actual oath is concerned, are 'certain (unspecified) jurists in all the four schools', the Ẓāhirīs (a now extinct school of law) and certain very early authorities; while, for the extension of this principle to its use as a 'quasi-oath' by way of threat or inducement, the authority is claimed of very early jurists such as ʿAlī, Shurayḥ, ʿAṭāʾ, al-Ḥakam ibn ʿUtayba, and the Ẓāhirīs. The provision that a pronouncement of divorce which is made double or triple by word or sign shall count only as a single, and therefore revocable, divorce (Article 3) is, however, even more radical, for this is contrary to *fatāwī* attributed to ʿUmar, ʿUthmān, ʿAlī, Ibn ʿUmar, Ibn Masʿūd, Ibn ʿAbbās and others accepted by all four schools. Indeed, this is a point in regard to which the authority of consensus (*ijmāʿ*) is frequently claimed. But the reform is supported not only by cogent arguments from the

Qur'ān but also by a statement attributed by Muslim to Ibn ʿAbbās (and also reported as from ʿAlī and Abū Musa'l-Ashʿarī) that a triple divorce pronounced in one sentence, or on a single occasion, was regarded as single and revocable in the time of the Prophet and that of Abū Bakr, and it was not until the Caliphate of ʿUmar that the latter decreed that henceforth it should be considered to be triple and irrevocable in order to discourage the growing frequency of its use. The views of Muḥammad ibn Isḥāq, Da'ūd al-Ẓāhirī, various doctors of Cordova, and later jurists such as Ibn Taymiyya and Ibn al-Qayyim, are also quoted in support of this reform.[21]

Examples of points in which the reformers have adopted a principle which is really of Shīʿī origin, but without any clear acknowledgement of this fact, can be found in the provision in Judicial Circular No. 53 in the Sudan and Article 37 in the Egyptian Law of Testamentary Dispositions, 1946, which declares that a testator's bequest to one of his heirs, provided this does not exceed the 'bequeathable third' of his net estate, is both valid and effective without this being in any way dependent on the consent of his other heirs—as is also true, under Article 13 of the Egyptian Law, of instructions in his will about how the various items in his estate are to be distributed between his heirs, provided only that the total pecuniary advantage this accords to some heirs over others does not exceed their proper entitlement by more than this same bequeathable third. This runs directly counter to what has been claimed to be a consensus of Sunnī jurists, based on their belief that the 'Verse of Bequests' in the Qur'ān (Sura 2:180) has been abrogated both by the 'Verses of Inheritance' (Sura 4:11 and 12) and by an alleged tradition which consists in (or includes) the terse phrase 'No bequest to an heir'—although this tradition has, in fact, far from convincing support and is amenable to more than one interpretation. But the reformers justified this bold innovation on three grounds: partly by the fact that some Sunnī

[21] For all these examples, see my article 'The Problem of Divorce in the Sharīʿa Law of Islam: Measures of Reform in Modern Egypt', in *Journal of the Royal Central Asian Society*, Vol. XXXVII, Part II (1950).

commentators had never agreed that the 'Verse of Bequests' had been completely abrogated; partly by an appeal to the views of 'other doctors' (as an euphemism for Shīʿī jurists); and partly by reference to the needs of society.[22] A somewhat similar example can be cited from the Syrian Law of Personal Status, 1953, where the provision in Article 129 (1) that a baby born to a married woman more than the minimum period of gestation after her marriage shall be regarded as the legitimate child of her husband 'unless non-access between the spouses can be clearly proved, as for instance if one of them is imprisoned or absent in a distant country for more than the period of gestation'. Here the Egyptian reformers resorted to the procedural expedient of forbidding the courts to entertain any claim to legitimacy put forward on behalf of a child born to a mother more than a year after her husband had been separated from her;[23] but the Syrians, in adopting this rule as a matter of substantive law, were giving effect to what was in fact the basic Shīʿī doctrine—although they combined this with an adoption of the Egyptian innovation of accepting a solar year as the maximum period of gestation. So this Syrian provision also represents an example of *talfīq*, or patching. There are also, of course, a number of examples of Shīʿī law explicitly made applicable to Sunnīs in the Iraqī Law of 1959; but that represents a somewhat special case, since more than half the population of Iraq are Shīʿīs, and the Law was specifically designed to introduce identical provisions for all Iraqīs where this seemed feasible. An outstandingly important instance of this can be found in the amendment to the Iraqī law which was made in 1963; for this repealed Article 74 of the Law of 1959 (which had, in effect, completely excluded the application of the Islamic law of inheritance, in *all* circumstances, in favour of a statutory enactment, of German inspiration, previously applicable only to rights of occupancy and use of Government-owned

[22] Cf. pp. 151–2 below, and my articles, mentioned above, in which both the Sudanese Circulars and the Egyptian Law are discussed in detail.

[23] Law No. 25 of 1929, Article 4. For this, and for the Syrian Law, cf. my articles mentioned above.

land), in favour of a provision which is fundamentally Shīʿī in origin, but with latitude for both Sunnīs and Shīʿīs to adopt their own approach in the detailed application of its basic provisions.[24]

When we turn to *talfīq* in the full meaning of that term, as the most extreme form of the expedient of *takhayyur*, we find that it came to be used more and more frequently after about 1940. In 1939, for example, Judicial Circular No. 49 in the Sudan had abandoned the dominant Ḥanafī doctrine, that the presence of a father's father will completely exclude any germane or consanguine brothers or sisters of the praepositus from a share in his inheritance, in favour of the variant Ḥanafī view, put forward by the 'Two Companions', Abū Yūsuf and Muḥammad al-Shaybānī (and also followed both by the Shāfiʿīs and, substantially, by the Mālikīs), that such brothers and sisters will not normally be totally excluded but will share with the father's father according to principles attributed to Zayd ibn Thābit. When, however, the Egyptian reformers came to tackle this same problem in the Law of Inheritance, they, too, decided that germane brothers and sisters ought not to be excluded in such cases, but provided that they should share in the inheritance with the father's father according to principles attributed, in the main, to ʿAlī ibn Abī Ṭālib, but combined with a preference, in one particular, for a doctrine attributed to Ibn Masʿūd—and this innovation was duly followed in the Sudan by Judicial Circular No. 51 of 1943.[25] Another instance of *talfīq* in the Egyptian Law can be found in the provisions of Article 6: 'There is no right of inheritance between a Muslim and a non-Muslim, but non-Muslims may inherit from each other. Difference of domicile is no bar to inheritance between Muslims; and it is also no bar between non-Muslims except where the law of the foreign state concerned forbids inheritance to foreigners'. This article represents a combination of the law common to all the Sunnī schools in regard to the bar to inheritance between Muslims and non-Muslims; the view of some jurists, as

[24] Cf. pp. 150–1 below, for a fuller discussion of this point.
[25] Cf. pp. 69f., 76, 152f. below, for a more detailed discussion.

against others, in not holding difference of religion between two non-Muslim relatives as any impediment to their mutual inheritance; and the doctrine of all Sunnīs, again, about the permissibility of mutual inheritance between Muslim relatives, whatever their domicile. But the more radical form of *talfīq* is involved in the rule applicable to non-Muslims who differ in domicile; for here most schools preclude rights of inheritance between one who is domiciled in a Muslim country and another who is domiciled in a non-Muslim country, because the latter is a potential enemy of the Muslim State, while the Mālikīs allow inheritance in such cases—and here the provision we are discussing adopts the Mālikī view where the law of the other country concerned would grant reciprocal treatment, but the doctrine of the other schools where it would not.

Two further examples must suffice. In the addendum added in 1959 to Article 143 of the Tunisian Law of 1956 the first paragraph provides that the doctrine of the 'return' to quota-sharers (where their shares do not exhaust the estate, and there are no agnates), which is accepted by almost all Sunnīs except the Mālikīs, should be introduced in Tunisia. But the remarkable point about this particular enactment is that none of these other schools puts the spouse-relict on a par with other quota-sharers in this respect, while the Tunisian enactment makes no such distinction.[26] The most obvious and radical resort to *talfīq* which can be cited, however, comes in the Egyptian Law of the Provisions of the Waqf, 1946 (which was followed, in several respects, by the Law of Family Waqfs, 1947, in the Lebanon). Here Article 1 provides that, for the future, 'the creation of a *waqf*, its revocation, any alteration in the application of its income or its conditions, or any exchange of its property by the founder, are alike invalid unless a declaration (*ishhād*) to that effect be made' before an appropriate court. This, in itself, represents an unequivocal administrative order;[27] and the element of *talfīq* consists (to quote the Explanatory Memorandum) in the fact that a *waqf* which 'lacks such *ishhād* . . . is regarded as invalid on the basis of the

[26] See pp. 71, 149, 151 below. [27] See pp. 163–4 below.

opinion of those early jurists who hold a *waqf* always invalid, while where the *ishhād* has been properly effected it is regarded as valid on the basis of the opinion of the generality of jurists. Again, an alteration in the application of its income or in its conditions is regarded as invalid, if not effected by means of such an *ishhād*, on the basis of the alternative Ḥanbalī opinion to the effect that the founder may not make such a change even if he stipulated the right to do so . . . , while if the suitable *ishhād* has been effected the alteration will be held valid on the basis of the law now applicable and similar provisions in other schools . . .' Article 5, moreover, introduces one of the major innovations of this Law when it decrees that 'A *waqf* of a mosque must be perpetual; a *waqf* in favour of some charity may be either temporary or perpetual, but if expressed in general terms shall be perpetual; while a *waqf* for any other purpose must be temporary and shall not extend to more than two series of beneficiaries . . . or sixty years after the death of the founder'. This represents a double form of *talfīq*. First, there is the combination of the doctrine of those jurists who allow a temporary *waqf* with that of the majority of jurists who regard any *waqf* as necessarily perpetual; and, secondly, there is the application of the view of the majority of jurists, who regard the *waqf* system as essentially valid, to a family *waqf* up till the time when the first two series of beneficiaries become extinct (or a period of sixty years comes to an end) after the death of the founder, coupled with the application of the view of a small minority of jurists, who do not recognize the validity of any *waqf* whatever, to that same *waqf*, or to any other family *waqf*, should the founder have made provision for it to last longer than the Law allows, or should the first two series of beneficiaries have become extinct, or sixty years have elapsed, since the founder's death.

(c) *The expedient of re-interpretation*

At times, however, even this distinctly artificial extension of the expedient of *takhayyur* was not readily available, and the reformers felt themselves compelled to resort openly to a new interpretation of the ancient texts—or, in other words, to a contemporary exercise of the right of independent deduction (*ijtihād*). It had, indeed, been widely argued, for a number of years, that it was wrong ever to have believed that the 'door of *ijtihād*' had been closed, for without this 'striving'[28] to apply the sacred law to the ever-changing circumstances of life it must inevitably become stagnant and moribund. Not only so, but modern Muslims were much better placed than their predecessors to exercise this faculty, since the opinions of early jurists were now much more easily accessible, through the printed page and world trade, than they were in the days of painfully copied manuscripts and tedious travel. It was only because these more *avant-garde* views were still challenged by the dead weight of traditional opinion—and particularly by a continual appeal to an allegedly authoritative *ijmāʿ*—that the reformers continued to resort, whenever possible, to what could still be represented as *taqlīd*, in however spurious a form.

But it was in regard to the vexed questions of divorce and polygamy that we find the outstanding examples of the reformers having recourse to a re-interpretation of the ancient texts. Considerable progress had, indeed, been made, by use of the expedient of *takhayyur*, in imposing certain limitations on the previously unrestricted scope of formulae of repudiation pronounced by a Muslim husband; but these had not, in fact, gone beyond an attempt to ensure that hasty and ill-considered words would not have the effect of bringing to a premature end a marriage which, on reflection, he might still wish to continue. Where, on the other hand, he was firm in his desire to repudiate his wife, there was nothing to deter him. But surely it was not beyond the wit of the reformers to devise some method of restraint?

One method of doing this could, in point of fact, be regarded as an example of *takhayyur* rather than neo-*ijtihād*. This consisted in legislation which gave the courts power to force a husband who repudiated his wife—particularly, of course, where he had no adequate justification, or where his action caused her particular

[28] This is the basic meaning of the term *ijtihād*.

hardship—to pay her a sum of money by way of financial compensation. This could be justified as representing what the ancient texts termed a *mutʿat al-ṭalāq*; for it was only the Ḥanafīs who interpreted this *mutʿa* as referring solely to a sort of substitute for dower due from a husband who divorced, before the marriage had been consummated, a wife whom he had married without naming any specified dower. The other Sunnī schools all understood this term as meaning a gift which a husband should always give a wife on repudiating her—unless, presumably, she had been seriously at fault; and the Mālikīs went so far as to regard this as a legal rather than a moral obligation, and to allow a wife to go to court to demand it. So legislation to this effect in Syria, Tunisia and Morocco—with certain comparatively minor differences—could certainly be regarded as a form of *takhayyur*. But this could scarcely be claimed in regard to legislation which provided that no formula of divorce would be effective if pronounced outside a court of law, and here a quite different justification was adduced. In the Qur'ān, the reformers argued, there is an explicit injunction that, should discord be feared between a husband and wife, two arbitrators should be appointed to attempt to reconcile them—a provision which had, in fact, already been utilized by the reformers where a wife demanded a judicial dissolution of her marriage because of cruelty on the part of her husband which she could not prove. In this case (as in Law No. 25 of 1929 in Egypt) the argument had turned on whether these arbitrators, or the court on their recommendation, could bring the marriage to an end, if reconciliation proved impossible, without being so authorized by the parties; and here the Mālikī, and a weaker Shāfiʿī, doctrine had been called in aid. But the new argument went further than this, and insisted that, in the very nature of things, some degree of discord must always precede divorce, yet in most cases no opportunity had been provided for arbitrators to be appointed and to attempt to salvage the marriage. The obvious solution, then, was to provide that no divorce would be effective except by consent of court, since this would give the court an opportunity to take appropriate action. Provisions to this effect were, in fact, included in the Tunisian Law of Personal Status, 1956, in the Iraqī Code of 1959 (although in this case with a proviso which largely robbed it of any real effect), in the Muslim Family Laws Ordinance, 1961, in Pakistan and in the Family Protection Act, 1967, in Iran. The Pakistani and Iranian reforms, moreover, included detailed provisions which go far beyond the scope of any ordinary exercise of *ijtihād* and fall, rather, under the heading of administrative instructions.[29] And in Singapore, again, provision has been made in the Administration of Muslim Law Act, 1968, that in default of agreement between the parties a divorce may be registered only by the Sharīʿa Court itself, where conciliation is always attempted.

It was in a somewhat similar fashion that the reformers addressed themselves to the problem of polygamy. This subject has been a matter of major concern in the reform movement since the turn of the century. It was in 1900 that an Egyptian writer, Qāsim Amīn, published a book entitled *Taḥrīr al-Marʾa* (The Liberation of Women), in which he upheld a high view of the marriage relationship, decried the evils of polygamy, and maintained that the Qurʾān in effect both allowed it and forbade it. Thus a man would be justified in marrying a second wife only in a few exceptional circumstances, such as where his first wife was an invalid or barren. Even so, polygamy was allowable in the sight of God (*diyānatan*) only where there was no fear of injustice, which could scarcely ever be the case. Like other permitted things, moreover, it could sometimes be classified as 'deprecated' (*makrūh*) or even 'forbidden' (*mamnuʿ*), according to circumstances, and in the contemporary world its evil influence on family life was obvious and almost invariable; so it was perfectly permissible for the Ruler, in the public interest, either to forbid it entirely or to subject it to conditions. As early as 1898, moreover, the same problem had been discussed in Egypt[30] by the most eminent of all the reformers, Muḥammad ʿAbduh, in a newspaper article. In the event, however, it was the Ottoman reformers who were the first to introduce any legislative reform in this matter. But, although they included a most moving passage in the

[29] Cf. pp. 65ff. below.

[30] Cf. pp. 101, 110ff. below.

Explanatory Memorandum which accompanied the Ottoman Law of Family Rights, 1917, about the evils inherent in polygamy, they in fact contented themselves with providing that a wife might validly stipulate in her marriage contract that, should her husband marry a co-wife, she could claim a judicial divorce[31]—and somewhat similar provisions have been included in many subsequent reforms.

It was, however, under the influence of Muḥammad ʿAbduh, although long after his death, that the Egyptian committee set up in 1926 to recommend reforms in the law of marriage and divorce included in its proposals not only an article to validate stipulations inserted by wives in their marriage contracts but also an article providing that a man who already had one wife should not be permitted to marry another woman without consent of court—which might withhold its consent unless it was satisfied that he was capable of treating two or more wives with equal justice and was in a financial position not only to support his existing dependants but to assume further obligations. The first of these conditions was based on the 'Verse of Polygamy' in the Qur'ān, which specifically forbids a man to marry a second wife if he has any fear that he may not be able to accord them equal treatment;[32] and the second on the interpretation given by Shāfiʿī himself to the last clause in that verse (namely, 'this would be better for you, that your children may not increase'). The innovation, therefore, was not so much in the principles invoked as in the proposal that they should be imposed by a human court rather than left to the conscience of the husband and the bar of eternity. In the event, however, these proposals were not included in Law No. 25 of 1929 because King Fu'ād refused to accept them—nor have they been promulgated in any subsequent Egyptian reform. But a

[31] Or even, in this Law only, that the other wife should be divorced. Cf. p. 49 above.

[32] It is only fair to observe, however, that the earlier jurists had argued, reasonably enough, that the Qur'ān must not lightly be regarded as contradicting itself; so the equal justice demanded by the 'Verse of Polygamy' must be interpreted in terms of those favours which a husband has power to control, and not the instinctive inclinations of his heart. Cf. Sūra 3: 128.

number of other countries have now decreed that a man may conclude a polygamous contract of marriage only with consent of court. In Syria it is the financial criterion, alone, which has been adopted; and this is a test which a court of law can apply without any great difficulty. In Iraq, on the other hand, the reformers were not content with this, but also introduced the criterion of any fear of unequal treatment (which compels the court to assume the uncongenial mantle of the prophet) and the further test of whether there is 'any lawful benefit' in the polygamous marriage (a provision which is presumably intended to cover cases in which the first wife is afflicted with sterility or sickness). But in 1956 President Bourguiba characteristically determined to go the whole way, and a provision was included in the Tunisian Law which prohibited polygamy altogether. He justified this, moreover, on two quite different grounds. The first (which I suspect was his real reason) was that there were certain institutions—such as slavery and polygamy—which made sense at an earlier stage in human development, but were offensive to the civilized conscience today. But he also gave the more conventional reason, which he knew would be much more acceptable to orthodox opinion, when he quoted the Verse of Polygamy to show that a man was expressly forbidden to marry more than one wife if there was any fear that he would not accord them equal treatment, and then observed that history had proved that no man other than a prophet was capable of such a feat.

The next development was in Morocco, where the reformers were considerably more cautious. First, they decreed that if a woman stipulated, at the time of her marriage, that she should be the only wife, this would give her a right to a judicial divorce if her husband then proceeded to contract a further marriage. This, as we have seen, is fully covered by the principle of *takhayyur*. Next, they included in the Code a general statement that, where any injustice was to be feared between co-wives, polygamy was not permitted; and they provided that, even where the first wife had not made any stipulation on this subject, she could still appeal to the court, should her husband marry another woman, to consider any injury which this might have caused her. But the first of these clauses is no more than a reiteration of the Qur'anic injunction, without any specific sanction if it goes unheeded, while the second represents normal Mālikī doctrine, which allows a judicial divorce for *ḍarar*, or injury, in such cases. A further clause was also included, however, providing that a marriage contracted with a second wife would not be valid at all if she had not been informed about the existence of the first marriage; and this seems to represent a mild form of *ijtihād*—based, presumably, on an extension of the principle of what might be termed tacit misrepresentation.

Reference has already been made to the Iraqī Law; but both here and in Tunisia a point of controversy arose as to whether a marriage contracted in defiance of statute law, and therefore subject to criminal sanctions, was—or was not—valid *per se*. In the Iraqī Law of 1959 marriage with a second wife, without consent of court, is expressly included in a list of invalid unions. But this aroused much fiercer opposition from orthodox circles than did the prohibition of polygamy under pain of legal sanctions; for they argued that it was one thing for the State to forbid the contraction of such marriages, in what it claimed to be the public interest, and to punish those who disobeyed the relevant statutory enactment, and quite another for anyone to deny that such a marriage, if actually concluded, was essentially valid under the Sharīʿa. So, as soon as a new regime came to power in Iraq, this last point was changed by Article 1 of Law No. 11 of 1963. In Tunisia, on the other hand, almost exactly the opposite situation has prevailed; for in the Law of Personal Status, 1956, polygamy was expressly forbidden, but the question of whether such a marriage, if concluded, would be valid or invalid was passed over in silence. As a result, there was a sharp division of opinion on the subject. In traditional circles it was argued that the Law included a list of invalid unions, but this made no mention of a marriage contracted in defiance of the prohibition of polygamy: by inference, therefore, such a marriage should clearly be regarded as valid. But official circles took the opposite view, on the ground that the Civil Code decreed that any contract which was contrary to public policy was null and void, and that the prohibition of polygamy in the Law of Personal Status was conclusive proof that a polygamous contract of marriage was contrary to the policy of the State. The reason why the invalidity of a polygamous union had been inferred, rather than explicitly spelt out, in that Law was in order not to arouse orthodox opposition. But, however this may be, the law has now been made plain by an enactment, in 1964, explicitly providing that any such contract of marriage is to be regarded as invalid *per se*.[33] Further details of legislation on this subject in each of the countries concerned, and also in Pakistan, Singapore and Iran, will be found in the next chapter.[34]

(d) *The expedient of administrative orders*

In one sense this is, of course, basic to all the preceding expedients. The procedural device, for example, can be brought into operation only by means of some law or regulation precluding the courts from entertaining litigation in specified circumstances. Reforms based on *takhayyur* or *ijtihād*, too, must necessarily be introduced by means of a legislative enactment or some form of executive decree. But there are also many examples of reforms being made in the substantive law, in so far as this is applied by the courts, by means of what may be termed administrative instructions or provisions, usually included in some legislative enactment, which find their justification not in the fact that they rest on any specific provisions in the Sharīʿa, however these may be interpreted or applied, but because the reforms concerned are regarded as beneficial and 'not contrary to the Sharīʿa'. This is explicitly spelt out, for instance, in the Explanatory Memorandum issued with the Syrian Law of Personal Status, 1953, where the sources from which its provisions were derived are listed as not only the Ottoman Law of Family Rights (as previously applied), certain Egyptian Laws (as suitably amended), Qadrī Pasha's Code, and a

[33] Cf. my chapter 'Modernization: Islamic Law', in *Northern Africa: Islam and Modernization* (ed. Michael Brett, Frank Cass, London, 1973), pp. 78 f.

[34] Cf. pp. 109 ff. below.

draft code put together by the Qāḍī of Damascus (Shaykh ʿAlī al-Ṭanṭāwī), but also 'such material as the Committee saw fit to adopt from some school other than that of the Ḥanafīs, and such regulations (*mawādd al-tanẓīm*), not contrary to the principles of the Sharīʿa, as it included'. It can even be argued that such provisions may be regarded as clothed with the authority of the Sharīʿa itself by reason of the injunctions in the Qur'ān that Muslims should obey their lawful leaders. A few examples of this expedient will illustrate the ways in which it has been used.

One of the first reforms to be introduced, in most parts of the Muslim world, was a new structure of courts. In both the Ottoman Empire and Egypt, for example, parallel systems of Mixed Courts for litigation in which foreigners were involved, Niẓāmiyya Courts (later renamed, in Egypt, Ahliyya Courts) to apply the new codes of statute law, and Sharīʿa Courts to administer the personal and family law of Muslim litigants, were all established. Not only so, but a special Code of Procedure for the Sharīʿa Courts, comprising no less than 190 Articles, was promulgated in Egypt as early as 1880; and this was followed by further codes in 1897, 1909/1910 and 1931. As a result, a whole system of Courts of First Instance, Courts of Appeal and a Court of Cassation has been set up, with the higher courts presided over by a bench of judges. Even in Saʿūdī Arabia—which has, in the main, held rigidly aloof from the whole movement of reform—commercial chambers or tribunals have been introduced; and the Sharīʿa courts, which still enjoy a comprehensive jurisdiction, have been so organized as to provide for appeals to be heard by a bench of judges. But no explicit authority can be found in the ancient texts for this beneficial reform.

In regard to evidence, moreover, Article 24 of the Egyptian Code of Procedure of 1897 states, in the most orthodox fashion, that 'Proof in the Sharīʿa is of three types: confession, testimony and refusal of oath'; but the next article explicitly provides that 'A confession in writing is the same as a confession by word of mouth'. Subsequent Articles extend this concession, and Article 27 summarizes the position in the words: 'The result is that documentary evidence is accepted provided it is free from suspicion of forgery or fabrication'. This may, indeed, be said to represent a return to the spirit (and letter) of the Qur'ān itself, where the reduction of contracts to writing is explicitly recommended; but it runs directly counter to the classical doctrine of the Sharī'a, where oral testimony was the basic rule, and documentary evidence was admitted only as essentially secondary evidence by means of a series of stratagems. Not only so, but the relative positions of oral testimony and documentary evidence have now been reversed, and in many cases the latter, alone, is accepted.

Again, the traditional system of examining the character of witnesses (*tazkiyya*) has today been abandoned in many countries, even in Sharī'a courts, in favour of the practice of putting them on oath and submitting their testimony to cross-examination;[35] but here there is some authority for the former in the Sharī'a, and the latter, too, was supported by Ibn al-Qayyim, in particular. Provision is also made in the later codes to ensure that the impugning of witnesses' characters (by the orthodox system of *tajrīḥ*) should be kept within strict limits. Under the traditional procedure, of course, it was normally the plaintiff alone who could (and must) call witnesses, after which it was open to the defendant only to impugn the character of these witnesses or to make some counter-claim in which he himself became the plaintiff; but now provisions are included in some modern Codes along the lines of Article 186 of the Egyptian Code of 1931, which expressly states: 'If one of the parties brings testimony to establish some point, the other party always has the right to prove that this is not true by every method of proof. All the rules of procedure regarding proof shall be followed with respect to the rights of both parties, without distinction.' It was in 1931, too, that the Egyptian

[35] This procedure was first introduced in Egypt by the Code of 1897, in which Articles 38 and 39 provide for the cross-examination of witnesses, and Article 40 for their being put on oath—but only at the request of the other party. It is noteworthy that the Lebanese Code provides for a Sunnī to put witnesses on oath as a matter of course, but for a Ja'farī *qāḍī* to do so only at his discretion (Article 89).

reformers, in Article 123, introduced the innovation of adding 'conclusive circumstantial evidence' to the three methods of proof which, alone, were previously accepted in Sharīʿa courts. And on this point the Lebanese Code is even more comprehensive, for Article 42 states that 'the methods of proof are what indicate and reveal the truth, namely oral and written confession, testimony, oath, circumstances, the report of experts and the investigations of the court', while the Syrian Code lists documentary evidence, oral testimony, circumstances, oath, inspection and expert knowledge. It also included, initially, the provision that 'The court shall assess the value of witnesses' testimony . . . and may accept the testimony of a single individual if it is convinced of its truth' (Article 62). But this innovation caused such an outcry among the orthodox, who were quite unwilling to accept Ibn al-Qayyim's interpretation of the relevant Qur'anic verses as representing the ideal to be aimed at rather than the minimum that a court might ever accept, that this clause was amended, in 1949, by Sharīʿa Order No. 88, which provides that in Sharīʿa courts 'the minimum testimony required by the Sharīʿa is a condition of judgment based on testimony, and the Qāḍī may not base his judgment on the testimony of a single witness except in the circumstances prescribed in the Sharīʿa'.

When we turn to the substantive provisions of family law, Article 145 of the Syrian Law of Personal Status provides that 'If a wife becomes disobedient and her children are more than five years old, the Qāḍī may place them with whichever of the spouses he sees fit, provided that he has regard to the welfare of the children in the light of the circumstances of the case'. Here the traditional law simply gives the husband the right to bring an action to enforce the 'obedience' (*ṭāʿa*) of his wife and her return to the marriage home; and the circumstances in which a wife who has become separated from her husband can claim the custody of the children of the marriage are precisely defined, and not left to the discretion of the court in terms of the welfare of the children.[36]

[36] So it is exceedingly doubtful if this beneficial reform can justly be described as 'not contrary to the Sharīʿa'.

Much the same attitude can be detected in Article 69, where the usual rule that a husband may not insist that any of his relatives, except a child under the age of discernment, should be accommodated in his wife's marriage home, is tempered by the addition of the words 'if it be established that they cause her any harm'. More significant still, a *qāḍī* in Syria not only has the right, as we have seen, to withhold permission for a man to contract a polygamous marriage, but Article 19 provides that 'If two betrothed persons are not suited to each other in regard to their ages, and there is no benefit in the proposed marriage, the Qāḍī may withhold his permission'; and a close parallel to this provision was included, two years earlier, in Article 6 of the Jordanian Law of Family Rights. But no direct authority for any such provision can be found in the classical texts, and the Explanatory Memorandum which accompanied the Syrian Law simply states: 'Seeing that a gross disparity between the ages of the spouses leads to a lack of stability in married life and to moral corruption, and the courts have become accustomed to withholding consent to such marriages, a provision has been included which permits the Qāḍī to refuse his consent thereto.'

Again, one of the major problems which have engaged the attention of the reformers is that of orphaned grandchildren who are totally excluded, under the Sharīʿa, from any share whatever in a grandparent's estate—however dependent they may have been on his or her support—if that grandparent is survived by a son.[37] The reason for this is the basic rule that 'the nearer in degree excludes the more remote', according to which the son will take the whole estate (in default of any other entitled claimant) and the orphaned grandchildren will get nothing. But this has now been remedied in Egypt, Syria, Tunisia and Morocco by the device of 'obligatory bequests'; for legislation has been introduced which makes it incumbent on the grandparent, in such circumstances, to make a bequest to these grandchildren of what their deceased parent would have inherited had he (or, in Egypt and Tunisia, she) survived, provided that this does not exceed the 'bequeathable

[37] For a more detailed discussion, cf. pp. 153 ff. below.

third'.[38] If, moreover, the grandparent fails to do this, the court is to act as though he had; and if, instead, the grandparent has made voluntary bequests to other people, the grandchildren's right will prevail. In the main, this most salutary reform is based on a somewhat extreme form of *takhayyur*, for it rests primarily on the authority of those commentators who maintain that the 'Verse of Bequests' was not wholly abrogated by the 'Verses of Inheritance', but is still obligatory on a Muslim at least in so far as a close relative who is not, in the circumstances, an heir is concerned—together with various dicta to the effect that, should a testator make bequests to others when his own relatives are in need, the money or goods concerned should be taken from these legatees and given to the heirs. But the fact is that there is no reference to grandparents, as such, in these authorities, which are general in their terms; and it is only by decision of the legislature—in the light of the foregoing principles and the needs of society—that the relevant provisions are restricted to this case alone.[39]

Yet another problem which is a matter of concern in some countries is the claims of the 'nuclear' family as against those of members of the extended family or tribal heirs.[40] Under Sunnī law the estate of a parent who is survived by a daughter and a distant agnatic cousin, for example, is divided equally between the two of them; but however much this may have made sense in a tribal society, where a man looked for protection and support from his agnates, it causes deep dissatisfaction in many urban communities today, where a man may scarcely know a distant cousin, or heartily dislike him. It seems, indeed, that in Iraq Sunnīs used, not infrequently, to change over to Shīʿī allegiance for this very reason, for in Shīʿī law the daughter would take the whole estate in such cases; and this was one reason for the total abandonment of the Islamic law of inheritance in the Irāqī Law

[38] It should be noted, however, that this is to be reduced by the amount of any gift which has been made to the grandchildren by the grandparent during his or her lifetime.

[39] For further details, cf. pp. 155f. below.

[40] For further discussion, cf. pp. 150ff. below.

of 1959, and for the adoption of broadly Shīʿī principles, in respect to all Iraqīs, in the amendment introduced in 1963. But in Tunisia, where the indigenous population is exclusively Sunnī, a different device was adopted. By an addendum added in 1959 to the Law of Personal Status, 1956, the doctrine of the *radd* or 'return',[41] which has always been accepted by the Ḥanafīs and Ḥanbalīs (and has also been adopted by most modern Shāfiʿīs), was introduced in a basically Mālikī environment, but with two unusual features. The first of these, to which reference has already been made,[42] was that no distinction was made in this regard between the spouse-relict and other sharers; and this can find at least minimal support among some of the early jurists. But the second was far more radical, for it provided that the presence of a daughter or son's daughter would exclude even a germane or consanguine brother from the *radd*—and also, by implication, a germane or consanguine sister. For this there is no semblance of justification in any school of Sunnī law; indeed, it involves a complete misuse of terms, for the proper concept of the 'return' has no place whatever, in such circumstances, in the Sunnī system of inheritance. This particular reform is unquestionably of Shīʿī origin; and it has been inserted in an otherwise Sunnī system by what could only be termed a singularly incongruous piece of *talfīq*—masquerading, in outward form, as an administrative regulation introduced to meet what may well be regarded, in contemporary Tunisia, as a very real social need.

Four other examples of this expedient—that is, of effecting reforms by means of innovations often alleged to be 'not contrary to the principles of the Sharīʿa'—may be cited, for they raise problems which are, in a sense, *sui generis*. The first comes from Iran, where the Family Protection Act, 1967, introduced some radical changes in the law of divorce.[43] Mention has already been made of countries in which no divorce is effective until after the parties have been to court and conciliation has been attempted;

[41] For an explanation of the doctrine of the return, cf. pp. 149f. below.
[42] Cf. p. 57 above.
[43] For further details, cf. pp. 112f., 119ff., 128ff. below.

so there is at least a partial parallel to the Iranian insistence that no divorce is possible until a 'Certificate of irreconcilability' has first been obtained. But it was a major innovation that such a certificate will never be given except on certain clearly specified grounds. In those cases in which the demand for divorce emanates from the wife, the semblance of orthodox Sharīʿa principles was ingeniously preserved by the provision of a standard contract of marriage in which the wife makes the stipulation that she should have a right to a divorce on these grounds; but it is significant that women who were married before this Act was passed, and who had made no such stipulations, are in practice, it seems, treated in precisely the same way. Where the demand emanates from the husband, however, the fact is that this was the first reform introduced in the field of Islamic law which makes it impossible for him validly to divorce his wife, however much he desires this and whatever financial compensation he is prepared to provide, unless he can base his demand on one or other of these specified reasons. So this constitutes a clear example of a reform, based on the fiat of the legislature and the welfare of the public, in which it is exceedingly difficult to maintain the principle that it is 'not contrary to the Sharīʿa'.

The second example comes from the Tunisian Law of 1956, where Article 19 decrees, in unequivocal and unqualified terms, that 'A man is prohibited from remarrying his triply divorced wife', for this runs directly counter to the consensus of Muslim jurists, based on Sūra 2:230, that a man may indeed remarry his triply divorced wife, but only if she has first been married to another man and then again divorced. The genesis of this curious provision lies in a sequence of historical facts. First, as a salutary reform, Muḥammad had introduced the concept of the *ʿidda* period, during which a man who had pronounced an impetuous formula of repudiation against his wife could revoke it and resume the marriage relationship. But it was soon found that husbands began to exploit their wives by first repudiating them, then revoking the repudiation just before the end of the *ʿidda*, and then again repudiating them—and thus keeping them in a continuous state of suspension, neither truly married nor really free, in the hope of extracting a financial consideration for the type of divorce known as *khulʿ*. So, to prevent this, instructions were given that a third repudiation would be regarded as final and irrevocable. Somewhat later, however, a woman came to Muḥammad saying that a marriage contracted in her youth had not been a success and the union had ended in divorce; but, since then, she had contracted a marriage with another man who had also divorced her, and she was now an older and wiser woman. Might she not, therefore, remarry her first husband? Permission was given; and this, it is said, was the origin of the Qur'anic provision that remarriage after a triple repudiation was allowable only if the woman concerned had experienced an intervening marriage. It was not very long, however, before this concession led to the revolting expedient that a husband who had triply divorced a wife from whom he did not really want to be parted would procure a man, called a *muḥallil*, who would marry her and then divorce her purely in order to make it lawful for him to remarry her. All jurists insisted that this intervening marriage must be consummated, although recourse was sometimes had to stratagems in an attempt to evade this; but some jurists altogether refused to recognize a marriage which was deliberately contrived for no other purpose than to facilitate remarriage after a triple divorce, and insisted that the intervening marriage, to be effective, must be contracted in good faith. It was this view which prompted the Jordanian reformers to provide, in Article 82 of the Jordanian Law, that this intervening marriage must not be concluded with even the unexpressed intention of making the woman lawful once more to her former husband (*qaṣd al-taḥlīl*). And it was, no doubt, in order completely to exclude the unsavoury devices to which recourse was often had in this context (devices, indeed, which Mālikī law not only deprecates but officially regards as ineffective) that the Tunisian reformers enacted this absolute prohibition of any remarriage of a husband with his triply divorced wife. When I visited Tunisia soon after this Law was promulgated, moreover, I found that some jurists were prepared to deny any contradiction between this legislative provision and the Qur'ān and to insist that Article 19 would not in fact prohibit such remarriage after a *genuine* intervening union—on the ground that the woman concerned should not then be regarded as the triply divorced wife of her first husband but the widow or divorcee of the second! It would seem, however, that this ingenious interpretation is precluded by Article 14, which specifically classifies a threefold divorce as a permanent rather than a temporary (or potentially temporary) impediment to marriage. So the significance of this Article in the Tunisian Law is that it constitutes a clear-cut departure from orthodox teaching. But this does not seem to have excited much opposition—partly, no doubt, because of the casuistry to which some of the *'ulamā'* resorted, and partly because impetuous and ill-considered repudiations have been largely eliminated in Tunisia by the fact that no divorce is now recognized unless it is effected in a court of law.

A third example is provided by very recent legislation in the People's Democratic Republic of the Yemen and the Republic of Somalia, in both of which a Family Law has been promulgated which includes a number of provisions for which no authority whatever can be found in the classical texts. The declared purpose of both these Laws was to enhance the status of women—so provision was made, *inter alia*, for both parties to a marriage to share, according to their means, in the expenses of their wedding, their matrimonial home, their own maintenance and that of their children; for the paramount consideration in any dispute about the custody of their children to be the welfare of the children concerned; and, in Somalia, for men and women to be given equal shares in inheritance.[44] But here the divergence from orthodox teaching is undeniable.

Our last example must be taken from Pakistan, where the whole approach to the introduction of reforms in Islamic law differs significantly from that of the Arab world. It has already been noted, in passing, that several of the provisions of the Dissolution of Muslim Marriages Act, 1939—promulgated, of course, in what

[44] Cf. pp. 191 ff. below.

was then British India—depart from the Mālikī models on which they were officially based much more radically than would have been acceptable in corresponding legislation in Middle East countries. After Independence and Partition, moreover, the attitude of the advocates of reform in Pakistan was thrown into bold relief by the fact that the Government appointed a Reform Commission which issued a circular, to all and sundry, asking them to express their opinions as to what reforms in family law were both in accordance with the principles of Islam and desirable in practice. Then, in the light of the replies they received, they published a series of proposals, to which the only member of the Commission who could be described as an *ʿālim*, or one learned in Islamic law, wrote a forceful note of dissent. In the event the proposals were only partially implemented; but the significant point is that it was regarded as acceptable for them to be drawn up by a Commission which could in no sense be considered expert in such a subject, and to be based (in part, at least) on what almost amounted to a popular vote of such men and women—most of them educated, in all probability, in the Western and essentially lay tradition—as troubled themselves to reply to the questionnaire. In Egypt, by contrast, the major reforms were proposed and drafted by a committee presided over by the Shaykh of the Azhar University, and made up, in more or less equal proportions, of experts in Islamic law and of practising lawyers; and the story is told that, at their first meeting, the Chairman told the practising lawyers that it was for them to say what reforms were needed, and then for him and the other *ʿulamāʾ* to say how these could be effected in a way which was consonant with the principles of the Sharīʿa!

Naturally enough, this difference of approach made itself felt, in Pakistan, not only in the proposals put forward by the Commission but also in the Muslim Family Laws Ordinance, 1961, which in part implemented these proposals. Reference has already been made to provisions in this Ordinance relevant to the law of divorce, although it may be remarked in passing that these reforms as a whole seem to constitute a major provocation to orthodox opinion without providing any very effective safeguard for the interests of a discarded wife.[45] But the difference between the Pakistani and the Arab approach is more obvious still in the matter of the financial interests of orphaned grandchildren; for here, as we have seen, four Arab countries have had recourse to the device of providing that they should receive 'obligatory bequests' from a deceased grandparent's estate in all those cases in which they would otherwise be completely excluded from inheritance, whereas the Pakistani Act cuts the Gordian knot by making unequivocal provision that they should have the right to represent their deceased parent in all such circumstances. This solution—which was, in fact, proposed in the Lebanon some twenty-five years ago, but aroused such opposition that it was never applied to Muslims in that country—may seem, at first sight, the obvious way to solve the problem; and this is, no doubt, the view taken by many educated Pakistanis. But there are two basic objections. On the practical level, it completely upsets the structure and balance of the Islamic law of inheritance—as may be seen from a simple illustration. Suppose there were only two claimants to an estate: a daughter, and the daughter of a predeceased son. In this case, under the Ḥanafī law, the daughter would initially take one-half and the granddaughter one-sixth, and then finally—by the doctrine of the 'return'—the daughter would receive three-quarters of the estate and the granddaughter one-quarter; whereas, under the Pakistani Ordinance, the position would be virtually reversed, for the granddaughter would step into the shoes of her deceased father and take two-thirds of the whole estate, leaving only one-third to her aunt. And the second objection is that, whereas the device of 'obligatory bequests' can find *some* justification and support in the classical texts, the introduction of a right of representation can find none whatever. On the contrary, it runs directly counter to a principle of law accepted by Sunnīs and Shīʿīs alike—and one from the application of which Muḥammad himself is said to have suffered.

In addition to this, it must also be noted that in a number of

[45] See pp. 127f. below.

countries statutory enactments which make no pretensions whatever to being based on Islamic principles have imposed important restrictions on the application even of the family law of Islam, or have effected changes in the way in which this law is applied. This is particularly true, naturally enough, of what was formerly British India, and of those countries in East, West and North Africa which were formerly under British or French rule. In British India, for example, the Caste Disabilities Removal Act, 1850, provided that 'So much of any law or usage . . . as inflicts on any person forfeiture of rights or property, or may be held in any way to impair or affect any right of inheritance by reason of his or her renouncing or having been excluded from the communion of any religion . . . shall cease to be enforced by law'— and similar provisions have been promulgated elsewhere. Again, the Indian Penal Code, 1860, included a section which made the consummation of marriage with a wife of very tender age a criminal offence—and, once more, a similar provision can be found in the criminal codes of certain African countries. In addition, a series of enactments has been promulgated, in India and several other countries, restricting child marriage as such. The Indian Evidence Act, too, has *inter alia* effected radical changes in the law of legitimacy, regardless of the religion of the parents, in the Indian sub-continent.[46] Other examples could be quoted from many different countries; but one of the most obvious is, perhaps, the impact the prohibition of slavery has had on the whole field of family law—in India, Africa and elsewhere.

(e) *The expedient of reform by judicial decisions*

In the Indian sub-continent, and all those countries which were formerly under British rule, there is yet another way in which changes have been effected, and are still being effected today, in Islamic law (in so far as this is applied by the courts): namely, by judicial decisions. To a minor degree this is, no doubt, true in other countries, too; but the fact is that the influence of judicial precedents, while by no means negligible in a Civil Law system,

[46] Cf. pp. 138ff. below.

has a unique position under the Common Law. At the one extreme stands the classical doctrine of Islamic jurisprudence, crystallized in the famous saying of the Caliph ʿUmar, when reminded that a judgment he had just given was diametrically contradictory to one he had given on identical facts some years before, that 'It is better to return to the right path than to persist in error'; and, at the other, the Common Law subservience to the doctrine of *stare decisis*. In some Muslim countries—such as Egypt and Tunisia—the Sharīʿa courts have now, of course, been abolished as a separate system, and all jurisdiction has been brought within the scope of unified national courts, where the continental attitude to case law officially prevails; and even in specifically Islamic courts it is idle to imagine that past decisions, particularly those of the higher courts, have no influence whatever. Under the Mālikī law as applied in the Maghrib, indeed, the authority of *ʿamal*, or the practice of the courts, is recognized even by the jurists. But it is fair to say that in this matter of the authority of judicial precedents the heritage of English law is unique.

Naturally enough, this phenomenon has two sides. In the past mistaken decisions have at times effected fundamental changes in what is aptly called 'Anglo-Muhammadan Law'—or Islamic law as applied by judges trained in the Common Law tradition and under an essentially English system of evidence and procedure. The outstanding example of this is the judgment of the Privy Council in *Abul Fata* v. *Russomoy* in 1894,[47] which was so contrary to the accepted principles of the Sharīʿa in regard to family *waqfs*, and touched the interests of Indian Muslims so closely, that in 1913 the Mussulman Wakf Validating Act was passed in an attempt to restore the *status quo*—and in 1931 another Act had to be passed to give the former enactment retrospective effect. Even so—and although everyone with any knowledge of the Sharīʿa knew that the Judicial Committee had misinterpreted the law in *Abul Fata*'s case—British courts in Aden, Kenya and Zanzibar all felt themselves bound by this decision, although they could easily have

[47] [1894] 22 I.A. 76.

'distinguished' it on more than one ground. As a result, legislation had to be promulgated in all these territories, as in India, to remedy the resultant situation. But the crowning folly was when, in 1952, an appeal from the Court of Appeal for Eastern Africa, in the case of *Fatuma binti Mohamad bin Salim* v. *Mohamed bin Salim*,[48] gave the Privy Council itself an ideal opportunity to reverse its previous judgment—or, at the very least, to distinguish it; but unhappily, under Lord Simmond's influence, their Lordships refused to do either.

Two other examples can be given, from what was then British India, of ways in which the Sharī'a has been either mutilated or reformed by judicial decision. As long ago as 1885 Mr Justice Mahmoud gave a highly questionable judgment, in regard to the devolution of the assets and liabilities of a deceased person's estate on his heirs at the moment of his death, which has prevailed to this day in both India and Pakistan. This judgment, which substantially reflects English law, may well be regarded as beneficial to society; but it runs directly counter to the principles of the Ḥanafī law which Mr Justice Mahmoud presumably thought he was expounding.[49] But the other example represents a genuine reform in the law which has recently, as we have seen, been effected by means of legislation in a number of Muslim countries; for the fact is that, over the years, the courts in India have consistently regarded conditions included in marriage contracts as valid and enforceable provided only that they were 'reasonable and not contrary to the provisions of the law'—a phrase that would apparently cover most of those conditions by means of which a husband stipulates that he will not exercise some of the rights that are traditionally accorded him in Ḥanafī law.[50] It seems clear, however, that the judgments that have been given in such cases sometimes represent a misunderstanding of the relevant principles in the Islamic texts and sometimes a deliberate disregard of a principle which seemed to the court to be manifestly

[48] [1952] A.C.I.

[49] Cf. *Jafri Begam* v. *Amir Muhammad Khan* (1885) 7 All. 822.

[50] Cf. Fyzee, pp. 104 f.

inequitable[51]—but not, in any instance, a conscious adoption of Ḥanbalī doctrine.[52]

More recently, however, judges in both Pakistan and India have on occasions, beyond any question, consciously assumed the mantle of reformers. It was by a series of judicial decisions, for example, that Muslim wives in Pakistan have been given the right to a judicial divorce, on repayment of their dower, on grounds which amount to incompatibility of temperament or breakdown of marriage. For justification, the judges concerned went back beyond the doctrines of the Ḥanafī jurists to their own interpretation of two Qur'anic verses (Sura 2:228 and 229), the first of which lays down the general principle that women should have rights similar to those that their husbands have over them, and the second of which refers specifically to the sort of divorce known in Islamic law as *khulʿ*—in which a wife agrees to give her husband some financial consideration for her freedom. In the case of *Balqis Fatima* v. *Najm ul-Ikram Qureshi*[53] the High Court of Lahore relied on the first of these verses when it held that, since a husband has full power to repudiate his wife at will, it would be unreasonable if the wife were not given a comparable right—although this must, in her case, remain subject to a decree of court which might require her to repay all the benefits she had received from the marriage. Even so, the law on this subject in Pakistan remained very much in doubt until 1967, when the Supreme Court, in the case of *Khurshid Bibi* v. *Muhammad Amin*,[54] upheld this very controversial decision. This time it was on the second of these verses that the court based its judgment, quoting the writings of certain early commentators to support the view that the words 'but if you fear that they (i.e. the spouses) cannot preserve the limits prescribed by God, then it shall be no sin for either of them in what she gives to get her freedom' gave the court authority to

[51] The same tendency to bend the rigid requirements of the law in favour of what seems more equitable may be seen in the way in which British courts have frequently dealt with litigation about the custody of children.

[52] In this context, cf. N. J. Coulson, *A History of Islamic Law* (Edinburgh University Press, 1964), pp. 191 f.

[53] P.L.D. 1959 Lah. 566.

[54] P.L.D. 1967 S.C. 97.

enforce a *khul*ʿ in cases of incompatibility, aversion or marriage breakdown, even against the will of the husband, on the ground that the 'you' in that verse refers to judges. In addition, it based its decision on a tradition in which the Prophet of Islam is said to have ordered a husband whose wife had taken an intense dislike to him, although he had not in fact ill-used her, to accept the return of her dower and then repudiate her.

From India, too, examples can be quoted of cases where courts have deliberately set out to reform the law. In *Itwari* v. *Asghari*[55] Dhavan J. held that, in India, the Islamic institution of polygamy was 'tolerated but not encouraged', so he refused to grant a husband who had married a second wife a decree of restitution of conjugal rights against his first wife who had refused to live with him—on the ground that, under the social conditions of India today, the taking of a second wife must be regarded as an insult to the first wife which was likely to cause her mental suffering and affect her health. Since, therefore, a husband must be taken to intend the natural consequences of his action, the taking of a second wife, in the absence of a 'weighty and convincing' explanation, raised a presumption of cruelty to the first, so it would be inequitable for the court to compel her to continue to live with him. Somewhat similarly, in the case of *Badruddin* v. *Aisha Begum*,[56] Oak J. remarked that, although a Muslim is permitted to have four wives, he did not consider 'having more than one wife is part of religion'. So he held that the fact that a Muslim husband had contracted a marriage with another wife gave the first wife just grounds for refusing to live with him, and granted her maintenance under Section 488 of the Code of Criminal Procedure. And Krishna Iyer J. upheld this judgment in the case of *Shahulameedu* v. *Subaida Beevi*,[57] where he attacked the institution of polygamy as 'the rather unholy practice of a conjugal quadrangle', alleged that it behoved the courts in India to enforce Section 488 (3) of the Code of Criminal Procedure in favour of all Indian women—Hindu, Muslim or otherwise—and

[55] A.I.R. (1960) All. 684.
[56] (1957) All. L.J. 300.
[57] 1970 K.L.T. 4.

maintained that the Qur'ān itself had 'enjoined monogamy upon Muslims and departure therefrom as an exception' permissible only in special circumstances.

It must be recognized, indeed, that there are circumstances in which this expedient of judicial intervention is a very effective way of introducing a reform which might arouse fierce opposition from some quarters, and even political contention, if it were incorporated in a legislative enactment which had to be debated in a legislature. A decision in a court would normally receive much less publicity, and might even pass almost unnoticed. Unless reversed by an appellate court or put on one side by statute law, moreover, the new doctrine might well, with the passage of time, come to be accepted and followed without question.

4. A RECONSIDERATION OF THE LAW AS A WHOLE

We have seen that the first stage in the reform movement, almost everywhere, was for the reformers to put whole sections of the Sharīʿa on one side, where this seemed necessary, in favour of contemporary codes derived from largely alien sources; and that, in the middle of the last century, this seemed preferable to many Muslims to any attempt to meddle with the divine law itself. It was better, they felt, to leave the sacred law precisely as it had come down to them, intact and inviolate, even if this meant in practice that they must accept another law in its place. It was, however, only in Turkey under Ataturk that Muslims were prepared to extend this principle to their family law; for elsewhere it was generally felt that this must necessarily remain essentially Islamic. When, therefore, the need for reforms in such matters as marriage, divorce and succession ultimately became unavoidable, the reformers were compelled to search for ways in which the Sharīʿa itself could be so interpreted and applied as to meet the needs of society; and we have been concerned with the expedients which they used to this end. This may be regarded as the second stage in the movement of reform.

It was inevitable, therefore, that the logic of events would, sooner or later, confront Muslims with a further question. If the principles of the Sharīʿa could in fact be interpreted, applied and even codified in such a way, then why should this be confined to the family law, while almost all other fields of the law were left to largely alien inspiration? Why should not an attempt, at least, be made to derive codes of law for every aspect of life from the rich soil of their own cultural heritage? Some, indeed, went so far as to assert that it would be possible to dispense entirely with any borrowings from the West, and to base the law of Muslim countries exclusively on principles drawn from the Sharīʿa.

One country where questions like this were debated was Egypt, where a new Civil Code was promulgated in 1948 to come into force at the abolition of the Mixed Courts on 15 October, 1949. Considerable publicity was, indeed, given to the fact that ʿAbd al-Razzāq al-Sanhūrī and the committee which put this code together had drawn extensively on 'the decisions of Egyptian courts, comparative legislation and the Sharīʿa' as sources by which the previous civil codes had been amended and enriched; that 'many of its general concepts and many of its detailed provisions' had been derived from the Sharīʿa; and that this strengthening of the links between the code and the Sharīʿa represented 'a retention of a spiritual heritage which deserves to be preserved and used'.[58] But ʿAbd al-Razzāq al-Sanhūrī himself declared, before a Committee set up by the Senate: 'I put it on record now that three-quarters, or five-sixths, of the provisions of this Law are based on the decisions of Egyptian courts and on the existing legislation.'[59] When, moreover, some members of this committee maintained that a suitable code could have been drawn up based on the Sharīʿa alone, Sanhūrī first claimed that he would yield pride of place to no man in his love for the Sharīʿa, then admitted that little new had in fact been borrowed exclusively therefrom, and finally stated categorically: 'I assure you that we did not leave a single sound provision of the Sharīʿa which we could have included in this legislation without so doing . . . We adopted from the Sharīʿa all that we could adopt, having regard to sound

[58] *al-Qānūn al-Madanī*: *Majmūʿat al-Aʿmāl al-Taḥḍīriyya*, Vol. i, pp. 20 and 159.
[59] Ibid., p. 70.

principles of modern legislation; and we did not fall short in this respect.'[60]

A short summary of the extent to which this Egyptian Civil Code—which has, in fact, been largely adopted in both Syria and Libya—has incorporated principles and precepts from the Sharī'a will be found in the next chapter. But passing reference must be made here to the fact that its chief architect also played the leading part in drafting civil codes for Iraq and Kuwait; and that the code he drafted for Iraq includes a great many more provisions based on the Sharī'a than does the Egyptian code. So the question inevitably arises whether he had undergone a subjective change of attitude in regard to the Sharī'a in the years between 1948 and 1953, or—more significantly—had found objective grounds for a belief that it could in fact provide the basis for a satisfactory code to cover all the exigencies of modern life. But although it is, of course, always possible that Sanhūrī had modified his views in some particulars, it seems clear that the basic explanation for the contrast between the two codes lies in the radical difference in the legal background of Egypt and Iraq respectively. In Egypt codes predominantly based on French law had been in operation for some seventy years, while in Iraq the principles of the Sharī'a, as codified in the Majalla, still prevailed. So the significant point, it seems to me, is not so much that Sanhūrī incorporated in the new Iraqī code much more of the Sharī'a than he did in Egypt, but rather that he abandoned it as often and as radically as he did in favour of quite different principles—and particularly so in matters such as contracts of a 'speculative' or allegedly 'usurious' character about which Muslim opinion is most sensitive.

A quite different example can be found in Pakistan—a country which owes its very existence to the fact that the majority of the Muslims in the Indian sub-continent believed that it was only in an independent State, which was at least in some sense Islamic, that they could ensure for themselves and their children the way of life which they most deeply desired. It is by no means clear, however, how Muhammad 'Ali Jinnah himself envisaged such a

[60] Ibid., pp. 85 etc.

State, and how Islamic he in fact meant it to be—or, indeed, how Islamic the people of Pakistan themselves want it to be. The problems to which this has given rise, and the possibilities in regard to the future, will be discussed in the last chapter of this book. They are epitomized in clauses in the 'Principles of Policy' such as 'No law shall be repugnant to the teachings and requirements of Islam, as set out in the Holy Quran and Sunnah, and all existing laws shall be brought into conformity with the Holy Quran and Sunnah'; and, again, 'Riba (usury) should be eliminated'. But phrases like this have hitherto given rise to controversy rather than consensus, debate rather than action; and the fact is that the criminal and civil law of Pakistan is no more Islamic today than it was at the inception of Independence.[61]

[61] Cf. pp. 174ff. below.

CHAPTER III

The Achievements and Results of Reform

IN previous chapters of this book we have discussed the background to the movement for law reform which has been flooding, almost like a tidal wave, through the vastly greater part of the Muslim world during the last 125 years, the pressures which prompted it, and the methods used by the reformers. It now remains to summarize what has in fact been achieved, to discuss the problems that still remain and to assess the prospects for the future. The task of the present chapter, then, is to depict the legal position which prevails today, in most of the relevant countries, in so far as the Sharīʿa is concerned—since it would clearly be impossible, in one short book, to attempt to describe in any detail the numerous codes of commercial, criminal and civil law, largely of Western inspiration, which have been promulgated in one country after another.

I. COMMERCIAL, CRIMINAL AND CIVIL LAW (OTHER THAN THAT OF THE FAMILY)

The Ottoman Commercial Code, which was promulgated as early as 1850, was squarely based on French law, and owes virtually nothing to the Sharīʿa. It prevailed at first throughout the whole Ottoman Empire, including Egypt, but it has been progressively replaced in several countries by more contemporary codes which are also predominantly of French inspiration. Quite recently, moreover, this code has again been called in aid, this time even in Saʿūdī Arabia, to govern those commercial activities which come within the jurisdiction of the new Commercial Tribunals (or 'Chambers'). In those parts of North Africa which were never part of the Ottoman Empire, moreover, French law—

or local legislation promulgated under French influence—largely prevails today in regard to commercial transactions; and this is also true, of course, of the former French colonies in central Africa and elsewhere. In countries which at one time formed part of the British Empire, on the other hand, the commercial law is based on the law of England. Some of the relevant topics are, of course, also covered by international conventions. In sum, the Sharīʿa as such has virtually no place today in the sphere of commercial law, in the strict sense of that term, in any part of the world.

Much the same is also true of the criminal law of Islam, except in parts of the Arabian peninsula—and even there the punishments inflicted do not always, by any means, follow the exact prescriptions of the Sharīʿa. Until little more than a decade ago the Islamic criminal law, as interpreted by Mālikī jurists, was also applied by the native courts of the more rigidly Muslim areas in Northern Nigeria—except that, in cases of deliberate homicide, the British colonial power would not allow the 'heirs of blood' themselves to execute the condemned man in precisely the same way (where exact reciprocity was possible) in which he had despatched their kinsman, and also, in the case of the prescribed punishments, had prohibited stoning and restricted flogging to the imposition of merely ritual lashes (as some later Mālikī jurists had themselves advised). But all this has now been relegated to the past by recent legislation, in which relics of the Sharīʿa survive in no more than two or three details. For the rest, the Islamic criminal law—in a considerably modified form—prevails today only in Afghanistan.

What happened was that, in the first half of the nineteenth century, embryonic criminal codes which represented a sort of compromise between Islamic and Western concepts were promulgated in the Ottoman Empire in general and Egypt in particular, while the application of Islamic criminal law was progressively curtailed in India. But the Ottoman Penal Code of 1858, the Egyptian Codes of 1875 and 1937,[1] and the Indian Penal Code of

[1] The Penal Code of 1875 was largely based on French law, but the Criminal Code of 1937 on Italian law.

1860 were based, almost completely, on the Civil and the Common Law respectively; and similar legislation has been promulgated in one after another of the countries which were formerly under European rule. What is true of the substantive criminal law is also, moreover, largely true of the law of criminal procedure. In the former Anglo-Egyptian Sudan, for example, both the Penal Code and the Code of Criminal Procedure represent an adoption of the corresponding Indian legislation with only minor amendments; and substantially identical codes, with trivial changes, have now been promulgated in Northern Nigeria by the enactment of the Northern Nigeria Penal Code in 1959 and the Northern Nigeria Criminal Procedure Code in 1960.[2] Elsewhere the relevant codes are based on French or Italian rather than English law. But, however this may be, there are very few parts of the Muslim world today where either criminal law or criminal procedure owe anything of significance to the Sharīʿa.

When we turn to the law of contract, tort and civil procedure, the situation is more complex. The Tunisian Code of Obligations and Contracts, 1906, represents the enactment of part of the 'Code Santillana'—an *avant-projet* of a civil and commercial code, based on Islamic jurisprudence, first published in 1899; but a somewhat similar code, prepared for use in Algeria by Marcel Morand and published in 1916, was never officially promulgated. The Egyptian Civil Code of 1948 is, however, of much more importance, for it has provided the basis of the Syrian Civil Code of 1949 and the Libyan Civil Code of 1954, and has exerted a vital influence on the Iraqī Civil Code of 1953. It is clear, moreover, that the Egyptian Code of 1948 substantially follows the pattern of the codes of 1875 and 1883, and thus derives the vast majority of its provisions from the Code Napoleon. But in the new code some of these provisions have been adapted in the light of decisions given in Egyptian courts in litigation arising from the previous codes; and a certain number of principles and precepts from the

[2] For a detailed comparison of the Sudanese and Northern Nigerian Codes, cf. A. Gledhill, *The Penal Codes of Northern Nigeria and the Sudan* (Sweet and Maxwell, London, 1963).

civil law of other countries, such as Germany, Italy and even Japan, have been included. What primarily concerns us here, however, is the debt which it owes to the Sharīʿa; and this can be summarized under four headings.

To begin with, the Sharīʿa is expressly included among the sources from which an appropriate rule or principle may be derived by the courts in default of a relevant provision in the code, for Article 1 enacts that 'The provisions of this Code govern all matters to which they apply in letter or spirit. In the absence of any provision that is applicable, the Judge shall decide according to custom and, in the absence of this, in accordance with the principles of the Sharīʿa. In the absence of any of these, the Judge will apply the principles of natural justice and the dictates of equity'. It is noteworthy, moreover, that the Explanatory Memorandum puts considerable emphasis on the importance of this provision and observes: 'The circumstances in which a Judge may not be able to find any relevant provision will not be few in number, so the court will in many cases go back to the Sharīʿa and seek inspiration from its principles—a fact which represents an outstanding victory for the Sharīʿa.'[3] In discussion before the Senate Committee on Civil Law, moreover, the further point was made that the Sharīʿa had deeply influenced the customs of the country, particularly in rural districts.[4] The Introduction to the Syrian Civil Code, again, emphasizes not only that 'custom and Islamic law' have been accorded a place 'consonant with their importance as a fundamental and flexible source from which an important part of any deficiency which may appear in this Code may be supplied', but also that the provision concerned does not limit such derivation to the authoritative view of any one school but allows it, without limit or restriction, from the whole scope of relevant Sharīʿa principles.[5] All the same, such statements seem to be directed more to their impact on public opinion and sentiment than to any practical application, for the phrase 'the principles of the Sharīʿa' is exceedingly nebulous, and

[3] *al-Qānūn al-Madanī*, Vol. i, p. 20.
[4] Ibid., p. 92.
[5] *al-Qānūn al-Madanī* (Syrian), p. 19.

resort to these principles is, in any case, postponed not only to both the letter and spirit of the Code but also to any relevant local custom.

There are, however, a few other articles which invoke the Sharīʿa in a way which seems much more likely to result in its practical application. Thus Article 32 in the Egyptian Code (which corresponds to Article 34 in the Syrian Code) provides that 'Missing persons and absent persons are subject to provisions enacted in special legislation; in the absence of such, the Sharīʿa will be applied'. Again, Article 915 (corresponding to Article 876 in Syria) enacts that 'The establishment of the heirs, the computation of their shares in the inheritance, and the devolution upon them of the property of the estate, is governed by the Sharīʿa and by legislative enactments concerning wills'. And it is significant that the Explanatory Memorandum remarks that Article 875 of the Egyptian Code (corresponding to Article 836 in Syria) has 'resolved two basic points of dispute in regard to inheritance, for it decrees that it is the Sharīʿa which is to be applied in regard to the inheritance of Egyptians even where they are not Muslims, and even if they have all agreed that the law of their sect is to apply; and it also makes the Sharīʿa applicable to all matters of inheritance, including the devolution of the ownership of the estate upon the heirs'.[6] With regard to testate succession, too, the Memorandum attached to the original draft declares that 'The Sharīʿa, and codifications and legislation based thereon, govern the substantive law of bequests . . . in regard to which Muslim and non-Muslim Egyptians are on an equal footing; while in matters of form the Code of Procedure for Sharīʿa Courts has laid down provisions to which all bequests must conform'.[7] At first sight much of this seems an unnecessary glimpse of the obvious in so far as Muslims are concerned, since questions of testate and intestate succession are regarded as falling within 'family law' in its wider connotation, and are thus specifically within the competence of what were at that time the Sharīʿa rather than the National Courts; but the purpose of these clauses is to clarify any

[6] *al-Qānūn al-Madanī*, Vol. vi, p. 200. Cf. also pp. 205 f. [7] Ibid., pp. 293 f.

possible confusion, to demarcate the competence of the respective courts and to provide for any case in which the National Courts are seized of litigation which involves some question of testate or intestate succession.

The next point to be noted is that the desire for conformity with the Sharīʿa is said to have had an influence on the choice made in this code between certain concepts in regard to which contemporary codes in Europe are divided. Examples of this which were specifically cited are an objective rather than subjective tendency in the treatment of obligations and contractual rights; the principles applicable to the concept of the abuse of rights; the legal consequences of exceptional and unpredictable events; and provisions about the assignment of debts. In the first case it is not suggested that this attitude is exclusively derived from the Sharīʿa: on the contrary, it is said to characterize, in general terms, the European codes which are of Germanic, as distinct from Latin, origin. But the claim is made that the principles of the Sharīʿa give support to the Germanic view; for although it is a maxim of the Sharīʿa that the intention of the parties, rather than the technical terms employed, must always be decisive, yet these intentions are to be judged by the expressions they used—as is shown, *inter alia*, by the details into which Muslim jurists commonly go in defining the exact meaning to be attributed to this expression or that—while the tests to be applied may again be said to be objective, since 'they are based on custom and practice'.[8] Much the same may be said of the provisions which cover the concept of the abuse of rights (Articles 4 and 5 of the Egyptian Code, and Articles 5 and 6 of the Syrian); for here the influence of the Sharīʿa, although by no means exclusive, is said to have been decisive—since the doctrine of the abuse of rights is 'applied in the most comprehensive way in that system, not only on the basis of a subjective test, as in most legal systems, but also on the basis of an objective test, since every right is limited by the social and economic purposes for which it was established'.[9] When we come, again, to the legal consequences of

[8] Ibid., Vol. i, pp. 20 ff. Cf. also pp. 30, 90 f., 131, 158, etc.

[9] Ibid., p. 21.

exceptional and unpredictable events, the Explanatory Memorandum admits that the primary source is both that 'principe de l'imprévision' recognized by the administrative, rather than the civil, courts in France (whereas the Court of Cassation in Egypt had previously followed the lead of the French civil courts in this matter and had quashed a contrary decision of the Egyptian Court of Appeal) and also Article 269 of the Polish Civil Code. But the Memorandum insists that the decisive factor in preferring this view was the support it receives from 'the concept of necessity in the Sharīʿa'[10] and from the principle, recognized therein, that a contract of lease may be nullified for good reason (*ʿudhr*).[11] In regard to the provisions about the assignment of debts, on the other hand, the Explanatory Memorandum states unequivocally that this is an innovation in the new Code which is 'purely Islamic in origin, although a parallel may be found in the Germanic codes'.[12]

Then again, certain principles and provisions have been borrowed more or less exclusively from the Sharīʿa which had no place in the previous codes. Examples of these may be found in the provisions regarding *majlis al-ʿaqd*, or the duration of that 'meeting' of the parties at which a contract is concluded[13] (although this example could equally well, perhaps, have been included among those cited in the previous paragraph, since the Explanatory Memorandum attached to the original draft admits that the terms of the article are derived, in the main, from English law, although the last sentence may fairly be said to represent a summary of the principles elaborated by Ḥanafī jurists);[14] and in the principles which govern legal capacity[15] (e.g. that a person who is 'devoid of discernment', because he is under seven years of age, feeble-minded or insane, is

[10] Ibid., p. 22.

[11] Ibid., p. 89. Cf. also Article 608 of the Egyptian Code and Article 575 of the Syrian.

[12] Ibid., Vol. iii, p. 136.

[13] Article 94 (Egypt), Article 95 (Syria).

[14] Thus any turning to another subject by the one to whom the offer was made is regarded as bringing the 'meeting' to an end; but not mere lapse of time without such change of subject.

[15] These are summarized in Articles 45–47, 110–16 and 118–19 (Egypt) and Articles 47–9, 111–17 and 119–20 (Syria).

regarded as totally incapable of exercising any contractual rights whatever; that contracts entered into by one who has reached the age of discernment but not that of majority[16] are regarded as valid when they are by their very nature necessarily advantageous, void when they are by nature necessarily disadvantageous, and subject to annulment 'if this is in the interests of the minor' when they may, in principle, be either profitable or detrimental; and that minors, insane persons, 'prodigals', etc. are governed by the rules relating to guardianship, or 'natural' or 'legal' curatorship, in accordance with the relevant rules). Other examples include provisions regarding the lease of *waqf* property[17] (no mention of which was made in the previous codes, although the Sharīʿa was always regarded as applicable; so the relevant principles were summarized in the new codes in so far they were likely to be relevant to the National, as distinct from the Sharīʿa, Courts); principles regarding contracts of *ḥikr*[18] (by which *waqf* land[19] in need of development may be let for a long period to a person who is prepared to finance this and to pay the owners an annual rent corresponding to current values by a contract which gives the lessee a right *in rem* over the land); principles governing the lease of agricultural land—and, in particular, the contract known as 'amodiation' (under which the lessor takes a fixed share in the crops) and the consequences of destruction of crops sown in leased land[20] (for, although there were parallels to some of these provisions in the previous Egyptian codes, to others there was either no parallel at all or some quite different provision). The contract of *muzāraʿa* (on the validity of which orthodox jurists are much divided) is also included for the first time. Yet further examples are provided by the right of a lessee to demand remission of rent if his crops are destroyed by *force majeure* (which represents a complete reversal of the law previously in force, and is attributed to the principles relevant to an oppressive rent, or *ījār murhiq*, in the Sharīʿa; the provisions

[16] This is fixed at twenty-one in Egypt, and eighteen in Syria.
[17] Cf. Articles 628–34 (Egypt) and 595–601 (Syria).
[18] Ibid., Vol. vi, pp. 560 ff. (in Egypt only).
[19] Although the contract *can* apply to other land also.
[20] Cf. Articles 610–27 (Egypt) and 577–94 (Syria).

regarding the termination of a lease on the death of the lessee and the annulment of a contract of lease on the ground of 'serious and unforeseen circumstances'[21] (where the latter, in particular, represents a new provision based on the principle of *'udhr*, or 'excuse', in the Sharīʿa); and provisions applicable to the release of debts by unilateral declaration.[22]

Finally, there are a number of provisions which were adopted from the Sharīʿa, either in whole or in part, in the previous Egyptian codes; and these have all been preserved, whether in their original or an amended form, in the new Egyptian and Syrian legislation. Outstanding examples include the principles applicable to such matters as dispositions of property during *maraḍ al-mawt*, or 'death sickness',[23] to *ghubn*, or lesion;[24] to deciding the party at whose risk the subject matter of a sale remains;[25] to planting or building on leased land;[26] and to the ownership of different storeys in the same house, or of a party wall.[27] More important than any of these, however, are a group of provisions about which it is specifically stated that they were adopted and derived from the Sharīʿa: e.g. principles relevant to the right of pre-emption (*shufʿa*);[28] provisions relevant to gifts;[29] and the basic provision of Sharīʿa law that 'There can be no inheritance until after the payment of debts'.[30]

In conclusion, three further points demand passing reference. First, it is interesting to note that, while it was distinctly claimed, in the Report of the Egyptian Chamber of Representatives, that 'The provisions of this draft Code have an individuality which makes them completely independent of the sources from which they were

[21] Cf. Articles 601 and 602 (Egypt) and 568 and 569 (Syria).

[22] Cf. Article 371 (Egypt) and 369 (Syria).

[23] Articles 477, 478 and 916 (Egypt) and 445, 446 and 877 (Syria).

[24] Articles 129, 425–27, 631, 845, 904 and 912 (Egypt) and 130, 393–95, 598, 799, 865 and 873 (Syria).

[25] Articles 437 and 438 (Egypt) and 405 and 406 (Syria).

[26] Article 592 (Egypt) and 559 (Syria).

[27] Articles 856–61 (Egypt) and 811–16 (Syria).

[28] Cf. Articles 935–48 in the Egyptian Code only.

[29] Articles 486–504 (Egypt) and 454–72 (Syria).

[30] Articles 899, 895 and 897 (Egypt) and 860, 856 and 858 (Syria).

derived. The purpose in referring to modern codes was not that the draft should be bound to these various codes in regard either to elucidation or development',[31] yet the Chairman of the Senate Committee on Civil Law made the equally categorical statement that 'The provisions derived originally from the Sharī'a must be elucidated by reference to the provisions of the Sharī'a'.[32] It is not at all clear, however, how far this distinction can—or should—be pressed. Secondly, the Report of the Committee on Civil Law includes the following observation: 'Let no one imagine that the multiplicity of sources, as set out above, has deprived the draft Code of that close cohesion and coherence which it should possess. The fact is that all these sources are similar in character; for the principles of the existing Code, and the case law which expands them, have lived side by side with the Sharī'a, and with the principles derived therefrom'.[33] But while it is true that two systems, one applying the Civil Code and the other based on the Sharī'a, have existed side by side in Egypt for some seventy years, and that there has inevitably been a certain interchange of ideas and influence, yet the fact remains that the two systems are widely different in origin, in character, and in a large number of their detailed provisions. Thirdly, the Explanatory Memorandum, after enumerating, with all possible emphasis, the debts which the draft Code owed to the Sharī'a, makes the additional claim that the victory of the Sharī'a is the more complete in that 'the substance of the draft Code could without much difficulty have been derived from its provisions'.[34]

But while it is true, of course, that a large number of the provisions of this code which have not been specifically attributed to the Sharī'a, whether primarily or secondarily, could find at least partial support in the *dicta* of this jurist or that (and that certain other provisions could, not unreasonably, be represented as an extension of principles known to the Sharī'a, rather than legislation contrary thereto), yet Sanhūrī himself made it clear, in the course of discussion before the Senate Committee on Civil Law, that to claim that such provisions were (or could be) in any real sense derived from

[31] *al-Qānūn al-Madanī*, Vol. i, pp. 71 f.

[32] Ibid., p. 116. [33] Ibid., p. 161. [34] Ibid., Vol. i, p. 20.

the Sharīʿa would be highly equivocal.[35] In a number of vital respects, moreover, the Code runs directly counter to the traditional interpretation of Islamic law in all the recognized schools—e.g. in regard to such matters as loans or investments which carry fixed rates of interest, betting and gambling, life annuities and insurance.

It would be impossible, within the scope of this book, to analyse the civil codes of other Muslim countries in any comparable detail. As we have already seen, the chief architect of the Civil Code of Iraq, 1951, was the same ʿAbd al-Razzāq al-Sanhūrī whose name and views we have already encountered in regard to the Egyptian Civil Code; but the Iraqī code includes far more articles which were originally derived from the Sharīʿa. The reasons for this were almost certainly objective rather than subjective, in the sense that the dominant consideration was the situation which prevailed in Iraq rather than any change of heart, on the part of Sanhūrī, about the Sharīʿa as such; for, when he began his work in Iraq, the only civil code in force in that country was the Majalla,[36] which was based on precepts and principles derived from the Sharīʿa. For the rest, the earlier Tanẓīmāt reforms in regard to commercial and criminal law had, of course, been in force in Iraq as an integral part of the former Ottoman Empire, together with the Land Law, the Tapu Law,[37] the Land Commercial Code and a system of 'Justices of the Peace' introduced under British influence. But with the passage of time this heterogeneous legal heritage had come to be in urgent need of revision and codification.

A first attempt was made in 1933, when a committee of local legislators studied the situation and presented a report; but this proved abortive, because of opposition from Muslim religious leaders. Then, in 1936, a second committee was appointed under the Acting Minister of Justice, with Sanhūrī (who was at that time a member of the faculty of the Iraq Law College) as one of its members, and gave serious consideration to two alternative expedients: that followed in Egypt, where European law had been

[35] *al-Qānūn al-Madanī*, Vol. i, pp. 82–90, etc.

[36] See p. 84 above.

[37] Land Registry.

substantially adopted, or the drafting of a distinctively Iraqī code designed to maintain an unbroken nexus between the past and the present (that is, between those traditional Islamic precepts and principles which were so deeply rooted in the social, religious and economic institutions of the people of Iraq, and those new concepts of Western origin, the adoption of which seemed to be essential in the light of a rapidly developing connection with European countries). In the event the second alternative was preferred, and Sanhūrī, assisted by Professor Munīr al-Qāḍī of Iraq, was asked to prepare a draft code. The work was interrupted in 1936, but in 1943 the Iraqī Government invited Sanhūrī, then back in Egypt, to return to Iraq and finish the work—aided, now, by the new Egyptian Code which was already in draft form.

An analysis[38] of the Iraqī Code of 1951 makes it perfectly clear that, in general terms, it consists in almost equal parts of articles derived from the Majalla (and a text entitled *Murshid al-Ḥayrān*), on the one hand, and the Egyptian Civil Code, on the other. Obviously, therefore, what might be termed the 'Islamic component' is far stronger and more pervasive than in the Egyptian Code; but it is significant that it is the basically French principles of the Egyptian Code which have prevailed in regard to such vexed questions as fixed rates of interest, insurance, and contracts of a 'speculative' nature.

In Kuwait, which attained full independence in 1961, Sanhūrī was again invited to draft a series of codes which may be said, in general terms, to represent a yet further development of the work he had already done in Egypt and Iraq. But the extra-territorial jurisdiction of the British Crown continued until 1971 in Bahrain, Qatar and the then 'Trucial States', in so far (broadly speaking) as non-Muslim immigrants and visitors were concerned; and the law applied in these British courts—alongside the Islamic and customary law which prevailed in the local courts—was derived from specific Orders in Council and imported Indian legislation. Now, however, Bahrain, Qatar and the 'United Arab Emirates' (i.e. the former

[38] A detailed analysis was, in fact, made by Mr K. Hafuth, one of my pupils, in a dissertation for the London Postgraduate Diploma in Law in 1962.

Trucial States of Abu Dhabi, Dubai, Sharjah, Ajman, Umm al-Qaiwain, Ra's al-Khaima and Fujairah) exercise exclusive jurisdiction as fully independent states. In Bahrain a considerable corpus of statute law exists, much of it dating from before independence; and both here and elsewhere legislative enactments will, no doubt, in future come to assume an increasingly important role. But whereas, in Kuwait, statute law covers almost every sphere of life outside the personal and family law of Muslim litigants, the Sharīʿa still occupies a considerably more significant place in all the other Emirates. In Bahrain, it is true, a clear distinction is made between the civil and the Islamic judicature and the Constitution lists the Sharīʿa as only one of the principal sources of law, although the Judicature Law of 1971 provides that, where the judge can find no legislative provision which is applicable, he shall base his decision on the principles of the Sharīʿa. In Qatar, on the other hand, the Sharīʿa is declared to be *the* principal source of law; yet a considerable volume of legislation exists (promulgated both before and after independence) which includes a Civil and Commercial Code—based, in the main, on the same Franco-Egyptian inspiration, and administered by civil courts. And in the United Arab Emirates (where the interim Constitution makes the Union legislature, rather than that of the individual Emirates, responsible for all major legislation—except, that is, for certain seemingly contradictory provisions in Article 149), the Sharīʿa is stated, as in Bahrain, to be a (rather than 'the') principle source of law, and a body of statute law—again, it would seem, based on Egyptian models—is in course of preparation. It is noteworthy, moreover, that Abu Dhabi, Dubai and Sharjah already have a system of courts which exercise civil and criminal jurisdiction alongside the traditional Islamic courts. In the Gulf, therefore, it is only in Oman that the Sharīʿa still reigns virtually supreme—and even there a Law has been promulgated to govern foreign investments, together with a Commercial Companies Law and a Banking Law under which a special Committee has been set up to hear and determine disputes.

The Persian Civil Code, 1939, represents yet another combination of Islamic and French principles which is far closer to the Sharīʿa (in its Shīʿī form) than is the case either in Egypt or Iraq. In Jordan and Israel, on the other hand, the Majalla is still substantially in force, although it has, of course, been amended in parts (particularly in Israel); while in Lebanon it has been extensively replaced by legislative enactments of essentially French inspiration. To the situation in what was formerly French North Africa reference has already been made.

In those territories which were once part of the British Commonwealth, the traces of Islamic law in matters of contract and tort are today of no great significance. In India and Pakistan the relevant law is almost entirely derived from the Common Law and local legislation of English inspiration, and the same is true of former British colonies in Africa and even of the former Anglo-Egyptian Sudan.[39] Individual Muslims, in several of these countries, no doubt still conclude contracts between themselves in accordance with the principles of the Sharīʿa, and a small minority resolutely adhere to the traditional prohibition of fixed rates of interest or certain contracts of insurance. But it is only in Saʿudi Arabia, North Yemen and Oman[40] that the Sharīʿa is still substantially in force in such matters; and even there a number of those stratagems in regard to its more inconvenient precepts, to which Muslims have resorted all down the centuries, are still, no doubt, in use. It may be cynical to remark that the rigid prohibition of any fixed rate of interest on a loan in Saʿudi Arabia, for example, has only resulted in far higher rates being demanded (and paid) to compensate the creditor for the risks he runs of not being able to enforce the transaction or even being prosecuted for making it; but this would in fact be true, at least among the more educated elements in the population. Two very recent developments, moreover, are significant of the way things are going today: contracts of insurance—previously restricted exclusively to the sphere of maritime commerce—are now, it seems, permitted in regard to

[39] For details, reference may be made to my *Islamic Law in Africa* (H.M.S.O., 1954; Frank Cass, 1970).

[40] Countries, indeed, which have always been substantially independent.

automobiles and other property, although not in regard to life assurance; and banks have begun to operate on the basis of what is really interest, although this is discreetly called 'commission' rather than the pejorative term *ribā'*, or 'interest'.[41]

2. MARRIAGE

When we turn to such matters as marriage, divorce, the paternity and guardianship of children, testate and intestate succession and the *waqf* system, reforms in the sphere of Islamic law which have been introduced by means of one or other of the expedients described in Chapter II are so interesting and significant that a separate section of this chapter must be allotted to each of these different aspects of family law.

According to the classical doctrines of the Sharī'a, a Muslim woman may not have more than one husband at the same time, but a Muslim man may have as many as four wives at once. In addition, the Ithnā 'Asharī branch of the Shī'a, alone, allows him to contract any number of temporary marriages, or 'marriages of enjoyment' (*mut'a*), while all schools allow a man to exercise rights of concubinage with his own female slaves. Any sexual intercourse outside these limits—or, rather, outside any 'semblance' (*shubha*) of these relationships—constitutes *zinā'*, or illicit sex relations, for which the prescribed punishment is death by stoning in the case of an offender who has ever consummated a lawful marriage, and one hundred lashes in the case of others. But these penalties can seldom lawfully be imposed in real life because of the extremely exacting standard of proof required, and also because of the principle that such punishments are averted by any circumstance of doubt—quite apart from the fact that the Islamic criminal law has today, as we have seen, an exceedingly limited application.

In pre-Islamic Arabia there were, it seems, several types of marriage, ranging probably from the patrilineal and patrilocal to the matrilineal and matrilocal—and including the so-called 'marriages of enjoyment' and various other arrangements which

[41] Cf. pp. 182, 185, 194f. below.

came very near to licensed prostitution. The most respectable form, however, was a patrilineal marriage in which the groom paid a dower for, or to, his bride. This has developed, no doubt, out of the widespread custom of paying bride-wealth to the tribe or family of the wife both as a consideration for their loss of her reproductive capacity and as a stabilization of the union; but it would seem that even before the advent of Islam the dower had come to be regarded in Arabia as properly belonging to the bride herself—although it was, in fact, commonly paid to her father. In any case this is a basic characteristic of the Islamic law of marriage, however much it is still disregarded in practice in some quarters. Muslim jurists often go so far as to employ the simile of a sale and regard the dower as a consideration for marital rights—a consideration that constitutes an essential element in every Muslim marriage. Nor is this repayable on divorce in Islamic law, once the marriage has been consummated, except by the wife's voluntary agreement[42]—even where it was she who was primarily to blame for the breakdown of the union.

It is against this background that we must view the two major innovations introduced after the advent of Islam. First, polygamy was limited to a maximum of four wives at a time, according to the classical interpretation of what is often called the 'Verse of Polygamy' in the Qur'ān. Even so, a man's indulgence in polygamy was made conditional on his confidence that he would be able to treat a plurality of wives with equal justice, and also (on one interpretation of the last clause in this verse) on his ability not only to support his existing dependents but to assume further responsibilities as well—but these conditions were regarded as incumbent on his conscience and enforced by the sanctions of religion, rather than by any human court. Secondly, divorce, although permitted, was stated (in a tradition attributed to the Prophet) to be the most hateful to God of all permitted things. Its rigours were, therefore, somewhat mitigated by the introduction of a waiting period (or *'idda*) during which a divorced or widowed woman was precluded from contracting another marriage; for this was designed not

[42] The one exception to this principle will be noted below.

only to avoid doubts about the paternity of children, but also to give the husband an opportunity to reconsider any hasty action and revoke the divorce at any time before the *ʿidda* came to an end.[43]

In Islamic law, moreover, marriage is regarded as a contract between two parties rather than any sort of sacrament. Its essential constituents are declaration (*ījāb*) and acceptance (*qabūl*), and no religious ceremony, however customary, is legally necessary. But Muslim jurists, after stating these essential constituents (*arkān*), commonly discuss under five different headings the conditions (*shurūṭ*) which must be fulfilled for a valid marriage.

First, they discuss those conditions which govern the conclusion of the contract (*shurūṭ al-inʿiqād*) as such, quite apart from whether, or not, it results in a valid marriage. These are that the declaration and acceptance must agree together, must be pronounced at the same 'meeting' of the parties, must be in terms adequate to effect an immediate union, and must issue from persons legally competent to conclude the contract. Here the major point which challenged the reformers was the fact that the classical doctrine of all schools of Islamic law allows a marriage guardian[44] to contract his minor ward in compulsory marriage, and that the Mālikīs, Shāfiʿīs and Ḥanbalīs also insist that the marriage of even an adult woman can be contracted only by her guardian (or someone else acting on his behalf). The Ḥanafīs, on the other hand, allow a woman who has attained majority to contract herself in marriage provided that she chooses a husband who is her 'equal' (*kufʾ*) in family, religion, profession and so forth, and that the dower involved is appropriate (*mahr al-mithl*); and they give even minors an option, when they reach their majority, of repudiating a marriage previously contracted on their behalf, except only when

[43] We shall see below, under the section on divorce, how this provision was sometimes abused in practice, and also how its purpose was largely frustrated by the jurists.

[44] But the schools differ among themselves in the list they give of potential marriage guardians and which of them may give his ward in *compulsory* marriage. See, in part, below.

the guardian who contracted it was their father or grandfather.[45] The other Sunnī schools totally exclude marriage by compulsion by anyone other than the father or father's father (or, in the Mālikī doctrine, the father's executor); but they extend such compulsion, in regard to a woman who has not previously been married, far beyond the age of majority. The Ithnā ʿAsharī Shīʿīs, for their part, agree with the Ḥanafīs in allowing an adult woman to contract herself in marriage, but they differ from the Ḥanafīs in permitting only a father or grandfather to contract a minor in compulsory marriage. In all schools, moreover, majority means the attainment of puberty (*bulūgh*) with adequate mental development (*rushd*)—the test in regard to puberty being the appropriate physical signs, but with the proviso that the minimum age is twelve for a boy and nine for a girl, and that puberty may be presumed when either boys or girls reach the age of fifteen (although some jurists prescribe other ages, such as eighteen for a boy and seventeen for a girl).

Thus the reformers were faced with two major problems: child marriage and compulsory marriage. The first of these inevitably posed a problem of considerable delicacy for the pious Muslim, since Muḥammad himself married one of his wives when she was very young indeed. But today there are few parts of the Muslim world where there are no restrictions on child-marriage. In some countries these restrictions are enforced by the criminal law, as in India and Pakistan, where the Indian Child Marriage Restraint Act, 1929, prescribes penal sanctions where the bridegroom has not reached the age of eighteen and the bride fourteen—an age raised to sixteen in Pakistan by the Muslim Family Laws Ordinance, 1961. In Egypt, on the other hand, there is no direct restriction on a guardian's right to give his minor ward in compulsory marriage; but the exercise of this right has been greatly discouraged by legislation that forbids marriage registrars to register any union in which the bride and bridegroom have not reached the ages of sixteen and eighteen respectively, and that precludes the courts from entertaining any matrimonial cause whatever where the

[45] With certain, somewhat detailed, qualifications.

parties have not reached these ages, or in respect of any disputed marriage which has not been registered.[46] Most of the Middle East countries, however, have followed the precedent set by the Ottoman Law of Family Rights, 1917, in prescribing the age at which a boy or girl attains full competence to marry[47] and the minimum age at which marriage is ever permissible[48]—and also in providing that the marriage of those who have reached these minimum ages but not that of full competence will be permitted only if they obtain leave of court (and also, in most cases, the consent of marriage guardians).[49] In Middle East countries it is in Egypt alone, therefore, that any recognition is given to the marriage of one who is not physically mature, except only that in the Sudan a girl who has not reached puberty but is at least ten years old may be given in marriage, with the consent of court, where there are grounds for anxiety about her morals.[50] As for the compulsory marriage of adult girls who have not been previously married, this was never, as we have seen, permissible in Ḥanafī or Shīʿī law; but the reformers have done their best to abolish it also in countries such as Tunisia, Algeria, Morocco and the Sudan, where the Mālikī law formerly prevailed. In Morocco and the Sudan[51] a marriage is still irregular unless the bride's father, whether in person or by agent, intervenes; but the bride herself must always be a consenting party—except that, in Morocco, the court is

[46] Except, only, for claims for legitimacy. Cf. Law of the Organization and Procedure of Sharīʿa Courts, 1931—together with Law No. 56 of 1923 in regard to the registration of marriages.

[47] For a boy eighteen in all cases, and for a girl eighteen in Iraq, seventeen in Jordan and Syria, sixteen in Algeria and fifteen in Tunisia and Morocco.

[48] Twelve for a boy and nine for a girl under the Ottoman Law, fifteen for a boy and thirteen for a girl in Syria, and fifteen and sixteen for both sexes in Jordan and Iraq, respectively.

[49] Except that no allegation of irregularity in this regard is to be entertained by the courts, in either Jordan or Syria, after pregnancy has become apparent—or, in Jordan, after the parties have reached the prescribed ages. Cf. Article 30 in the Jordanian Law, and Article 40 in the Syrian. It seems clear, moreover, that much the same principles were in fact applied under the Ottoman Law, which is still in force in the Lebanon.

[50] Cf. Judicial Circular No. 54 of 1960, Article 8.

[51] Cf. Articles 4, 9 and 12 of the Moroccan Code, and Article 1 of Judicial Circular No. 54 of 1960 in the Sudan.

empowered to give a girl in compulsory marriage to a suitable suitor and protector if her morals are in jeopardy. The role of the marriage guardian has been virtually restricted, therefore, to that of protecting the interests of wards who are physically mature but have not reached the age of statutory majority—which coincides, in most countries, with the age of full competence to marry, but has been fixed at twenty in Tunisia and twenty-five in Morocco. But even in these cases, in which the consent of the guardian is normally essential, an overriding power is vested in the courts—which may permit marriage, even against the wishes of the guardian, where it considers this to be in the interests of the parties concerned.

The second category of conditions discussed by Muslim jurists are called *shurūṭ al-ṣiḥḥa*: that is, those conditions which determine whether a contract, impeccable in its basic essentials, actually concludes a valid marriage. Chief among these is the requirement that the parties must not be within the prohibited degrees of consanguinity, affinity or foster relationship. In addition, a man is prohibited from being married at one and the same time to two women who would be debarred from marrying each other if either of them happened to be a male; and a man who already has four wives may not marry a fifth while the other marriages persist. While, moreover, a Muslim man may marry a woman who is a Muslim, a Christian or a Jewess, a Muslim woman is precluded from marrying anyone except a Muslim. A further requirement of a valid marriage, in Sunnī but not in Shī'ī law, is the presence of two eligible witnesses.[52] Some Ḥanafī jurists habitually classify marriage contracts under the three categories of valid (*ṣaḥīḥ*), irregular (*fāsid*) and void (*bāṭil*), and accord certain legal effects to the intermediate category. It seems preferable, however, to postulate that no irregular or void marriage has any validity whatever in Islamic law unless it is consummated; but that, if it is, any children

[52] The only exception to this is that the Mālikīs dispense with the need for such testimony where adequate publicity is given to the occasion when the wife is conducted to the marriage home. Where the original witnesses to a marriage are not available, moreover, all schools will accept hearsay evidence, or evidence of repute.

will be regarded as legitimate where the circumstances were such that some jurists would have regarded the union as a valid marriage, or where the parties were themselves acting in good faith (however mistakenly)—and in these cases the woman must observe the *'idda* period when the parties are separated and is usually entitled to an appropriate dower, while some jurists hold that the union will give rise to the bar of affinity in regard to any future marriage contracted by either party.[53]

The only points which demand mention under this heading in the context of recent reforms are that it is noteworthy that even in Turkey, where the Sharī'a has been completely abandoned, a provision has been inserted in the Civil Code which retains the distinctively Islamic impediment of foster relationship—although no corresponding provision, curiously enough, has been included in the Turkish Family (Marriage and Divorce) Laws of 1951 and 1954 which govern the family relationships of Turkish Cypriots.[54] It is also important to note that Muslim men or women may, in India, conclude a marriage with any partner, regardless of his or her religion, under the terms of the Special Marriage Act, 1954, provided that neither party is a lunatic or has a spouse living, and that the groom has reached the age of twenty-one and the bride that of eighteen; and this Act includes special provisions not only governing divorce, but also succession, in such cases.

The third category of conditions commonly discussed in modern textbooks are those which are termed *shurūṭ al-nufūdh*: that is, those which determine whether a contract of marriage is not only valid but effective. The reason for this is that Ḥanafī jurists regard a considerable number of contracts (including contracts of marriage) which are concluded by one who has reached the 'age of discernment', but not that of majority, as essentially valid but suspended

[53] This is set out in detail, with a minor slant towards specifically Mālikī principles, in Article 22 of the Tunisian Law of Personal Status, 1956. Cf. also Article 16 of the Family Law, 1974, in South Yemen, which lists the legal effects of an invalid marriage as legitimacy of issue, the bar of affinity and the obligation to observe the *'idda*.

[54] Cf. my article 'The Family Law of Turkish Cypriots', in *Die Welt des Islams*, N.S., Vols. 3 and 4 (1958), pp. 161–87.

on his or her guardian's consent: if the guardian gives his consent, the contract becomes effective, while if he does not, then it is null and void. Similarly, a contract of marriage concluded by a slave was regarded as suspended on his owner's consent, and a contract concluded on another person's behalf by an unauthorized person (*al-fuḍūlī*) as suspended on the consent of the principal party; and this would also, of course, apply to an agent who acts in a way which is beyond his authority. But these conditions scarcely come within the ambit of recent reforms except for the obvious parallel between them and those legislative provisions which permit the marriage of those who have reached the minimum age for marriage but not that of full legal competence, provided always that the necessary consent—whether of court, guardian or both—has been given.[55]

The fourth category of conditions on which Muslim jurists commonly insist in this context are called *shurūṭ al-luzūm*: that is, conditions which determine whether a contract of marriage is binding; for there are certain circumstances in which even a contract of marriage which is both valid and effective may be revoked. Such, for example, is the case under Ḥanafī law where a minor has been given in marriage by anyone other than a father or father's father; for the minor then has an option of repudiating the marriage (called *khiyār al-bulūgh*) on reaching puberty. Such too is the case, on one view,[56] where an adult Ḥanafī woman gives herself in marriage to one who is not her 'equal', for her agnatic guardian may, in such circumstances, apply to the court to have the marriage terminated (as he may also, in the traditional law, if she gives herself in marriage to an 'equal' for an inadequate dower—unless the husband is willing to make this up to what is regarded as an appropriate sum). In the doctrine of the other Sunnī schools these questions can never arise (except only where the husband has deceived the wife's marriage guardian about his status), since it is the guardian alone who can contract his female ward in marriage; and in Shīʿī law the question of equality in marriage has no place. But jurists of all schools regard a valid and effective marriage

[55] Cf. pp. 49f. and 104 above.

[56] On the other view, such a marriage is regarded as irregular *ab initio*.

contract as subject to annulment if the husband is unable to consummate the marriage or (in the majority view)[57] if, unknown to his wife, he is afflicted at the time of marriage with some disease of mind or body which would make married life dangerous—or even, in some cases, if he becomes so afflicted at a later date.

A number of reforms have been introduced, in one country or another, in these matters. In India and Pakistan, for example, a minor girl given in marriage even by her father or paternal grandfather now has the right, under Section 2 (vii) of the Dissolution of Muslim Marriages Act, to repudiate the marriage when she reaches the age of eighteen—provided only that she has not previously signified her consent to the union. Under the Ottoman and Syrian Laws, again, a marriage guardian is precluded from exercising his right to demand the annulment of his ward's marriage to a man who is not her equal in any case in which her pregnancy has already become apparent.[58] In Morocco a guardian may still refuse his consent to his ward's marriage with one who is not her equal, but no longer has the right, under the Code of 1958, to oppose her marriage for an inadequate dower which she herself is willing to accept; and in Tunisia he is precluded from any interference, whether on grounds of equality or dower.[59] It is clear, therefore, that a guardian's right to insist that his ward receives her 'proper' dower seems to be almost obsolete today. In the Moroccan Code the question of equality in marriage is still expressly stated to be the 'special right' of both the bride and her guardian; but there can be no doubt that the general tendency in the contemporary Muslim world is for courts to consider any such question primarily in terms of the interests of the parties to a marriage rather than those of their families, as can be seen in judicial decisions in India and Pakistan.

Finally, modern jurists discuss those conditions, termed *shurūṭ*

[57] But not in the generally accepted view of the Ḥanafīs, whose school claims such widespread allegiance.

[58] Cf. Article 50 in the Ottoman Law and Article 30 in the Syrian (which simply states that the right of annulment on grounds of inequality lapses if the wife becomes pregnant).

[59] Cf. Articles 6–15 of the Moroccan Code, and Articles 3–10 of the Tunisian.

al-sijill, which determine whether a contract of marriage may properly be registered. In a sense this is a wholly new departure initiated by the reformers, for in the traditional system there was no such requirement. But here the reformers were able to quote the authority of the Qur'ān itself to establish the desirability of reducing contracts to writing; and it is noteworthy that the principle that marriages must be registered either by the courts or by special officials forms the basis of many of the most important contemporary reforms. It is partly in this way, for example, that the reforms in regard to child marriage and marriage by compulsion have been effected—by means of legislation precluding courts or registrars from registering a marriage where the parties have not reached the prescribed ages, where they have not signified their personal consent, and where, in appropriate circumstances, the court or marriage guardians have not given their consent.[60] Any infraction of these rules normally incurs a penal sanction on all those responsible; and in some countries no unregistered marriage is recognized by the courts, at least unless or until pregnancy becomes apparent. Article 6 in the Family Law of South Yemen, indeed, states unequivocally that 'A marriage will not be regarded as effective unless (a) it has been registered before the appropriate official, and (b) the husband and wife have signed the deed and the register of marriage'. This insistence on registration has, moreover, been called in aid in Jordan, Syria and South Yemen to prevent marriages being concluded in which there is a gross disparity in age between the parties, unless there is some genuine benefit in the union;[61] and also, in several countries, to prohibit or restrict polygamy—which is still very common in some parts of the

[60] Cf. Ottoman Law of Family Rights, 1917, Articles 37, 4–7 and 52; Jordanian Law of Family Rights, 1951, Articles 17 and 4–5; Syrian Law of Personal Status, 1953, Articles 40 and 15–20; Tunisian Code of Personal Status, 1957, Articles 5–6; Moroccan Code of Personal Status, 1958, Articles 41–43, 6–9 and 12; and Algerian Law No. 63-244 of 1963.

[61] Cf. Article 6 of the Jordanian Law (which also insists that the consent of the younger party must not have been given 'under compulsion or duress'), Article 19 of the Syrian Code and Article 9 of the South Yemen Law (which forbids a marriage in which there is a difference of twenty years between the parties unless the wife has reached the age of thirty-five).

Muslim world, although it is today comparatively rare in countries such as India, Pakistan, Tunisia, Egypt and Iran.

Reforms in regard to the practice of polygamy have been discussed at some length in the previous chapter,[62] so here I must confine myself largely to actual legislation which has been enacted (or, in some cases, merely proposed). As already noted,[63] two articles on this subject which were included in a legislative draft approved by the Egyptian Government in 1927 were eventually omitted from Law No. 25 of 1929 by the personal decision of King Fu'ād—partly, at least, on the grounds that polygamy in Egypt was largely confined to the *fellaḥīn*, where its continuance was alleged to be justified both by economic conditions and the birth rate. Even so, the Ministry of Social Affairs put forward similar proposals in 1943 and 1945, only for them to be shelved once more; and in spite of endless discussion and several draft codes, no legislation on this subject has yet been promulgated in Egypt. It was in fact in Syria that the suggestion of Muḥammad ʿAbduh[64] which is the better suited to legal determination was first included in a legislative enactment, for Article 17 of the Syrian Law of Personal Status, 1953, provided that 'the court may withhold permission for a man who is already married to take a second wife where it is established that he is not in a position to support them both'. But Article 18 in the Tunisian Law of Personal Status, 1956, was far more radical, and tersely decreed that 'Polygamy is prohibited' (and the full import of this prohibition was spelt out in 1964 when it was explicitly provided that a contract of marriage with a second wife would not only make those concerned liable to criminal sanctions but would be regarded as invalid *per se*).

Polygamy was forbidden in Turkey, of course, under Ataturk, when the Sharīʿa was abandoned in favour of a slightly amended form of the Swiss Civil Code; and it is also forbidden to Turkish Cypriots. More recently, in the new Constitution of the 'Shia Imami Ismailis', or the Ismāʿīlī Khōjas of East Africa, Article 223 provides that 'polygamy is strictly prohibited', and Article 224 (a)

[62] Cf. pp. 49, 59, 61 ff. above. [63] Cf. p. 62 above.
[64] Cf. p. 63 above.

that a marriage may be solemnized between two members of the community only if 'neither party has a spouse living at the time of the marriage'.[65] For the rest, recent legislation on this subject in Muslim countries is less drastic than the complete prohibition enshrined in the Tunisian reforms but commonly goes somewhat further than the Syrian law. Thus in the Moroccan Code of 1958 Article 30 provides that: '(1) Polygamy is not permitted if there is any fear that co-wives will not be treated with equal justice. (2) A woman whose husband marries another wife, but who has not made a stipulation for an option of divorce in such circumstances, may petition the Qāḍī to investigate any injury she may have suffered. Nor may a husband marry a second wife unless she has been made aware of the fact that the man who wishes to marry her is already married to another woman.' Article 31, moreover, decrees that 'A woman has the right to make a stipulation in her marriage contract that her husband should not marry a co-wife, and that, if the husband does not observe this stipulation, she should have the right to demand that her marriage should be dissolved.' In Iraq in 1959, moreover, the reformers went a little further than this, although not so far as in Tunisia, when they provided in Article 4 that 'Marriage with more than one wife is not allowed without permission of court, and such permission shall not be given unless the following two conditions are fulfilled: (a) that the husband has the financial competence to support more than one wife; and (b) that there should be some lawful benefit in this second marriage'; in Article 5 that 'Polygamy is not permitted if there is any fear that co-wives will not be treated with equal justice, and the decision in this matter shall be left to the Qāḍī'; and in Article 6 that 'Anyone who makes a contract of marriage with more than one wife contrary to the provisions in Articles 4 and 5 shall be punished by imprisonment for not more than one year, or by a fine of not more than 100 dinars, or by both'.[66]

[65] Cf. my article 'The Isma'ili Khojas of East Africa', in *Middle Eastern Studies*, Vol. 1, No. 1 (1964), p. 26.

[66] For a few comments on the provisions of these two Laws, cf. pp. 63–4 above.

In Pakistan the Muslim Family Laws Ordinance, 1961, provides in Article 6 that 'No man, during the subsistence of an existing marriage, shall, except with the previous permission in writing of the Arbitration Council, contract another marriage, nor shall any marriage contracted without such permission be registered under this Ordinance'. An application for such permission, moreover, must 'state the reasons for the proposed marriage, and whether the consent of the existing wife or wives has been obtained thereto'. On receipt of this application, the Chairman of the Arbitration Council 'shall ask the applicant and his existing wife or wives each to nominate a representative and the Arbitration Council so constituted may, if satisfied that the proposed marriage is necessary and just, grant, subject to such conditions, if any, as may be deemed fit, the permission applied for'. A man who contracts another marriage without permission, moreover, is not only subject to criminal sanctions but must 'pay immediately the entire amount of the dower, whether prompt or deferred, due to the existing wife or wives'. Both in what was then West Pakistan and East Pakistan Rules were promulgated, moreover, 'to carry into effect the purposes of this Ordinance'. In Singapore, again, Article 90 of the Administration of Muslim Law Act, 1968, provides that no marriage shall be solemnized under that Act if the party to be wedded is married to any other person, except by a 'Kathi'[67] or with his written consent—after satisfying himself that 'there is no lawful obstacle according to the Muslim law or this Act to such marriage'. The Act does not specify what these obstacles are, but I understand that all such cases now have to be referred to the 'Chief Kathi' himself, and that permission is in fact seldom given. So this is an outstanding example of law reform by what is virtually administrative action.

The Family Protection Act, 1975, in Iran (which repealed and replaced a somewhat similar enactment of the same name promulgated in 1967, together with certain articles in the Civil Code of 1937) is chiefly remarkable for the reforms which have been effected in the law of divorce; but it is noteworthy in this context

[67] I.e. *Qāḍī*.

that Article 17 permits a wife to petition for a divorce in *any* case in which the husband marries another wife—and this would, it seems, include a *mutʿa* or temporary marriage with another woman. In addition, Article 16 decrees that a husband has no right to take a second wife unless the first wife either consents to the marriage or is herself unable or unwilling to co-habit, has become insane or afflicted with some incurable disease, has been sentenced to imprisonment for not less than five years, has become 'addicted' (i.e. to drink, drugs or gambling), has deserted the family, has become sterile or has disappeared. Article 17 adds that in all cases the court must also be satisfied that the husband is capable of supporting more than one wife and treating a plurality of wives with equal justice; and, should he contract a second marriage in defiance of these provisions, then both he and his second wife (if she was aware of the contravention) are liable to imprisonment for six months—although the second marriage, it seems, would itself be legally valid. The clause in this Article about equality of treatment must, presumably, be taken to apply even to the case where a man marries one 'permanent' wife and one *mutʿa* wife. But even in the case of two 'permanent' wives, the provision is not wholly without difficulty in a Shīʿī country; for the Ithnā ʿAsharī law provides that a wife's maintenance should be reckoned exclusively by reference to her own social and financial status, so a man who marries one wife from an aristocratic and wealthy family, and another from a humble and impoverished home, would normally be required to maintain the first in quite a different style from that appropriate to the second. It is also noteworthy that this article has been cited in Irān as virtually making any future *mutʿa* marriages, if polygamous, subject to penal sanctions,[68] since the courts are today unlikely to give permission for such a union.

But the most recent enactment about polygamy comes in the Family Law, 1974, in South Yemen and in Somalia, 1975. In the

[68] Although it seems unlikely that many Iranian wives would in fact invoke the criminal law against husbands who indulged in a *mutʿa* marriage for the duration, for instance, of a visit to the holy cities of Qum or Mashhad. Cf. my article 'Reforms in Islamic Law in Irān', in *Iqbal Review*, Vol. 12, No. 3 (1971), pp. 16 ff.

former[69] Article 11 (a) provides that 'Marriage with a second wife is not permitted without the written consent of the appropriate district court, and the court has no right to give such consent unless one of the following circumstances has been established before it:

(a) a medical certificate that the wife is barren—with the proviso that the husband did not know this before marriage;

(b) a medical certificate that the wife is suffering from a chronic and infectious illness—with the proviso that it is not curable'.

It must also be remembered in this context that it is both legal and morally correct, in Islamic law, for a man to have sexual relations not only with his wives but also with his female slaves. With the abolition of slavery—most recently, in Saʿūdī Arabia—such concubinage has largely come to an end. But Muslim jurists in Northern Nigeria would still, in all probability, recognize as legitimate a child born to a man by a woman who would have been his slave, or even by a woman 'given' to him by the person whose slave she would have been, had slavery not been abolished; and the woman herself, although 'free' according to the law of the land, would still be regarded as his *jāriyya*, or female 'slave', in terms of personal relationship. Elsewhere in West Africa, moreover, a distinction is made, on much the same basis, between 'free' wives and 'slave' wives—i.e. women of a lower social class—in a way which represents a complete perversion of true Islamic law on this matter.[70]

3. MARRIED LIFE AND ITS TERMINATION

There is comparatively little on the subject of married life as such in recent legislative reforms in the Muslim world, but a great deal about the circumstances which justify its termination—whether by divorce, judicial dissolution or putative widowhood.

Broadly speaking, the marital relationship envisaged in the traditional law may be summed up in terms of a wife's duty to obey her husband in every lawful demand he may make—provided only

[69] It seems, moreover, that the provisions of the latter, which is not yet available to me, are broadly similar.

[70] On this whole subject, cf. my *Islamic Law in Africa*, pp. 215, 234, 237 etc.

that he has given her her 'prompt' dower—in consideration for his duty to provide her with suitable maintenance and support. The respective rights and duties of the spouses (including the husband's right to marry additional wives, to decide where the family home shall be, and strictly to control his wives' social and professional activities) are, moreover, regarded by most of the schools of law as prescribed by the divine Lawgiver and not susceptible to any variation, at the will of the parties, to which expression may validly be given in stipulations or conditions inserted in the contract of marriage—except that there was a certain difference of opinion between the jurists as to the circumstances in which a husband might compel his wife to move to an alien environment. According to the majority view, the only stipulations inserted in a marriage contract which are valid and enforceable are those which serve merely to reinforce or particularize one or another of the established rights or duties of marriage, such as to the amount and nature of the dower. Any conditions designed to safeguard or improve a wife's position—such as a stipulation that her husband will not marry a co-wife, will not forbid her to practise her trade or profession, or will not submit her to personal chastisement—were regarded as invalid and unenforceable by all except the Ḥanbalīs.[71] In the other schools it was only by the device of inducing the husband to pronounce a conditional divorce which would come into operation in specified circumstances, or to delegate to her the right to divorce herself in such circumstances, that a wife (or her father) could give legal teeth to stipulations or promises about how she should be treated. But the Ḥanbalīs regard as valid any stipulation in a marriage contract by which a husband undertakes not to do something which the Sharīʿa normally permits but does not require as part of the essence of marriage.

Recent legislative reforms in the Muslim world have followed this Ḥanbalī principle in validating provisions, which differ somewhat from one country to another, in order to improve the position of married women. Reference has already been made to Article 38 in the Ottoman Law of Family Rights, 1917;[72] and the Jordanian

[71] Cf. pp. 49, 79f. above. [72] Cf. p. 49 above.

Law of 1951 gives this same Ḥanbalī principle a somewhat wider application when it provides in Article 21 that 'If a stipulation of benefit to one of the parties is included in the contract, this must be respected—e.g. a stipulation that the wife should have the right to divorce herself, that her husband should not make her leave the town where he agreed that she should live, or that he should not marry a co-wife: provided that in any case of dispute such stipulation must have been registered in the marriage certificate. If, then, the husband disregards these stipulations the marriage shall be dissolved at the request of the wife.' I am told, moreover, that the insertion of such stipulations in marriage contracts is today the rule rather than the exception in upper class families in Jordan, and is becoming increasingly common in all classes. But the Syrian Law of 1953 is much more detailed, for Article 14 provides that 'If a contract of marriage is coupled with a condition which conflicts with the legal nature of marriage or its purposes, or enforces something which is legally forbidden, then the condition shall be void and the contract valid'. If, however, it is 'coupled with a condition which enforces some benefit to the wife which is not legally forbidden and neither affects the rights of another nor restricts the liberty of the husband in those matters permitted to him by law, then the condition is valid and binding'. Again, 'If the wife makes a condition in a contract of marriage which does so restrict the liberty of the husband or affect the rights of another, then the condition, though valid, is not binding on the husband; but if he fails to observe it, then the wife who made it has the right to demand the dissolution of the marriage'. And the Moroccan Code, after declaring in Article 38 that conditions contrary to the essence or purposes of marriage are void, explicitly states that 'It is not contrary to the purposes of marriage that a wife should stipulate the right to concern herself in the public interests of the country'. Yet again, Article 6 in the Iraqī Law of 1959 provides that 'A lawful stipulation included in a contract of marriage shall be recognized and must be observed',[73] and that 'A wife may demand the

[73] But this phrase may mean much or little, since it gives no indication whatsoever as to what stipulations are, in fact, to be regarded as 'lawful'.

dissolution of the marriage if her husband does not observe a stipulation she has inserted in the contract'. Much the same position has also been reached in India and Pakistan, but by judicial decisions rather than legislative enactments—provided only that the stipulations are regarded by the courts as reasonable and not contrary to the provisions or policy of the law.

It is noteworthy, moreover, in this context, as in the sphere of family law in general, that modern reforms are not designed solely and exclusively to give ill-used wives a degree of relief from traditional male domination. The underlying philosophy is partly to enable Muslim wives to play a more effective part in public and social life, and partly to give them a greater measure of control over their own circumstances and those of their children. That their growing emancipation implies an increased responsibility is expressly stated in the Tunisian Law when it provides, in Article 23, that a wife who has private means must share in the support of her family. But the Family Law of South Yemen goes much further, for Article 17 states that the married couple shall 'take their share in bearing the expenses of the marriage and the requirements of the marriage home according to their respective means'; Article 20 that both husband and wife shall 'take their share in bearing the costs of their common life after marriage, and if one of them is not able to do this the other is bound to pay the expenses and bear the burdens of their married life'; and Article 22 that 'the father and mother shall take their share in supporting their children according to their means, and if this is impossible for one of them, the other alone must be responsible for their support'.[74] The general concept of marriage which the reformers had in mind is summarized in Article 33 (2) of the Moroccan Code which states that the reciprocal rights and duties of the spouses include 'Good treatment, mutual respect and affection, and the safeguarding of the interests of the family'.[75] And the South Yemen Law even goes so far as to declare in Article 2 that 'Marriage is a contract between a man and a

[74] And again the Family Law of Somalia, 1975, seems to be broadly similar.

[75] Cf. my article 'Reforms in Family Law in Morocco', in *Journal of African Law*, Vol. 2, No. 3 (1958).

woman who are equal in rights and duties, the basis of which is mutual understanding and respect and the purpose of which is the creation of a stable family as the foundation of society'.

It was, indeed, the fact that Muslim husbands all too often failed to accord their wives this sort of treatment which first impelled the reformers to intrude into the sacrosanct sphere of family law. It was as early as 1915 that the Ottoman Sultan issued two imperial edicts granting an ill-used wife the right to demand a judicial dissolution of marriage where she had been deserted by her husband or where she found that her husband, unknown to her, was afflicted with some dangerous disease. Similar provisions duly reappeared, two years later, in the Ottoman Law of Family Rights, 1917, which is still in force (with certain amendments) in Israel and the Lebanon. Articles 122–5 in this Law give a Muslim wife the right to claim a dissolution of marriage if her newly married husband proves to be, or subsequently becomes, afflicted with some grave disease 'which makes it impossible for her to remain with him without injury'—such as elephantiasis, leprosy, syphilis or madness (but not, e.g. blindness), as the Lebanese version of the Law specifically states. As in the case of his inability to consummate the marriage (which is the only reason, apart from the 'option of puberty', which gives a wife the right to the annulment of her marriage under the traditional Ḥanafī law), the court must grant the husband a year's respite for treatment if his condition is such as to give hope of a cure, or decree an immediate dissolution of marriage if his condition is regarded as incurable; but the wife is disqualified from claiming this relief if she married with a knowledge of the husband's affliction or if she consented to continue the marriage relationship after the disease developed—but not by mere delay in bringing or pressing her demand. Similarly Article 126 provides that a wife may be granted a judicial dissolution of marriage if her husband disappears, goes away and does not return, or becomes missing and she cannot obtain maintenance. In addition, the Ottoman Law makes provision in Article 130 for a judicial divorce, after a suitable investigation by two (or, if necessary, three) arbitrators, where the wife alleges that her husband has treated her in a way which makes the continuance of the union impossible—but with the proviso that the court may deprive her of her deferred dower, or make her pay back not more than half of her dower where the whole has been handed over, if it appears that she alone was responsible for the breakdown of the marriage. Subsequent reforms in Egypt, the Sudan, Jordan, Syria, Tunisia, Morocco and Iraq go considerably further. There are, of course, minor differences in points of detail between the relevant provisions, but broadly speaking there are four different reasons for which a Muslim wife may today claim a judicial divorce or dissolution of marriage in these countries.

First, for certain 'defects' of body or mind which either prevent the husband from consummating the marriage or which make married life dangerous. Reforms to this effect have been introduced in Egypt,[76] the Sudan,[77] Jordan,[78] Syria (but in a much more restricted form),[79] Iraq,[80] Singapore[81] and India and Pakistan.[82] No reforms of this sort were needed in either Tunisia or Morocco, since the traditional Mālikī law makes provision for such cases.[83] But in Iran the Family Protection Act of 1975 gives a long list of circumstances which may be regarded as justification for a demand for a 'certificate of impossibility of reconciliation' as the essential pre-requisite for *any* divorce; and these include insanity, sterility, inability or unwillingness to have normal sexual intercourse, affliction with one of a number of specified diseases or with some 'addiction' which is prejudicial to family life, imprisonment for not less than five years, desertion of family life, the commission of an offence (or following some occupation) 'repugnant to family

[76] By Articles 9–11 of Law No. 25 of 1920.

[77] By Articles 2 and 4 of Judicial Circular No. 28 of 1927.

[78] By Articles 86–88 of the Law of Family Rights, 1951.

[79] By Articles 105 and 106 of the Law of Personal Status, 1953.

[80] By Article 44 of the Code of Personal Status, 1959.

[81] By Article 49 (d) and (e) of the Administration of Muslim Law Act, 1968.

[82] By Articles 2 (v) and (vi) of the Dissolution of Muslim Marriages Act, 1939.

[83] Cf. my articles 'Recent Developments in Sharī'a Law' v and VIII, in *The Muslim World* (Oct. 1951 and July 1952); 'The Problem of Divorce jn Sharī'a Law', in *Journal of Royal Central Asian Society*, Vol. XXXVII, Part 2 (1950); and those on the Sudan, Syria, Morocco and Iraq to which reference has been made above.

honour', or the absence of some special qualification the possession of which was made a specific condition of the marriage.[84] All these circumstances apply equally to both parties; but it is also noteworthy that the wife may apply for a certificate of impossibility of reconciliation where the husband marries a second wife, where the court holds that he has failed to treat a plurality of wives with equal justice, or where he has failed to support her.[85] Somewhat similarly, the Family Law of South Yemen provides that *either* party may request a judicial divorce if the other is afflicted with an incurable disease which makes married life impossible (provided this was not known before marriage).[86] Under the traditional Sunnī law, on the other hand, little or no provision was usually made in regard to defects in the wife, and the husband was normally left to deal with such cases by the exercise of his unfettered right of repudiation—although Article 54 (4) of the Moroccan Code, for example, specifies the action which a husband may take if he finds his wife afflicted with one of a number of diseases or defects; and here the point at issue is not the termination of the marriage, since he could always have divorced her under the traditional law, but the subsidiary question of his liability for dower.

Secondly, for failure of maintenance. Here there are considerable differences between one code and another regarding whether the basic criterion is the husband's inability or unwillingness to provide maintenance, what action is to be taken when he has the means but refuses to do anything about it, what precisely is to be done when he cannot be traced, what minimum maintenance must be provided to prevent a revocable divorce becoming decisive, etc.[87]

[84] Cf., in all cases, Article 8.

[85] Cf. my article 'Reforms in Islamic Law in Iran', in *Iqbal Review*, Vol. 2, No. 3 (1971)—for the law prior to the new Act of 1975.

[86] Article 29 (1) (a).

[87] The relevant provisions may be found in Articles 2–9 of Judicial Circular No. 17 (probably of 1916) in the Sudan; Articles 4–6 of Law No. 25 of 1920 in Egypt; Articles 98–100 of the Jordanian Law; Articles 110 and 111 of the Syrian Law; Articles 39 and 40 of the Tunisian Law; Article 53 of the Moroccan Code; Article 45 of the Iraqī Law; Article 49 (a) of the Singapore Law; Article 2 (ii) of the Dissolution of Muslim Marriages Act in India and Pakistan; Article 1129

Thirdly, for cruelty or intolerable treatment—although there are differences between one country and another as to whether, and in what circumstances, a judicial divorce may be granted by the court directly or only on the recommendation of two arbitrators, the circumstances (if any) in which the wife must pay her husband some financial compensation, and what precisely constitutes intolerable treatment or cruelty. In Egypt, for example, the latter is expressly made to depend on the social status of the parties; in India and Pakistan the Dissolution of Muslim Marriages Act provides a considerable list of circumstances which must, presumably, be regarded as constituting intolerable conduct; and in the Iranian Family Protection Act clauses covering 'any addiction which according to the finding of the court is prejudicial to the foundation of family life and makes the continuation of married life impossible', desertion of family life, conviction by final judgment of 'an offence repugnant to the family honour or prestige of the wife' and the marriage of another wife without the first wife's consent, presumably fall under this heading. In Pakistan, moreover, an addition inserted in the Dissolution of Muslim Marriages Act by Article 13 of the Muslim Family Laws Ordinance, 1961, gives the wife the right to demand a dissolution of marriage where 'her husband has taken an additional wife in contravention of the provisions of the Muslim Family Laws Ordinance, 1961'; in Morocco, Article 30 (2) of the Code provides that a wife whose husband has married a second wife may 'refer her case to the court to consider any injury which may have been caused her'; and in South Yemen, Article 29 (2) provides that a wife whose husband has been given consent of court to marry a second wife may herself request a judicial divorce for that reason.[88]

of the Iranian Civil Code; and Article 29 (1) (c) of the Family Law in South Yemen (although this provides that *either* party may request a judicial divorce if he or she needs support and the other, who could provide it, fails to do so).

[88] Detailed provisions in regard to intolerable treatment can be found in Articles 14 and 15 of Judicial Circular No. 17 in the Sudan; Articles 6–11 of Law No. 25 of 1929 in Egypt; Articles 96 and 97 of the Jordanian Law; Article 109 of the Syrian Law; Articles 56 and 30 (2) of the Moroccan Code; Article 40 of the Iraqī Law; Article 2 (viii) of the Dissolution of Muslim Marriages Act in

Fourthly, for deprivation of her husband's company for a considerable period of time. Again, there are many differences in points of detail between one country and another in this matter—e.g. in regard to the relevant period of deprivation (one, two or three years), whether the husband's absence must be without legal justification, whether his imprisonment for a specified period is included in this regard, and whether or not the wife must expressly allege that she has suffered hardship or been exposed to the danger of falling into immorality by reason of this deprivation.[89]

Such are the four grounds on which a wife can claim a judicial dissolution of marriage in almost all the countries concerned. But there are other such grounds which are peculiar to one country or another. In Morocco, for example, it will be remembered that a contract of marriage with a second wife must not be concluded unless or until she has been made aware of the fact that her intended husband is already married to another woman. But it is the Tunisian Law which has introduced the most sweeping reform in this context, since a wife may there insist, under Article 31 (3), on a judicial divorce—for any reason or none—provided she is prepared to pay her husband such compensation as the court may decree. It is noteworthy, moreover, that several other countries allow a judicial divorce to be granted on grounds of marital discord—and

India and Pakistan; Article 1130 of the Iranian Civil Code; Article 13 of the Muslim Family Laws Ordinance in Pakistan; and Article 29 (1) (d) of the Family Law in South Yemen (although this is applicable to both parties to the marriage).

[89] The relevant legislation was introduced in the Sudan by Article 13 of Judicial Circular No. 17 (but this was limited, by Article 1 of Circular No. 28 of 1927, to cases where a divorce for failure of support was not available); in Egypt by Articles 12–14 of Law No. 25 of 1929; in Jordan by Articles 89 and 90 of the Law of Family Rights; in Syria by Article 109 of the Law of Personal Status; in Morocco by Articles 57 and 58 of the Code of Personal Status; in Iraq by Articles 41 and 43 of the Law of Personal Status; in Singapore by Article 49 (b) and (c) of the Administration of Muslim Law Act; in India and Pakistan by Article 2 (ii), (iii) and (iv) of the Dissolution of Muslim Marriages Act; in Iran by Article 8 (iv) of the Family Protection Act, 1975; and in South Yemen by Article 29 (1) (b) of the Family Law (although this, again, is applicable to both parties to the marriage). And much the same result has been achieved, as we have seen, by judicial interpretation.

commonly provide that, where it is the wife who seems to be primarily to blame, she may be ordered to refund her dower, in whole or in part.[90] And in Pakistan, again, a wife may, in most cases, obtain a divorce for incompatibility of temperament or breakdown of marriage—but on the basis of case law rather than legislation.[91]

With regard to the other side of the coin—that is, the previously unfettered right of a husband to repudiate his wife—it is clear that the reformers have made much less progress. It is true that in the majority of the countries under discussion most of the wilder extravagences of the Ḥanafī law of divorce have now been remedied—and a divorce formula pronounced by a husband under the influence of compulsion, drink or uncontrollable passion, etc., is no longer regarded as valid or binding.[92] No legislation to this effect has been introduced in India, although it is probable that the courts would give judgment accordingly; and the provisions about the prior necessity for reference to a Union Council in Pakistan (under the Muslim Family Laws Ordinance) and to a Muslim Court in Singapore (under the Administration of Muslim Law Act), for the issue of a 'certificate of impossibility of reconciliation' in Iran (under the Family Protection Act) and for a decree of court in Tunisia and South Yemen (under the Law of Personal Status and the Family Law, respectively), clearly make any specific mention of these detailed points superfluous.

Considerably more radical are the provisions promulgated in some of these countries that a formula of repudiation pronounced as a mere oath[93] or threat should be regarded, at least in some

[90] But not in Egypt. For 'discord' see above, under intolerable treatment.

[91] Cf. *Balqis Fatima* v. *Najm al-Ikram Qureshi* (P.L.D. 1959 Lah. 566); *Sayeeda Khanum* v. *Muhammad Sami* (P.L.D. 1952 Lah. 13); *Ghulam Sakima* v. *Umar Baksh* (P.L.D. 1964 S.C. 456); *Khurshid Bibi* v. *Muhammad Amin* (P.L.D. 1968 Lah. 413); and *Siddiq* v. *Sharfan* (P.L.D. 1968 Lah. 413). Cf. also my article 'Reforms in the Law of Divorce', in *Studia Islamica*, Vol. XXI (1970), pp. 46 f.

[92] Provisions to this effect may be found in Articles 104 and 105 of the Ottoman Law; Article 1 of the Egyptian Law of 1929; Article 1 of Judicial Circular No. 41 of 1936 in the Sudan; Articles 68 and 69 of the Jordanian Law; Article 89 of the Syrian Law; Article 49 of the Moroccan Code; and Article 35 of the Iraqī Law.

[93] E.g. 'by the triple divorce'—a phrase used as an oath in any context.

circumstances,[94] as invalid; that this should also be true of a formula expressed in terms which need not necessarily imply divorce; and that a 'triple' divorce pronounced on one and the same occasion (whether in explicit terms, or in some other way) should be treated as only a single, and therefore revocable, repudiation. But provisions to this effect can be found in Egypt,[95] the Sudan,[96] Jordan,[97] Syria,[98] Morocco,[99] and Iraq.[100] There is no comparable legislation in India; and the much more sweeping terms of the Law of Personal Status in Tunisia, the Muslim Family Laws Ordinance in Pakistan, the Administration of Muslim Law Act in Singapore, the Family Protection Act in Iran and the Family Law in South Yemen, make detailed provisions of this sort unnecessary.

Yet further steps have been taken in a few countries to discourage Muslim husbands from divorcing their wives even when this is their considered desire. In Syria, for example, Article 117 of the Law of Personal Status, 1953, provides that 'If a man divorces his wife and it becomes plain to the Qāḍī that the husband was treating his wife wrongfully by divorcing her without reasonable cause, and that the wife would suffer damage and poverty thereby, the Qāḍī may give judgment in her favour against her husband, having regard to the latter's financial standing and also to the degree to which he has wronged her, of compensation not exceeding the amount of a year's maintenance for one in her position, in addition to the maintenance due to her during her *'idda* period . . .'. Again, Article 60 of the Moroccan Code of 1958 enacts that 'Every husband who takes the initiative in repudiating his wife must give her a consolatory gift (i.e. a *mut'a*) in proportion to his means and her circumstances, except in the case of a wife whose dower was

94 I.e. when the husband does not really want the union to be ended, in the Egyptian, Sudanese, Jordanian and Syrian Laws, but in *all* cases of future or suspended divorce, in Morocco and Iraq.

95 Articles 2–4 of the Law of 1929.

96 Articles 2–4 of Judicial Circular No. 41 of 1936.

97 Article 70 of the Law of Family Rights, 1951.

98 Article 90 of the Law of Personal Status, 1953.

99 Articles 50–2 of the Code of 1958.

100 Articles 36–7 of the Law of 1959.

specified but who was repudiated before the marriage was consummated'. It is also noteworthy that in Singapore Article 52 (2) of the Administration of Muslim Law Act, 1968, provides that 'A woman who has been divorced by her husband may apply to the Court for a consolatory gift or *matta'ah* and the court may . . . order payment of such sum as may be just and in accordance with the Muslim law' in the case of any divorce which is not by mutual consent; and that this is also true in Selangor, Kelantan, Trengganu, Pahang, Malacca, Negri Sembilan, Kedah, Perlis and Brunei.[101] Article 31 of the Tunisian Law of 1956, moreover, provides that where it is the husband who insists on ending a marriage—just as is the case where it is the wife who is intransigent in this matter—the court should decree what financial compensation he must pay her.[102] All these reforms should be given a warm welcome, for it remains true, in the vast majority of Muslim countries, that 'The Muslim wife lives under the perpetual threat of divorce. She never knows when this may happen. Even her husband himself may not know when this may happen; for a husband who swears an oath by "the triple divorce", or who makes divorce conditional on something which someone else may do, does not himself know when his wife may be divorced. Thus the happiness of the married couple, of their children and of the family may depend on some act extraneous to the will of the head of the family or the will of the mistress of the family'.[103] This is why legislation has been

[101] Cf. Selangor Administration of Muslim Law Enactment, 1952, Article 130; Kelantan Council of Religion and Malay Custom and Kathis Courts Enactment, 1953, Article 149; Trengganu Administration of Islamic Law Enactment, 1955, Article 107; Pahang Administration of the Law of the Religion of Islam Enactment, 1956, Article 130; Malacca Administration of Muslim Law Enactment, 1960, Article 125; Negri Sembilan Administration of Muslim Law Enactment, 1960, Article 125; Kedah Administration of Muslim Law Enactment, 1962, Article 125; Perlis Administration of Muslim Law Enactment, 1963, Article 94 (but here the wording is slightly different); Brunei Religious Council and Kathis Courts Enactment, 1955, Article 148.

[102] Cf. also Article 30 of the Family Law of South Yemen.

[103] Cf. the Explanatory Memorandum issued with the Moroccan Code. It is quite common, in some Muslim countries, for a man to swear 'by the triple divorce' that what he says is true; and this means that, strictly speaking, his wife is divorced if he is telling a lie.

promulgated in recent years, in a number of countries, to restrict —or, in Morocco and Iraq, even to abolish—the validity of formulae of suspended or conditional divorce; but the position of a Muslim wife is still exceedingly precarious, so any attempt to provide financial resources for a divorced wife is a significant step in the right direction. But the fact remains that the financial compensation which the relevant legislation at present allows, or the courts currently award, is far from adequate. It is only among the Ismāʿīlī Khōjas of East Africa that a more realistic sum would, in all probability, be awarded, although Article 273 of their Constitution of 1962 simply provides that 'If, upon dissolution of any marriage, the Council is of the opinion . . . that the husband was responsible for the breaking up of the marriage, it may award to the wife such monetary compensation as it may deem just and reasonable in addition to the Mohr' (*sic*).

A further step in the direction of restricting a Muslim husband's almost unlimited power of repudiation has been taken by legislation designed to ensure that no divorce is effective unless or until the intervention of the courts has been invoked. In Tunisia, for example, Article 30 of the Law of 1956 provides that no divorce pronounced outside a court of law will have any legal validity whatever; and in Iraq, too, the Code of 1959 made an attempt to insist on the same principle by providing in Article 39 that 'He who desires to divorce his wife must bring an action in the Sharīʿa court asking that this should be made effective, and must seek a judgment accordingly'; then largely emasculated this requirement by the proviso: 'If it is not feasible for him to take the matter to court, then he must register the repudiation during the '*idda* period'; but finally recovered its nerve and provided that the *ḥujja* or document which establishes the existence of the marriage 'will be recognised so long as it has not been nullified by the court'. It is also interesting to note that in Kenya the Report of the Commission on the Law of Marriage and Divorce, 1968, proposed that legislation should be enacted providing that divorce should be only 'by decree of a court of competent jurisdiction', whatever the religion of the parties, and after the matter 'has been referred to a conciliatory body and that body has failed to settle the dispute'; that it should not be on the basis of 'specific matrimonial offences but the general ground that the marriage has broken down'; and that the circumstances which may be considered as evidence of such breakdown 'should be precisely the same whether the petitioner were the husband or the wife'.[104] Rumour has it, moreover, that a comprehensive code of the law of personal status which has been in draft and under periodic revision in Egypt for some years—although repeatedly shelved—includes a provision that divorce should be only by judicial decree.

A similar purpose lies behind the reforms which have been introduced in Singapore and Pakistan. In the former, Article 50 of the Administration of Muslim Law Act, 1968, decrees that 'Before making an order or decree for talak, fasakh, cherai-taalik or kholo', the Sharīʿa Court may 'appoint in accordance with the Muslim law two arbitrators', who 'shall endeavour to effect a reconciliation between the parties'. For some years, moreover, it seems that the good offices of a 'Woman Muslim Social Case Worker' had been regularly used to try to bring the parties together again, and that her efforts have been successful in an astonishingly high proportion of cases. In Pakistan, again, Articles 7 and 8 of the Muslim Family Laws Ordinance provide that no divorce, in whatever form, is regarded as effective until ninety days after it has been reported to the Chairman of the appropriate Union Council, who must always form a panel of arbitrators and attempt to reconcile the parties. If this succeeds, then the formula of divorce, whatever its form, will be totally disregarded. It was, indeed, stated in *Ali Nawaz* v. *Mohd. Yusuf*[105] that the object of Article 7 'is to prevent hasty dissolution of the matrimonial status. If the husband himself thinks better of the pronouncement of *talaq* and abstains from giving a notice to the Chairman, he should perhaps be deemed . . .

[104] Recommendations Nos. 108, 110, 113 and 115. Cf. my article 'Comments (on Draft Law of Marriage and Divorce for Kenya) with reference to the Muslim Community', in *East African Law Journal*, Vol. v, Nos. 1 and 2 (1969), pp. 5–20. These Recommendations have now, moreover, been given legislative effect in the Tanzanian Law of Marriage Act, 1971 (cf. pp. 200f., 205ff. below).

[105] P.L.D. 1963 S.C. 59.

to have revoked the pronouncement'. Section (3) of this Article, moreover, 'precludes the *talaq* from being effective as such for a certain period, and within that period, consequently, it could not be said that the marital status of the parties had in any way been changed'.

But the most radical reforms which have hitherto been enacted in this matter, on any national level, are those of the Iranian Family Protection Act and the South Yemen and Somali Family Laws. The first of these not only insists that a wife must obtain 'a certificate of impossibility of reconciliation' before she may take any further steps with regard to the dissolution of her marriage, but that a husband must follow precisely the same procedure. This in itself would go no further than those provisions for delay and conciliation which exist elsewhere; the completely new factor in the Iranian legislation was that the husband's request for the issue of the necessary certificate, no less than the wife's, may be made *only* on one of a number of specified grounds—and that these specified grounds are, at first sight, precisely the same whether it is the husband or the wife who takes the initiative. Curiously enough, moreover, a detailed study of the Iranian Act of 1967 suggests that the grounds available to a husband are more, rather than less, restricted than those available to a wife; for, although the circumstances specified in the Act as justifying a petition for the requisite certificate are all expressed in terms of either party to the marriage, the Act provides that these circumstances are in addition to the grounds for the dissolution of a marriage included in the Civil Code—and reference to the Code reveals that provision is made for a wife to petition for divorce in circumstances in which nothing is provided about the rights of a husband (naturally enough, since he previously enjoyed an unfettered power of repudiation). Examples of this may be found in Article 1130, where it was provided (as we have seen) that the court should compel a husband to divorce his wife where he does not provide for her 'indispensable dues' and it is impossible to induce him to do so; where he ill-treats her to such an extent that a continuance of married life 'becomes insupportable'; and where a contagious disease, curable only with difficulty, makes married life dangerous. And while it might be thought that the courts would in all probability grant a certificate of impossibility to a husband, too, on similar grounds, in spite of the legislative silence on these points—since the whole spirit and ethos of the Act require reciprocity, and to refuse a certificate in such circumstances would appear unreasonable—I was advised that the court might well hesitate to do this unless or until the Act is amended; as, indeed, it duly was by an Act of the same name in 1975.[106] In South Yemen the Family Law not only forbids, and refuses to recognize, any divorce which has not been granted by the appropriate court—after the case has been referred to a 'People's Committee' to attempt conciliation—but also, as in Iran, precludes the court from permitting a divorce to either party except on specified grounds[107] (and, even so, Article 26 decrees that the court may only permit a single, and therefore revocable, divorce on any one occasion). And in Algeria, too, legislation was introduced in 1959 providing that divorce could be effected only by judicial decree on certain specified grounds—on the demand of husband or wife, or on their joint demand.[108]

But, however this may be, the basic point is that in no country in which the Sharīʿa still prevails in the sphere of family law, other than Algeria, Iran, South Yemen and Somalia, is a husband ever precluded from divorcing his wife, if he is determined to do so, provided he takes the necessary action and is prepared, if necessary, to pay such compensation as a court may decree. It is only in the Ismāʿīlī communities of East Africa that we find a similar provision, for Article 275 of their Constitution unequivocally enacts that a marriage 'shall not be capable of being dissolved, during the joint lives of the parties, otherwise than in accordance with the following provisions'—and then specifies a number of grounds (such as

[106] Even so, two additional grounds are available to a wife alone: that the husband has married a second wife, or has failed to treat a plurality of wives with equal justice (Articles 17 and 8).

[107] Cf. Article 25.

[108] Ordinance of 4 February, followed by regulations in a decree of 17 September. Cf. J. Schacht, *An Introduction to Islamic Law* (O.U.P., London, 1964), p. 98.

adultery, desertion, imprisonment, failure to consummate the marriage or to perform marital obligations without reasonable cause, cruelty, insanity, a disease which makes married life dangerous, renunciation of the Ismāʿīlī faith, or being of unknown whereabouts) all of which apply equally to husband and wife, and two further grounds peculiar to the wife alone (failure by the husband to provide maintenance, or the fact that he became impotent subsequent to the marriage and has continued to be so). But there are, of course, certain fundamental differences between this Constitution and both the Iranian and the South Yemen and Somali Laws: first, that the national enactments, alone, constitute legislation in the full sense of that term; and, secondly, that the former applies only to Ismāʿīlīs, who may always evade its provisions if they are willing to face excommunication from what is, in fact, a very tightly knit community.

There are a few other matters which should also be mentioned in passing under this general heading of reforms in regard to married life and its termination. The Qur'ān, for example, provides in Sūra 4:38 that a husband whose wife is 'rebellious' (*nāshiz*) should first rebuke her, then (if she persists) banish her to sleep in a separate room, and finally, if this too is ineffective, submit her to personal chastisement. The schools of law differ among themselves about the definition of the term 'rebellious' (e.g. whether it is confined to refusal of some demand that the husband may lawfully make upon her, or whether it includes *any* form of wrongdoing) and also about the limits which must be set to the chastisement that he may lawfully inflict (e.g. whether it must not be 'excessively' severe, or must merely stop short of causing the fracture of a bone!); but to go beyond these limits, whatever they may be, would constitute 'injury' or cruelty (*ḍarar*) rather than lawful punishment. It is significant in this context, moreover, that the Egyptian reformers accepted a criterion[109] which varies in accordance with the class and background of the parties concerned, for Article 6 of the Law of 1929 provides that 'If a wife alleges that her husband ill-treats her in such a way as to make it impossible for people of their class to

[109] Cf. p. 121 above.

continue the marriage relationship, she may request the Qāḍī to separate them'; and this implies that the infliction of pain or humiliation—whether by word or deed—which would be acceptable in some social circles, would be considered intolerable in others. Further points of some interest (but no great significance) can be found in such matters as the different ways in which the Ottoman and the Jordanian Law of Family Rights, respectively, treat the vexed question—in so far as Ḥanafī law is concerned—of the nature and legal effects of 'irregular' (*fāsid*) and 'void' (*bāṭil*) contracts of marriage,[110] the circumstances in which a wife is entitled to refuse to accompany her husband to a new locality,[111] and many other details; but to comment on all these would be both tedious and superfluous in this context.

Little need be said about dower (*mahr* or *ṣadāq*). In some countries it has become common for fathers to make such excessive demands for dower (particularly in regard to daughters who have received an expensive education) as to make it exceedingly difficult for a young man to find a suitable wife. This is obviously undesirable, and attempts have at times been made to impose statutory limits on the dower which may be asked or paid.[112] Elsewhere the practice has grown up for the courts to disregard, in any subsequent litigation, an excessive dower specified in a marriage contract merely as a status symbol for the bride or her family. More recently, again, a tendency has occasionally appeared for the rising generation to repudiate the whole concept of dower as an unworthy anachronism.

But questions of maintenance (*nafaqa*) are much more pertinent. In Egypt, for example, Article 1 of the Law of 1920 provides that 'The maintenance of a wife who has submitted herself to her husband, even if only putatively (*ḥukman*), is a debt owed by the husband from the time when he fails to support her, provided she is entitled thereto, without this being dependent on any decree or

110 Articles 52–8 and Articles 28–30, respectively.

111 Articles 71 and 33, respectively.

112 E.g. in South Yemen, where Article 18 of the Family Law provides that dower (prompt and deferred together) must not exceed 100 dīnārs.

agreement between the parties—and this debt will lapse only by payment or release'; while Article 2 states that 'In the case of a divorced wife who is entitled to maintenance, her maintenance is a debt, as in the preceding article, from the date of her divorce'. This represents a radical departure from the very complex details of the relevant Ḥanafī law (according to which arrears of dower were not regarded as a debt at all unless a particular sum had been agreed between the parties or decreed by court—and, even so, this debt was liable to lapse in a number of different circumstances) in favour of the much simpler and more satisfactory doctrine of the other Sunnī schools. Again, Article 16 of the same law provides that 'A wife's maintenance shall be calculated by reference to her husband's wealth or poverty, regardless of her own condition'—which represents an adoption of the Shāfi'ī (and an alternative Ḥanafī) doctrine in place of the Mālikī (and previously accepted Ḥanafī) principle that the relevant criterion should be the mean between the financial and social status of both husband and wife. Similar reforms have been introduced in several other countries. In the Sudan, Article 1 of Judicial Circular No. 17 of 1915 (which anticipated the Egyptian reforms by some five years) is more explicit than Articles 4 and 5 of the Egyptian Law of 1920 when it provides that 'If a husband has property out of which his wife's maintenance can be obtained, a decree for the maintenance to which she is legally entitled will be executed therefrom, whether it be money, movables or immovables'; but Article 8 of Circular No. 28 of 1927 is more conservative than the Egyptian Law, and arrears of maintenance still lapse in the Sudan on the death of either party unless the wife has been given leave of court to raise her maintenance on credit. It is noteworthy, however, that the Egyptian reformers found that this Law of 1920, which decreed that arrears of maintenance constitute a debt against the husband from the date when he first failed to provide it, opened the door to exceedingly dubious claims for maintenance alleged to have been due over many years; so the precaution was taken of including a clause in the Code of Procedure of 1931 which forbade the courts to entertain such claims in regard to any period in excess of three years prior to the suit. This, too, was adopted in the Sudan,[113] and provides a further example of the procedural expedient of effecting a reform by the denial of judicial relief in specified circumstances. But minor differences and anomalies abound—as, for instance, in the fact that Article 56 of the Jordanian Law follows Article 16 of the Egyptian Law of 1920 in decreeing that a wife's maintenance shall be calculated by exclusive reference to her husband's means, but follows Articles 92 and 95 of the Ottoman Law in making arrears of such maintenance actionable only after decree of court or mutual agreement on a specified sum; and that the Syrian Law seems to oscillate, in this respect, between the decisive doctrine of the Egyptian reforms and the more cautious Jordanian provisions, but includes the interesting innovation (for which there seems to be no authority in the classical texts) that even in an irregular or *fāsid* marriage the 'wife' is entitled to maintenance 'so long as she is ignorant of the irregularity of the union'.[114]

Maintenance is also due to a wife during the *ʿidda* following divorce, but not the *ʿidda* which follows widowhood. The latter must be kept for four months and ten days where the widow is not pregnant, but there is a difference of opinion whether the *ʿidda* of a pregnant widow always ends with the birth of her child. Article 48 (3) of the Iraqī Code, for example, has adopted the Shīʿī view that her *ʿidda*, in such cases, should last either four months and ten days or until delivery, whichever is longer. Again, Article 127 of the Syrian Law explicitly provides that where the husband of a woman who is already observing her *ʿidda* following revocable divorce dies, she should start to observe the full *ʿidda* of widowhood, but if she is observing the *ʿidda* following a decisive divorce she should observe the *ʿidda* of widowhood *or* that of divorce, whichever is longer.[115] The *ʿidda* ordinarily to be observed after divorce or dissolution of marriage, however, represents a

[113] By Circular No. 45 of 1936.

[114] Article 51 (3). Cf. also, in this context, Articles 76, 78, etc.

[115] Whereas Article 48 (a) of the Iraqī Code apparently opts for the *ʿidda* of widowhood in both cases, and Article 36 of the South Yemen Law prescribes the *ʿidda* of widowhood in the first case and completion of that of divorce in the second.

much more controversial matter. First, no such *ʿidda* whatever is incumbent if the parties have never had an opportunity[116] to consummate the marriage; and no maintenance is due during the *ʿidda* which follows a dissolution of marriage consequent on some criminal act by the wife or even, in the Mālikī and Shāfiʿī view, which follows any irrevocable divorce where the wife is not pregnant. The Ḥanafīs, on the other hand, give a divorced woman the right to maintenance for the duration of her *ʿidda* whether the divorce was revocable or irrevocable, and regardless of whether she is pregnant or not. It is noteworthy in this context, moreover, that the Iranian Family Protection Act, 1975, provides that, where a divorce has been granted by the court on the ground of some matrimonial offence, the innocent party, if not financially viable, is entitled to receive maintenance from the guilty party, if he is able to provide this, until the innocent party remarries or the financial position of either party changes. But the major complexity, all over the Muslim world, concerns the length of the *ʿidda*. Where the woman is pregnant this ends with delivery of the child; and where she has not attained puberty, or has definitely reached her menopause, it lasts for three calendar months; but in between these two ages the *ʿidda* lasts, in the traditional doctrine, for three *qurūʾ*—a term interpreted by some jurists as meaning menstrual periods and by others as the interval between such periods. But where the woman claims to have had three *qurūʾ* in a very short time, or—as is more commonly the case—where she alleges, over a long period, that she has not completed them, there is a divergence of view not only in the doctrine of the various schools but also in the solution reached by different reformers. In Egypt the reformers opted, in the Law of 1920, for the Mālikī view that the *ʿidda* should *normally* come to an end after a year in such cases (i.e. that a woman should wait for nine months and then, if she had had no period, continue her *ʿidda* for a further period of three months); but in Article 17 of the Law of 1929 they resorted, instead, to the pro-

[116] I.e. have neither actually consummated the union or had what is termed a 'valid retirement' or time of privacy (*khalwa ṣāḥīḥa*) when the union could have been consummated.

cedural expedient of providing that 'No claim for maintenance during an *'idda* shall be heard in regard to a period of more than a year from the date of divorce'—and in Syria this was made a matter of substantive law in Article 121. But this was anticipated by the statement in the Explanatory Memorandum issued with the Ottoman Law of 1917 that 'the Imām Mālik held that a wife's *'idda* (in such cases) is a period of three months after she has waited nine months from the time when it first became incumbent', and by the strangely erroneous application of this principle, in the form of an *'idda* of nine months only, in both the Ottoman and, as it would seem, the Jordanian Law.[117] Several of these Laws also prescribe that no claim that a woman has experienced three *qurū'* is to be accepted until a period of three months has elapsed,[118] which rests on Mālikī, Ḥanbalī and some Shāfi'ī authority rather than the view held either by Abū Ḥanīfa (who opted for 60 days) or that of his Two Companions (who postulated 39 days only). Characteristically enough, moreover, the Tunisian Law covers the whole subject by the terse provision in Article 35 that 'A divorced wife who is not pregnant must observe an *'idda* of three complete months'.[119] At first sight this would seem to be another instance of a departure from the clear teaching of the Qur'ān, which makes *qurū'* rather than calendar months the basis of calculation except in regard to women who have not reached puberty or have ceased to menstruate; but it can, it seems, find very tenuous support in the view of those who recommend that argument and deception in regard to such an intimate subject can best be excluded by accepting some such rule as a practical expedient.

Two further points must be mentioned in this section. First, it is noteworthy that, in the Indian sub-continent, the draftsmen of the Dissolution of Muslim Marriages Act, 1939, felt it necessary to add, at the end of eight different 'grounds for a decree of dissolution of marriage' in Article 2, a further provision which reads: 'on any

[117] Cf. Articles 140 and 102, respectively.

[118] Cf. Article 139 of the Ottoman Law.

[119] Cf. Article 31 of the South Yemen Law, which prescribes 90 days in such cases.

other ground which is recognised as valid for the dissolution of marriage under Muslim law'. Such grounds would, of course, include the various forms of divorce by mutual consent (*khulʿ*, *mubāra'a* and *ṭalāq ʿalā māl*), in regard to which the reformers made very few innovations—although it should be observed in passing that Article 96 of the Syrian Law provides that *either* party may retract a declaration of *khulʿ* at any time before the other party has accepted it; Article 98 that where the consideration for the *khulʿ* is something other than the dower, this consideration is binding and both parties are also released from any obligation regarding dower or maintenance; Article 99 that where the parties do not name any consideration, the *khulʿ* shall take effect and both parties shall be released from the rights of the other regarding dower and maintenance; and Article 103 that where a man stipulates in a *khulʿ* that he shall have charge of his child during the period of custody (*ḥaḍāna*), the *khulʿ* shall be effective but the stipulation void. But they would also comprise the ancient procedures of *īlā'* (oath of continence), *ẓihār* (injurious comparison) and *liʿān* (mutual imprecation).[120] In so far as either or both of the first two of these procedures should be considered as itself constituting a distinctive form of dissolution of marriage, rather than actions or words which are likely to precipitate a divorce, they may be dismissed as virtually extinct today; but this is certainly not true of *liʿān*. In its classical setting this was designed to provide the one and only way in which a husband who had grounds for suspecting his wife of infidelity, but was unable to produce the requisite four adult, competent, male Muslim witnesses—to having seen the very act of adultery—by whose testimony alone this infidelity could be proved, could accuse her, and repudiate her child, without exposing himself to the severe penalty specifically prescribed for *qadhf* (that is, slander of her chastity). Now that the Islamic criminal law has virtually no application outside the Arabian peninsula, however, what was originally a procedure by which, at one and the same time, an accusing husband could avoid being condemned

[120] The husband swears to his wife's adultery and the wife to her chastity, each imprecating the curse of God if this is a lie.

for *qadhf*, and a wife who denied the accusation could avoid the still more fearsome penalty prescribed for adultery (*zinā'*), chiefly survives as a means of denying paternity—and, as such, properly belongs to the next section of this chapter. It is noteworthy, however, that in the Indian sub-continent the procedure primarily provides a way by which a wife who claims to have been falsely accused of infidelity by her husband may go to court and claim the dissolution of her marriage.

Finally, provision has been made in several countries for a decree of putative widowhood to be given in certain specified circumstances, after which a wife may remarry as soon as she has completed the *'idda* of widowhood. In some cases, moreover, the reformers have prescribed what is to happen if the missing husband subsequently reappears and wishes to reclaim his now re-married wife. But this decree of putative widowhood must be clearly distinguished from a judicial divorce given on the ground that the wife concerned is unable to obtain her lawful maintenance from a husband who has disappeared and left no assets out of which an order for maintenance can be made, or on the ground that her husband has left her alone for so long that, although she has adequate means of support, she is suffering from desertion and even exposed to temptation to unchastity.

An excellent example of provisions regarding decrees of putative widowhood can be found in the Egyptian reforms of 1920 and 1929. Articles 7 and 8 of the Law of 1920 provide that a wife whose husband is lost or missing, even though he has left property out of which her maintenance can be obtained, may bring the matter before the court, which will make official enquiries about his whereabouts; then, should four years pass without news, it will give her permission to observe the *'idda* of widowhood and then remarry. If, however, the missing husband subsequently turns up, she will still belong to him unless her new husband has already consummated the marriage with no knowledge of the other's survival. This represents an adoption of pure Mālikī doctrine in place of the Ḥanafī rule that the missing husband must not be presumed dead until all his contemporaries have died (which was, itself, a simplification of the rule preferred by Abū Ḥanifa, Abū Yūsuf and Muḥammad al-Shaybānī who postulated 120 years, 110 years and 105 years after his birth, respectively). It is noteworthy, moreover, that Article 92 in the Jordanian Law of 1951 is essentially similar, except that it concedes that the four year period without news may be cut down, in time of war, to one year after the return home of the conflicting armies and their prisoners. But in 1929 Article 7 of the Law of 1920 was rescinded in Egypt and replaced by Articles 21 and 22 of the new Law, which provide that a missing person shall be declared dead, in the eyes of the law, four years after his disappearance if the circumstances make his death probable, or at the discretion of the court, after all possible enquiries have been made, in all other circumstances—although Article 8 of the former law, about the position which obtains should the missing husband subsequently reappear, has remained in force. This substantially represents the Ḥanbalī doctrine. No mention is made of this matter in the Tunisian, Syrian, Moroccan and Iraqī reforms.

4. CHILDREN AND FAMILY RELATIONSHIPS

(a) *Questions of paternity*. On this subject the law actually in force today in a number of different countries differs very considerably from the traditional doctrine of all the Sunnī schools. But the most radical departure of all, in any country where the Islamic family law is in general applied, may be found in the 'Anglo-Muhammadan Law' which still prevails in India and Pakistan (together with certain other parts of the Commonwealth), for here the terms of the Indian Evidence Act have served largely to substitute an essentially English, rather than Islamic, approach to this subject.

Under the Sharīʿa the fundamental criterion of legitimacy is the *conception* of the child during lawful wedlock. As a result, the determination of the legitimacy or otherwise of a child born to a woman during her marriage or after its termination is governed largely by whether the birth occurred not less than the recognized minimum period of gestation after the marriage was contracted and not more than the maximum period of gestation after its termination by widowhood or divorce. The minimum period, as accepted by all schools of law, is six months; but there is no such agreement about the maximum period, where the Ḥanafīs postulate two years, the Shāfi'īs and Ḥanbalīs four, the Mālikīs five years or even more, and the Shī'īs —much more realistically—nine or ten months. But there are further differences. One of these is that the presumption of legitimacy begins to run, in the Ḥanafī doctrine, six months after the contract of marriage whether, or not, it was possible for the parties to have had access to each other by any means other than the miraculous, while in the other Sunnī schools it begins to run six months after the marriage only if there was at least a possibility of mutual access between husband and wife—and, in the Shī'ī doctrine, the presumption of legitimacy applies, right throughout the marriage, only where the spouses could have had physical access to each other at the appropriate time. But it is noteworthy that a child conceived outside lawful wedlock is also regarded as legitimate if there was such a semblance, or *shubha*, of marriage as would have been accepted as lawful wedlock by some jurists, even though the parties concerned knew perfectly well that the union would not be regarded as lawful according to their school of law—and also in circumstances in which no jurist would regard the union as legitimate, provided the parties concerned were acting in innocence, as a result of a genuine misapprehension or mistake.[121] In addition, an acknowledgement (*iqrār*) of paternity is accepted as giving rise to a substantive relationship in all circumstances in which this acknowledgement cannot positively be proved to be false. For example, an acknowledgement of lawful paternity will suffice to establish the legitimacy of a child born less than the minimum period of gestation after the marriage of his mother to the one who made the acknowledgement, since conception *could* have occurred prior to their valid contract of marriage in some way which would not constitute illicit sex relations, and a child born to a woman to whom the man concerned *could not* have

[121] But in such cases the minimum period of gestation begins to run not from the contract of marriage but its consummation.

been validly married at the time of conception will also, in some cases, be accepted as his legitimate child if he so acknowledges him, since his act of intercourse with the mother might have been due to a genuine mistake. It is, however, essential to realize that Islamic law does not regard such acknowledgement as a means of legitimizing the illegitimate (although it is, beyond question, sometimes used for this purpose), but rather as a means of establishing a legitimacy which was always a fact, although this could not be *proved* in any other way.

But in the Indian sub-continent all this was radically changed by Section 12 of the Indian Evidence Act, which provides that a child born during the continuance of a valid marriage, or within 280 days after its termination, is conclusively presumed to be legitimate unless there was no access between his parents when he could have been begotten. In 1880, in the case of *Muhammad Allahdad* v. *Muhammad Ismail*,[122] the question of whether this section of the Indian Evidence Act supersedes the rules of Islamic law was still regarded as open; but subsequent decisions have made this perfectly clear. In India and Pakistan, therefore, the criterion of legitimacy depends, as in English law, on the date of a child's birth, not its conception; the maximum period of gestation has been fixed at 280 days; and an acknowledgement of paternity is not regarded as valid if the acknowledgor *could* not have been validly married to the child's mother—or if he can, in fact, be proved not to have been so married—at the time when the child was born.

In the Arab countries, on the other hand, the substance of the Islamic law of paternity still prevails, although there have been a few significant reforms. It was the Egyptian legislation of 1929 which set the pattern for most of these enactments, for the reformers recognized the absurdity of a child being regarded as the legitimate offspring of a man who had, indeed, contracted a marriage with the child's mother, but had never met her, from the time of the marriage until the birth of the child, in any way which could give the couple access to each other—or, indeed, if the child was born nearly two years after the parties had been divorced or the husband had died.

[122] (1888) 10 All. 289, 339.

In short, the Memorandum asserted, the application of the traditional Ḥanafī rules 'encouraged people to allege the legitimate paternity of illegitimate children—a fact about which there had been many complaints'. So Article 15 of the Law of 1929 now provides that 'No disputed claim of paternity shall be heard in regard to the child of a married woman where there had been no access between her and her husband from the time of the contract of marriage; nor to the child of a married woman who gave birth to him a year after her husband had left her; nor yet to the child of a divorced or widowed woman born more than a year after the time of her divorce or widowhood'. And the Syrian, Tunisian, Moroccan and South Yemen legislation has substantially adopted these principles, for in all these countries one year has been accepted as the maximum period of gestation[123] as a rule of substantive law—rather than, as in Egypt, a procedural requirement[124]—but with the precaution, in Morocco, that Article 77 goes on to provide that 'If the year comes to an end and there is any doubt about pregnancy, then the party concerned should refer the matter to the Qāḍī to seek the aid of medical experts . . .'.

Some of these countries have also prescribed means by which a husband may repudiate a child with which his wife is pregnant, or to which she has already given birth, without resorting to the *liʿān* procedure. Thus the Tunisian Law provides in Article 75 that 'If a husband disowns the child with which his wife is pregnant, or which is attributed to him, this repudiation will not be effective without a decree of court, and in such a matter all legal means of proof may be used', while Article 76 adds: 'If the court confirms the repudiation of paternity, according to the terms of the previous article, it shall pass a decree of illegitimacy and of physical separation between the spouses'. And the provisions of Article 90 of the Moroccan Code are almost identical.

When we turn to the custody (*ḥaḍāna*), guardianship (*wilāya*) and support (*nafaqa*) of children, there are certain tendencies evinced by

[123] Cf. pp. 47, 55 above and footnote 124 below.

[124] Cf. Articles 128 ff. in the Syrian Law, Article 69 in the Tunisian Law, Article 76 in the Moroccan Code, and Articles 37 and 39 in the South Yemen Law.

recent legislation, and a number of specific provisions, which demand notice. One of the most beneficial of these tendencies is that the rigid rules which used to govern the age at which the custody of young children by a mother, grandmother or other female relative ended, and they were handed over to the father, have been somewhat relaxed; for, in the words of the Explanatory Memorandum issued with the Egyptian Law of 1929, experience had shown that at these ages (seven for a boy and nine for a girl) 'a boy or girl may not be able to dispense with such custody and may be in danger if handed over to others, especially if their father is married to someone who is not their mother. For this reason there have been many complaints from women whose children have been torn from them at this age'. In these circumstances, Article 20 of this Law provided that 'The Qāḍī may give permission for women's rights to the custody of a boy to be extended from the age of seven up to nine, and of a girl from the age of nine up to eleven, if it appears that their welfare so requires'—and this reform was adopted in Jordan in the Law promulgated in 1951. In the Sudan, Judicial Circular No. 34 of 1932 went much further and abandoned Ḥanafī principles altogether in favour of those of the Mālikī school to which the vast majority of the Sudanese people in fact belong; and according to these principles the custody of boys extends till puberty, and of girls till the beginning of their married lives. But the Tunisian Law of 1956, curiously enough, has adopted the Ḥanafī rather than the Mālikī doctrine in this matter, in spite of the fact that the vast majority of Tunisians belong to the Mālikī school, and specifies the age of seven for a boy and nine for a girl—although Article 67 adds the proviso 'unless the judge sees that it would be more beneficial for him (i.e. the minor, whether boy or girl) to remain with the one who has custody'. In Iraq, too, the Ḥanafī principles have been followed rather than the far *less* beneficial Shīʿī doctrine in this matter; but again Article 57 provides that any dispute in regard to the period of custody shall be decided by the Qāḍī 'in the interests of the child', and that he may permit the extension of this period 'if it appears that the interests of the child so require'. The Moroccan Code follows

Mālikī principles, naturally enough, so Article 108 provides that the period of *ḥaḍāna* normally ends at puberty in the case of a boy and the commencement of married life in the case of a girl; but it is significant that Article 65 expressly states that a divorce by mutual consent must not be arranged on terms which 'affect the rights of the children if the wife is in straightened circumstances'. The Syrian Law of 1953 gives the court an even wider competence, since Article 145 provides that 'If a wife deserts her husband and her children are more than five years old, the Qāḍī may place them with whichever of the spouses he sees fit, provided that he has regard to the welfare of the children in the light of the circumstances of the case'. Somewhat similarly—but in more detail—Article 46 of the Family Law of South Yemen provides that 'A boy shall remain in his mother's custody up to the age of ten and a girl up to the age of fifteen, even if the mother has married; but the court may always decide otherwise if the mother (or her husband, if she has married) is shown to be totally unfitted to provide such custody—in the light of the facts of the case supported by social investigation'. In India and Pakistan both the Ḥanafī and Shīʿī law on this subject are still, in general, followed by the courts, with the period of custody ending at seven for a boy and puberty for a girl in the first case, and at the age of two for a boy and seven for a girl in the second; but there can be little doubt that the interests of the child would normally receive sympathetic, if perhaps somewhat inadequate or ineffective, consideration. But, however that may be, it was expressly provided in the Guardians and Wards Act, as long ago as 1890, that in appointing a *guardian*[125] the court should be guided '(i) by what, consistently with the law to which the minor is subject, is for the welfare of the minor; (ii) by the age, sex and religion of the minor, by the character and capacity of the proposed guardian, and the wishes of a deceased parent; and (iii) by the preference of the minor himself, if sufficiently old to form a preference'.[126]

[125] As distinct from one who has the right of custody.

[126] Cf. A. A. A. Fyzee, *Outlines of Muhammadan Law* (O.U.P., 3rd edn., 1964), p. 189.

It must be noted, moreover, that in Islamic law a distinction is made not only between custody and guardianship, but also, in some cases, between a guardian of the person and a guardian of property. A distinct order of priority is prescribed for each, together with detailed rules as to the respective competence, for example, of a father or some other relative (or, indeed, the father's executor), and even of a father known for good judgment or one who is known to be feckless or unreliable. It would be tedious to enter into details in this context; but it is important to observe that even when the mother has custody of her young children their father enjoys basic rights of guardianship and is responsible for their maintenance—and also, in suitable circumstances, for paying his divorced wife wages for her care of them, or for the suckling of those who need this. It is significant, moreover, that recent reforms go much further than the traditional doctrine in specifically including medical expenses among the items which a husband or father who is responsible for the maintenance and support of wife or children must provide. Article 65 in the Jordanian Law of 1951, for example, explicitly provides that:

(*a*) The fee of a midwife or doctor who is summoned for a wife's confinement is the absolute responsibility of the husband, whether the marriage is still subsisting or not.

(*b*) If a wife or minor child who is entitled to maintenance falls ill in such a way as to require a doctor or treatment, then the fee of the doctor or the cost of the treatment is the responsibility of the husband or father, on a par with maintenance, and shall be calculated by reference to his circumstances, be he rich or poor.

(*c*) Where children's maintenance is incumbent on their father he is also responsible for the cost of their education, and the pursuit of knowledge is to be regarded as one of the reasons which make a major son's maintenance incumbent on his father . . .

(*d*) If the father is destitute and cannot pay the fee of a doctor, the cost of treatment or the expenses of education, whereas the mother is in easy circumstances and able to pay these, she may be compelled to do so, on the basis that they shall be a debt against the father which she may reclaim if he subsequently becomes better-off; and the same shall also be true if the father is absent.

All this substantially represents the traditional law, except for the explicit mention of medical expenses (especially in regard to wives) and the fact that the duty of maintaining children whose father cannot support them (and who have no means of their own)[127] is laid unequivocally on their mother rather than on their paternal grandfather. The Moroccan Code makes the same point, but without any reference to a subsequent claim against the father, when Article 129 provides that 'If the father is unable to support his child and the mother is well-off, then she is responsible for his support'; Article 47 of the Tunisian Law explicitly states that 'Where the father is in straightened circumstances, the mother is to be preferred to the paternal grandfather in supporting her child'; and Article 22 of the South Yemen Law imposes the obligation to support children unequivocally on both parents according to their means.[128]

The rules which govern the duty to support other relatives—e.g. parents, brothers and sisters—are distinctly complex and differ from school to school. Generally speaking this duty falls only on such relatives as are in reasonably easy circumstances. The Ḥanafīs limit this duty, moreover, to relatives who are within the prohibited degrees of marriage (or would be if they were of different sexes), while the Ḥanbalī principle is to make the relevant criterion the right to inherit. It is noteworthy, therefore, that a tendency has appeared in recent legislation for the Ḥanbalī principle to be substituted, in part at least, for the Ḥanafī doctrine.[129] In the Iraqī Law this principle has been given full application, for Article 62 explicitly states that 'The maintenance of every indigent person who cannot earn his living is incumbent upon any relatives who would inherit from him, and who are themselves in easy circumstances, in proportion to the right of each to inherit'. Article 61, moreover, is equally explicit about the duty of children to support their parents when it enacts that 'It is incumbent on a child who is

[127] In Islamic law a husband is always responsible for his wife's maintenance, however wealthy she may be; but a child's maintenance may be provided from his own resources, if he has any.

[128] Cf. p. 74 above. And the Somali Family Law, 1975, apparently concurs.

[129] Cf. Articles 114 (4) and 119 of the Jordanian Law.

in easy circumstances, whether major or minor, to support his indigent parents, even if they are able to earn, unless the father manifests a determination to be idle'[130]—although this, in fact, represents the normal Ḥanafī doctrine. But it is noteworthy that the Syrian Law goes somewhat beyond normal practice when it provides, in Article 151, that 'A guardian who is within the prohibited degrees of marriage to his female ward may insist that she should live in his house if she be less than forty years old, even though she has been previously married. If she refuses to comply, without lawful cause, she shall have no right to maintenance.'[131]

5. TESTATE AND INTESTATE SUCCESSION

To Muslims the Islamic law of succession lies at the very heart of the Sharīʿa. The precise fractional shares in an estate to which a variety of relatives are entitled are expressly prescribed in the Qur'ān itself and are technically called *farā'iḍ*, which is one form of the plural of the Arabic term (*farḍ*) used for a duty imposed by divine command. The Prophet of Islam is, indeed, reported to have said that an understanding of *ʿilm al-farā'iḍ* constitutes one half of the sum total of revealed knowledge (*ʿilm*). The Islamic law of inheritance is a continual source of pride to Muslim scholars, who take enormous delight in finding the correct solution to the most intricate—and even improbable—problems by a meticulous application of its all-embracing but highly complex principles; and reforms in this branch of the law were much less urgent than in such matters as marriage and divorce. So it was not until 1943 that the Egyptian reformers tackled most of the relevant problems by promulgating a fairly comprehensive code entitled *Qānūn al-mīrāth* (the Law of Inheritance)—although a few of the detailed reforms it included had already been put into force in the Sudan under the influence of eminent Egyptian jurists who had held the

[130] Cf. Article 34 of the South Yemen Law, which makes no distinction between father and mother in this respect.

[131] Cf., for this whole section, my article 'Recent Reforms in Sharīʿa Law IV', in *The Muslim World*, Vol. XLIII, No. 3 (July 1951); my articles on the Jordanian, Syrian, Tunisian, Moroccan and Iraqī Laws, mentioned above; and Fyzee, *Outlines of Muhammadan Law* (O.U.P., 3rd edn., 1964), pp. 180 ff.

post of Grand Qāḍī in that country. For, however admirable the Islamic law of inheritance may be in general, there are a few basic points, and a comparatively large number of details, in which it is not altogether suited to the circumstances of modern life. In this brief summary we must, of necessity, confine our attention almost exclusively to basic questions; but a few more detailed points will also be mentioned in passing when they seem to be of special significance.

There is certainly no aspect of family law in which the Sunnīs and Shīʿīs[132] have reached such radically different results as in the law of inheritance, and it is interesting to observe that it is the Shīʿī system which seems, in general, much more suited to the circumstances of today. Yet in point of fact both Sunnīs and Shīʿīs took as their starting point authoritative sources which were almost identical; and the wide disparity between the conclusions they reached is basically due to a fundamental difference in their approach to the nature of the reforms effected by the Prophet of Islam—whether this, in its turn, is to be explained primarily on political or dogmatic grounds. The essence of this difference was that the Sunnīs accepted the pre-Islamic system of agnatic succession, or tribal heirs, as still relevant and operative, except in so far as it had been modified—in certain very radical respects—by the Islamic reforms, whereas the Shīʿīs regarded the agnatic system as having been completely superseded, and set out to erect a totally new system of inheritance on the basis of the Qur'anic provisions.

The system of agnatic succession, as this seems to have existed in pre-Islamic Arabia, was that a man's heirs were confined to males who were related to him through the male line. Priority between them was decided by three considerations: first, that descendants were given priority to ascendants, and ascendants to collaterals (and, among collaterals, descendants of the father to descendants of any more remote ancestor); secondly, that within each of these 'orders' or classes the nearer in degree was preferred to the more remote; and thirdly, that where two claimants were equal in respect to

[132] Cf. Chapter I, p. 10 above.

both order and degree, then one related through both parents was preferred to one related only through his father. Thus a son, or even a son's son, was given priority over a father; a father, or even father's father, over a brother or nephew; and a brother of the full blood over a brother of the consanguine blood. In default of close relatives even the most distant agnatic cousins would inherit, for it was on a man's agnates that, in a tribal society, the primary responsibility to aid or avenge him lay. It is for this reason, indeed, that it is exceedingly likely that, originally, a father was given priority over a minor son, and that adult brothers were in all probability preferred to the father's father. But, however that may be, women had no right to inherit as such, although a dying man's request that part of his property should be given to a daughter, mother or wife would, no doubt, normally have been honoured by his agnatic heirs.

It was to extend and reform this system that the Islamic reforms were introduced. Under these, nine quota-sharers were specifically mentioned in the Qur'ān, six of whom were women: mothers, daughters, wives, and sisters of the full, consanguine and even uterine blood—and to these the son's daughter and the 'true'[133] grandmother were added, on the principle of analogy, by Sunnī jurists. The other quota-sharers were males, three of whom were named in the Qur'ān: husbands, uterine brothers (who were not, of course, agnates) and fathers (who would be entitled as quota-sharers only when ousted by a son or son's son from inheriting as the nearest agnate)—and here, too, Sunnī jurists added the paternal grandfather on the principle of analogy. Sons, and brothers of the full or consanguine blood, were not mentioned at all in this system except where there were also daughters or sisters, when it was provided that the male claimant should take twice the share of the corresponding female; otherwise they would naturally take their appropriate entitlement as nearest agnate in the Sunnī view, or—but much less obviously—as next of kin (*dhū qarāba*) in the Shīʿī doctrine. But there were, of course, many further compli-

[133] I.e. a grandmother between whom and the deceased no non-agnatic grandfather intervenes.

cations, including rules which specified what may be termed those 'primary' heirs who could never be excluded, those 'substitute' heirs who would take the place of primary heirs in appropriate circumstances, and those 'secondary' heirs (e.g. relatives who were neither agnates nor quota-sharers) who were allowed to inherit, in the doctrine of some schools, in default of better entitled claimants.

Such, in brief and inadequate outline, is the Sunnī system. The first essential is to give any entitled quota-sharer his or her prescribed share (which varies, in many cases, according to their number and the presence or absence of certain other relatives of the deceased), and then to allot the remainder to the nearest agnate—be he son, father, brother or even distant cousin. If there is no agnate, however remote, then any quota-sharers will first take their prescribed shares and then divide the residue between them, proportionately, by the doctrine of the *radd* or 'return' (from which only the widow or widower is excluded in the traditional doctrine). And in default of either agnates or quota-sharers other relatives (sometimes inaccurately termed 'Distant Kindred') are, in the doctrine of most schools, entitled to inherit, on a system of priorities which varies from school to school and even, in the Ḥanafī school, between the 'Two Companions'.

But the Shīʿīs made no attempt to superimpose the Islamic reforms on the tribal system of Arabia. Instead, they constructed an entirely new system on the basis of the Qur'anic provisions. In the event, they divided all relatives into three classes: first, a class composed of descendants (whether agnates or not), together with father and mother; next, a class made up of brothers and sisters and their descendants, together with grandparents and great grandparents; finally, a class which comprises uncles and aunts (and great uncles and aunts) and their descendants, on both the paternal and the maternal side. Any claimant from the first class will exclude all others, and any claimant from the second class will exclude one from the third; but the husband or wife will in all cases be entitled to his or her share. Again, of course, there are many complications; but the way in which this system is made to cover all cases is basically by a wide application of the principles of representation and the 'return'.[134]

It seems probable that it is the Sunnī system which represents the closer approximation to what was originally intended; but it is the Shīʿī doctrine which is more suited to the nuclear family which has today largely ousted the extended family of tribal society. A vivid example of this is provided by the case of a man whose only relatives are a daughter and a distant agnatic cousin; for here the Sunnī system gives the daughter only her prescribed quota-share of one-half and allots the other half to the distant cousin, while the Shīʿīs give the whole estate to the daughter (who first takes her quota-share, and then the remainder by the doctrine of the return). And whereas, in a tribal society, the Sunnī system had, no doubt, much to commend it, since a man would often be compelled to rely on his agnatic relatives, however distant, to come to his aid, in the urban life of today people often object strongly to half their estates going to some distant cousin whom they may never have met or may even detest.

In a number of countries the reformers have, therefore, found different ways and means of furthering the interests of the nuclear family. The most radical reform of all was introduced, naturally enough, in Iraq, where rather more than half the population are Shīʿīs, and where a number of Sunnīs are alleged to have espoused Shīʿī allegiance precisely because the Shīʿī system of inheritance was better suited than the Sunnī to their family circumstances. In its original form the Iraqī Law of 1959 even went so far as completely to abandon the Islamic law of inheritance, and to adopt in its place the law (itself largely of German origin) which was previously in force in the Ottoman Empire to regulate rights of succession to the use of Government land. Two reasons were given for this astonishingly bold innovation: first, that the differences between the Sunnī and Shīʿī systems of inheritance were so radical that they could not be reconciled; and, secondly, that neither the one nor the other—unlike the relevant statute—accorded women equal shares

[134] I.e. where the fixed shares of those heirs who are entitled to inherit do not exhaust the estate.

with men. But as soon as the 'tyrant' ʿAbd al-Karīm Qāsim was overthrown in 1963, this section of the Law of 1959 was repealed and replaced by an amendment which made the general structure of the Shīʿī system of inheritance applicable to all Iraqīs (although *within* this basic framework of three mutually exclusive classes of heirs the Sunnīs still apply their own principles to the detailed division of an estate between individual claimants). In Tunisia, too, the reformers took steps to safeguard the interests of the nuclear family by adding, in 1959, an addendum to Article 143 of the Law of Personal Status, 1956; but, instead of adopting the Shīʿī system as a whole, they adapted the Mālikī law previously in force by not only introducing the doctrine of the 'return' (which is not accepted in the Mālikī system), but by extending it to the spouse relict on an equal footing with the other quota-sharers (which is contrary to the practice of all the recognized schools) and also expressly providing that a daughter or son's daughter 'shall take the residue of the estate by the return even in the presence of an agnate in his own right, such as a brother or uncle'. This means that a daughter or son's daughter will effectively exclude any collateral whatever, and will first take her quota-share and then any residue of the estate there may be—in a way which is certainly analogous to the Shīʿī system in this one respect but which lacks, in the isolated and attenuated way in which this has been effected in Tunisia, any traditional authority or precedent whatever.

Another reform—introduced in both Egypt and the Sudan as well as Iraq—which has tended to favour the interests of the nuclear family in a much less direct way, is a provision which gives a testator complete freedom to make a bequest to one of his heirs, if he so wishes, provided only that this does not exceed the 'bequeathable third' of his whole estate.[135] This has always been the Shīʿī doctrine; but the Sunnī schools either exclude a bequest to an heir in all circumstances, as in the Mālikī system, or make its execution dependent on the consent of the other heirs after the death of the testator, as in the Ḥanafī doctrine. But this was changed in the Sudan by Judicial Circular No. 53 of 1945 and in Egypt by

135 Cf. pp. 54f. above.

Article 37 of the Law of Testamentary Dispositions of 1946, while the Iraqī Law of 1959 made this principle applicable to all Iraqīs. This not only introduces a much needed element of flexibility into the rigidity of the Sunnī doctrine which previously prevailed, but makes it possible for a man to bequeath one-third of his estate to a wife, daughter or other member of his nuclear family in addition to her prescribed share, and thus to reduce the proportion of his estate which other—perhaps distant—relatives would otherwise inherit. In the case of a wife this is particularly welcome, since the fixed share to which she is entitled is woefully inadequate. And it is also noteworthy in this context that in the Sudan Judicial Circular No. 26 of 1925 decreed that the spouse relict should be entitled to the whole estate of one who leaves no other heirs and no 'acknowledged kinsman', while in Egypt a corresponding provision in the Law of Inheritance, 1943, gives the spouse relict priority over an acknowledged kinsman also—as is also the case in Syria, under the Law of 1953.[136]

A further reform which has been introduced in Egypt and the Sudan also has the effect, on occasion, of favouring the interests of the nuclear family at the expense of somewhat more distant relatives: namely, certain legislative provisions in regard to the position of full or consanguine brothers and sisters when they find themselves in competition with a father's father. In the doctrine of Abū Ḥanīfa—as distinct from that of the other Sunnī schools, the Shīʿīs or even Abū Ḥanīfa's Two Companions[137]—the survival of the deceased's father's father entails the complete exclusion of any of his brothers or sisters from a share in his estate; and then, when the father's father dies, *his* whole estate will go to any surviving son—with the result that a full or consanguine brother or sister of the first deceased will, in effect, be completely excluded by an uncle (or, if no uncle in fact survives, may have to share with a number of different cousins). But this was changed in the Sudan by Article 2 of Judicial Circular No. 49 of 1939, which introduced the doctrine of the Two Companions and the other Sunnī schools in place of that of Abū Ḥanīfa in this respect; then, when the Egyptian

[136] Articles 30 and 288, respectively.

[137] Cf. Chapter II, pp. 69f. above.

reformers—in Article 22 of the Law of Inheritance, 1943—preferred a different, and considerably more complex, way of effecting a broadly similar reform, this was introduced in the Sudan by Judicial Circular No. 51 of 1943, which rescinded the previous Circular. And substantially similar provisions were introduced in Syria, too, by Article 279 of the Syrian Law of 1953. No such reform was needed, of course, in Tunisia, Algeria[138] or Morocco, where the Mālikī law already covered this matter.

A much more important reform which has been effected, in widely different ways, in Egypt, Syria, Tunisia and Morocco, on the one hand, and in Pakistan, on the other, is designed not to further the interests of the nuclear family as such, but to fill the major lacuna in the Islamic law of inheritance in both its Sunnī and Shīʿī form. This lacuna is the inevitable consequence of a rigid

[138] In Algeria a distinctive legal system called *Droit musulman algérien* was developed during the years of close integration with France—including, of course, certain reforms in family law which culminated in Ordinance No. 59-2747 of February 1959 and Decree No. 59-1082 of September of the same year. But after Independence the Algerian National Assembly declared, on 31 December 1962, that existing laws should remain in force with the exception of all that was of 'colonial or discriminatory inspiration' or which 'compromised Algerian independence', and the Constitution of September 1963 emphasized the need to hasten the liberation of women 'in order that they may take their share in the management of public life and the development of the country, and has declared that "all citizens, of both sexes, have the same rights and duties"'. Since then two draft reforms in the field of family law, in 1963–4 and 1966 respectively, have been drafted and discussed. That of 1963 included provisions designed to preclude premature or compulsory marriage and to prohibit divorce other than by judicial decree; and that of 1966 was designed to limit polygamy to cases where the husband has sufficient means and where there was some 'legitimate benefit' in the second marriage. But neither of these draft Laws (which in fact included many of the provisions of the previous legislation) has actually been promulgated, so the present position is somewhat obscure. What is clear is that a specific Law of 29 June 1963 decreed that marriages must be contracted before a court, and that the bride and bridegroom must have reached the ages of sixteen and eighteen respectively; and also that the provision introduced in 1959 that divorce must be finalized before a court, which will investigate the circumstances where the wife contests the repudiation, has been retained—but it is noteworthy that, under the Constitution, the former discriminatory provision that this should not apply to Kabyles is no longer operative, and the law is now the same both for Sunnīs and Ibāḍīs.

application of the basic principle that 'the nearer in degree excludes the more remote'; for this means that a man or woman's orphaned grandchildren, who may have been completely dependent on their grandparent during his lifetime, will be excluded from any share whatever in his estate by the survival of any of that grandparent's sons.[139] This age-old rule (from which, it would seem, Muḥammad himself must have suffered) may have been comparatively innocuous at a time when family solidarity was sufficiently strong and when an uncle might perhaps be trusted to treat orphaned nephews and nieces on a par with his own children; but it is clearly ill-suited to the ethos and circumstances of today. The simplest way to fill this gap, at first sight, would be to give such grandchildren the right of representation: that is, the right to step into the shoes of their deceased parent and inherit what he would have inherited had he survived the grandparent. This solution was mooted in the Lebanon some years ago but was eventually abandoned, in so far as Muslims were concerned, because of the opposition which the proposal aroused; and it was, in fact, adopted in Pakistan as part of the Muslim Family Laws Ordinance, 1961. Clearly, it has much to commend it, for it is eminently straightforward and practical. It might be thought, moreover, that it would achieve exactly the same result as would have prevailed if the deceased parent had in fact survived until one minute after the death of the grandparent (instead of dying, perhaps, two minutes earlier); but under the Islamic law of inheritance this would by no means always be true. A far more important objection to this solution, however, is the fact that it may radically alter the basic principles of the Islamic system of inheritance, as can be shown by a simple example. Let us suppose that the praepositus is survived only by a daughter and the daughter of a predeceased son. In such a case the Sunnīs would initially allot the daughter one-half of the estate and the son's daughter one-sixth; and then, by the doctrine of the return, the daughter would eventually take three-quarters and the son's daughter one-quarter. But in Pakistan, under the Muslim Family Laws Ordinance, the son's daughter, stepping into the shoes

[139] Cf. pp. 69f. above.

of her deceased father, will take two-thirds of the estate and will reduce the daughter to one-third only.

It is precisely because this apparently simple solution wreaks such havoc with the basic principles of the law that a far more subtle solution was found to the problem by the Egyptian reformers, who relied on the assistance of the *'ulamā'* of the Azhar in devising reforms which not only met the needs of society but which could find *some* support, at least, in the classical texts. This solution was incorporated in the Law of Testamentary Dispositions rather than the Law of Inheritance, for it took the form of what are termed 'obligatory bequests'. Ample authority could be found for the proposition that the Qur'ān itself commands a Muslim to make a bequest in favour of any needy relatives (a command which had never been abrogated, as some would say, in regard to those who would receive no share in his inheritance); and an early jurist could be quoted as stating that if anyone did not obey this command, and left a bequest to someone else instead, the court should take this away from the stranger in favour of the needy relative. So the Egyptian reformers decreed that a grandparent who has orphaned grandchildren *must* make them a bequest of what their deceased parent would have taken had he or she survived, provided always that this does not exceed the 'bequeathable third' and that the grandparent has not made a gift of the same value to the orphaned grandchildren *inter vivos*.[140] If, moreover, he has failed to make such bequests, then the court must act as though he had; and if he has made other bequests instead, then the obligatory bequests must be given priority. These provisions were, moreover, substantially adopted in Tunisia by the Law of 1956 (with very minor changes), while they were accepted in Syria in 1953, and Morocco in 1958, with the major difference that the Syrian and Moroccan reforms are limited to the orphaned children of a predeceased son or son's son, and make no provision whatever for the children of a predeceased daughter or son's daughter.[141] The argument on which

140 While, if he has made them a lesser gift *inter vivos*, then the obligatory bequest is to be reduced by this amount.

141 Cf. Articles 78–80 of the Egyptian Law, Articles 191 and 192 of the Tunisian

the Syrians and Moroccans base this limitation is, of course, the fact that, should *all* the praepositus' children have died, it would be only the descendants of his sons who would inherit, whether as agnates or quota-sharers, while his daughters' descendants would be excluded as so-called 'Distant Kindred'; while the argument put forward by the Egyptians and Tunisians is that a daughter or son's daughter is herself always entitled to inherit, so why should orphaned children be deprived of what their mother would have taken?

Space forbids more than the most cursory mention of a few further points in regard to the law of testate and intestate succession. In the pure Sharīʿa, whether among Sunnīs or Shīʿīs, there have always, for example, been certain impediments to inheritance—such as the fact that the would-be heir is a slave, that he has caused the death of the praepositus, that he differs from him in religion, or even (in the case of two non-Muslims) that he differs from him in domicile. Today we may ignore the problem of slavery, except to observe that there are still some parts of the world where it is not, perhaps, entirely irrelevant; but the other three impediments demand passing comment.

It is, I think, characteristic of the new approach that the highly questionable Ḥanafī principle which debars from inheritance any heir who has caused the death of the praepositus in any direct way, however unintentionally, but does not debar one who has deliberately contrived his death in some indirect fashion, has now been abandoned—in Egypt and several other countries—in favour of the much more intelligible Mālikī doctrine that the criterion is whether, or not, the heir intended to cause his death, not the way in which it happened. It seems absurd, for example, to allow an heir who has deliberately planned the death of the praepositus by leaving on his table poisoned chocolates, in the hopes that he will eat them, to profit from his villainy, but to debar one who has accidentally shot

Law, Article 257 of the Syrian Law and Articles 266–9 of the Moroccan Code. For a much more detailed discussion, reference may be made to my article 'Recent Reforms in the Islamic Law of Inheritance', in *International and Comparative Law Quarterly*, Vol. 14 (1965), pp. 356–61.

him when out deer-stalking. But this was changed in Egypt by Article 5 of the Law of Inheritance, 1943, which reads: 'One of the impediments to inheritance is that the heir should have deliberately caused the death of the praepositus, whether as principal, accessory or a false witness whose testimony led to sentence of death and execution, provided the act was without justification or excuse and that the one who did it was sane and not less than fifteen years of age. Among excuses will be included the case of one who exceeds his lawful right of self-defence.'[142] Similarly, Article 17 of the Egyptian Law of Testamentary Dispositions, 1946, states that a legatee must not have caused the death of the testator intentionally—whether as principal, accessory or false witness—with the identical exceptions.

In the classical law, a difference of religion between a deceased person and his heir has always been regarded as an absolute bar to inheritance among the Sunnīs, but not to the validity of a bequest; and the Shīʿīs took the same view where the praepositus was a Muslim and the heir a non-Muslim—although they were always prepared to allow a Muslim heir to inherit, whatever the religion of the deceased. It is only where statute law (with no claim whatever to have any basis in the Sharīʿa) has intervened that any breach has been made in this rule—except for those areas of very mixed religious allegiance where customary law in practice prevails. Examples of statutory intervention can be found in the Caste Disabilities Removal Act, 1850, in what was then British India, and in the Marriage, Divorce and Succession (Non-Christian Asiatics) Ordinance, 1923, in what was then Tanganyika Territory, for Article 6 (1) of the latter expressly provides that 'so much of the law of any religion as deprives any person of a right of succession to property by reason of that person having renounced or having been excluded from the communion of any religion or having been deprived of caste shall not be in force in the Territory'. The Administration (Small Estates) (Amendment) Ordinance of 1947, also in Tanganyika, and the Asiatics (Marriage, Divorce and Succession) (Amendment) Ordinance of 1929 in what was then Nyasaland, include a similar exception in Article 18 (4) and

[142] Cf. Article 264 of the Syrian Law, etc.

Article 6 (1) respectively; but it is clear that these Ordinances found their inspiration, in so far as this clause is concerned, in the Indian Act of 1850.[143]

The impediment of 'difference of domicile' applies only[144] where the deceased is a non-Muslim subject of a Muslim State (that is, a *dhimmī*) and his would-be heir a non-Muslim subject of a non-Muslim State (that is, a *ḥarbī*); for here both the Ḥanafīs and Shāfi'īs exclude any right to inherit, on the ground that a *ḥarbī* must always be regarded as an actual or potential enemy of that part of the world which is under Muslim rule (that is, *Dār al-Islām*). The Mālikīs, on the other hand, do not regard difference of domicile as any bar to inheritance even between non-Muslims, but—unlike the Ḥanafīs—deny any mutual rights of inheritance between the adherents of two different non-Muslim religions. It is in this context that Article 6 of the Egyptian Law of Inheritance comprehensively provides: 'There is no right of inheritance between a Muslim and a non-Muslim, but non-Muslims may inherit from each other. Difference of domicile is no impediment to inheritance between Muslims; and it is also no impediment between non-Muslims except where the law of the foreign State concerned forbids inheritance to foreigners.' This last clause seems to constitute an eminently sensible compromise, based on a fairly extreme form of *talfīq*.

The new principles regarding the maximum period of gestation[145] have, moreover, been given their proper place in the law of testate and intestate succession. It is basic in the law of intestate succession, for example, that a claimant must have been in existence in fact or in law (that is, actually born or presumed to be *en ventre sa mère*) at the time when the praepositus died; so a claim made by an alleged heir who was born more than a solar year after the death

[143] But it must be remembered that it is only in comparatively few countries today that the estate of a non-Muslim would be administered under Islamic law at all.

[144] Except under the Syrian Law, in which Article 264 (c) precludes inheritance even between Muslims, in such cases, where there is no reciprocity in the law of the other country concerned.

[145] Cf. pp. 47, 55, 138ff. above.

of the praepositus may not be entertained by the courts in Egypt, and will be deemed invalid under the substantive law of several other countries. Precisely the same principle applies, moreover, to a claimant born to a divorced wife of the praepositus more than a year after he decisively divorced her—or, indeed, to any other claimant whose relationship with the praepositus depends on his legitimate status if he is born more than a year after his 'parents' have been separated. Where, on the other hand, a claimant's parents are still living together when the praepositus dies, it is the minimum, rather than the maximum, period of gestation that most jurists accept as the criterion; for if he was born after this, then he *might* not have been conceived at the time of the praepositus' death. All the schools agree, moreover, that the minimum period of gestation is six months; so the only controversy in this context is that certain Ḥanbalī jurists insist that the proper criterion in such cases is the normal rather than the minimum period of gestation; for they argue that, where a child is born less than nine months after the praepositus died, there is, in most cases, a distinct probability that he had already been conceived—so they prefer to accept the possible injustice to the other heirs involved in upholding such a claim rather than the probable injustice to the claimant in denying it. This principle has been adopted in the Egyptian Law of Inheritance, 1943, and the Tunisian Law of Personal Status, 1956, both of which provide that a child born to a married woman within 270 days of the death of the praepositus will be presumed to have been *en ventre sa mère* at the time of his decease.[146] Almost identical principles are, moreover, applicable to testamentary dispositions, where the legatee must normally have been in existence, in fact or in law, at the time when the testator died.[147]

Space forbids a discussion of the considerable number of other changes in the law of testate and intestate succession, as this was previously administered in one country or another, which have

[146] Cf. Articles 42–4 of the Egyptian Law, Article 150 of the Tunisian Law, and (in part) Articles 299–301 of the Syrian Law.

[147] Cf. Articles 35 and 36 of the Egyptian Law of Testamentary Dispositions, Article 236 of the Syrian Law, etc.

been effected in recent years by means of legislative provisions. In Egypt and Syria, for example, a baby is now entitled to inherit only if wholly born alive, contrary to the Ḥanafī doctrine previously followed; and in Egypt, again, the Ḥanafī doctrine that an embryo which is regarded as putatively (*taqdīran*) born alive—and therefore entitled to inherit and pass inheritance—has been similarly abandoned in favour of the law of the other Sunnī schools. The Tunisian Law, naturally enough, incorporates similar provisions; but it is noteworthy that the Tunisian reformers have followed the Egyptian Law in providing that the *ghirra*, or blood-money which is payable in respect of the dead embryo, is now—contrary to the doctrine of all four schools—to be regarded as belonging to the mother, as though she had lost part of her own body, rather than to the heirs of the still-born child. Both the Egyptian and the Syrian Laws, again, have largely adopted the doctrine attributed to Abū Yūsuf in regard to the rights of inheritance of the so-called 'Distant Kindred' in place of the considerably more complex rules advocated by Muḥammad al-Shaybānī. In regard to the law of bequests, moreover, the Syrian Law has followed the Egyptian legislation in providing that the sort of condition on which a bequest may validly be made dependent is 'one in which there is some legal benefit to the testator, to the legatees, or to some other person, and which is neither forbidden by, nor contrary to the purposes of, the Sharīʿa'; in permitting bequests either of *ʿayn* or *manfaʿa* (corpus or usufruct) to legatees who are not yet in existence, or some of whom are not yet in existence, and in the way in which it regulates them; and in regard to the rules applicable to bequests to legatees of a definite or indefinite number, to bequests to embryos, and to bequests of the usufruct of property in which the testator has made changes or additions. In certain other respects, moreover, the Syrian reformers have gone further than the Egyptians: e.g. in making *any* bequest to a foreigner subject to the principle of reciprocity of treatment, regardless of whether the foreigner is a subject of a Muslim or non-Muslim country; and in providing that it is a condition of the acceptance of a bequest that it should not only follow the death of the testator, but should be 'within thirty days thereof, or of the legatee's learning of the bequest'. In Egypt, moreover, these Laws of both testate and intestate succession have been made applicable to all Egyptians, regardless of their religion; and in several countries any claim to a bequest which is denied by the heirs will not be enforced by the courts in default of proper documentary evidence.[148]

But at this point it is essential that a major caveat should be entered. All over the world there is a yawning gulf between the law that lawyers learn and expound and the way in which this law is—or is not—applied in real life; and this is particularly relevant to legislative reforms which many people may not understand or of which they may be totally ignorant. But if this is true in a sophisticated and largely literate society, it is obviously far more so in a backward and illiterate milieu. In the Muslim world, therefore, it is one thing to introduce reforms in regard to matters such as marriage, divorce and inheritance and quite another to ensure that village women, in particular, are aware of their rights or have the opportunity—or even the temerity—to claim them; and there can be no doubt that many of the reforms discussed in this book remain, in some areas at least, of little more than academic—and also, one hopes, of educative—relevance. Real life does not always turn out even in the way that sociologists predict, however, as can be seen in Turkey where the Swiss Civil Code remained almost a dead letter in the villages of Anatolia for many years, and informal (or Islamic) marriages were much more highly regarded than those contracted under the new law. Then came the Korean war, Turks from all over the country were enlisted in the army, and people

[148] Cf., for this whole section, N. J. Coulson, *Succession in the Muslim Family* (C.U.P., 1971). Also my articles 'Recent Developments in Sharīʿa Law' VII and VIII—on Testamentary Bequests and Intestate Succession, respectively—in *The Muslim World* (Jan. and April 1952); 'The Syrian Law of Personal Status', in *Bulletin of the School of Oriental and African Studies* (1955); 'The Tunisian Law of Personal Status', in *The International and Comparative Law Quarterly* (1958); 'Recent Reforms in the Islamic Law of Inheritance', in *The International and Comparative Law Quarterly* (1965); and 'Islamic Law of Intestate and Testate Succession and the Administration of Deceased Persons' Assets', in *Islamic Law in India* (The Indian Law Institute, 1972).

began to realize that for a soldier to draw married rates of pay, or for his widow to draw a pension, he must have been married under the Code![149]

6. WAQFS AND GIFTS

The law of *waqf*, as it has developed down the centuries, is distinctively Islamic and still very widely applied. In one country after another, moreover, it has been found necessary to promulgate legislation designed to regulate the way in which *awqāf* are administered, and to prevent some of the abuses which are characteristic of so many of these family or charitable endowments and their private administrators. The responsibility for supervising the way in which these *mutawallīs* or *nāẓirs* perform their duties rests, in Islamic law, primarily on the courts; but in some countries a special Ministry of Waqfs has been set up and given certain statutory powers. It would be tedious to attempt to describe the relevant legislation in any detail; but it is significant to observe that as early as 1854 Muḥammad ʿAlī in Egypt issued a famous decree forbidding the creation of any further *awqāf*—although this decree seems to have been limited, in practice, to certain types of land, to have been frequently evaded, and soon to have become a dead-letter. It is also significant that in 1926 a law was passed in Turkey, some months before the abandonment of the Sharīʿa in general, providing for the liquidation of all *awqāf*; and that in Egypt, in the very same year, the relevant committee of the Chamber of Deputies, in presenting its report on the budget of the Ministry of Waqfs, made some pungent criticisms of the system and observed that 'These and other considerations make it incumbent on Parliament and those who watch over the country's economic and social affairs to consider whether the system ought, or ought not, to continue'. Thus the battle was joined between those who defended the system and those who urged its total abolition. But soon a middle party emerged, pledged neither to its total abolition nor to its preservation in its existing form, but rather to its radical reform. For

[149] Cf., for Turkey, my article 'The Movement towards Codification in Turkey, Cyprus and the Arab World', in *Indian Year Book of International Affairs* (1958), pp. 131 f.

a number of years the issue was in doubt; but finally the 'Law of Rules Relevant to Waqfs' was promulgated in Egypt in 1946—and it is noteworthy that in 1947 many of the provisions of this Law were adopted in the Lebanon, with minor alterations, in the Law of Family Waqfs.

These two Laws include a considerable number of exceedingly interesting reforms, a few of which demand mention and comment. Article 1 of the Egyptian Law, for example, enacts that 'From the date when this Law comes into force, the creation of a *waqf*, its revocation, any alteration in the application of its income or its conditions, or any exchange of its property by the founder, are alike invalid unless a declaration (*ishhād*) to that effect is made by the competent person before one of the Sharīʿa courts . . .'; and Article 6 of the Lebanese Law is very similar. This provides yet another instance of the growing tendency, in one point after another, to insist on proper documentary or official evidence—even in Egypt, in this case, as a substantive, rather than merely procedural, reform. But Article 5 is much more radical when it enacts that 'A *waqf* of a mosque must be perpetual; a *waqf* in favour of some other charity may be either temporary or perpetual; while a *waqf* for any other purpose must be temporary and shall not extend to more than two series of beneficiaries . . . If, on the other hand, a *waqf* for other than charitable purposes is made temporary by a specified time limit, this must not exceed sixty years after the death of the founder. The founder of a *waqf* prior to this Law, moreover, may make this *waqf* temporary in accordance with the foregoing provisions where he has the power of revocation.' This represents a positively revolutionary change in the law of *waqf* as this was previously accepted and administered, for it rang the death knell on family perpetuities. It found its juristic basis, moreover, in an extreme form of *talfīq*, since it applied the view of the vast majority of jurists (who supported the *waqf* system) to such endowments as fell within its terms, yet relied on the opinions of a small minority of lawyers (who took the diametrically opposite view) in regard to those endowments that did not conform to the new rules—which were, themselves, completely contrary to the generally accepted doctrine. And the Lebanese Law similarly insists, in Articles 8–10, on family *waqfs* being limited to two series of beneficiaries, although it does not provide for them to be limited by a term of years.[150]

In somewhat the same vein, Article 11 of the Egyptian Law provides that, in future, 'a founder may revoke his *waqf*, in whole or in part, and may also alter the application of its income or its conditions, even if he purported to deprive himself of this right, provided that such alteration shall be effective only within the terms of this Law . . .'; and again the Lebanese Law, Article 7, is broadly similar. Article 17 of the Egyptian Law, moreover, covers what happens to the *waqf* property when the *waqf* comes to an end, and provides that it shall revert to the founder if still alive, but that, where he has already died, it shall in some circumstances become the property of the beneficiaries, and in others of the heirs of the founder at the time of his death. Here the Lebanese Law is less complex, for Article 10 provides that property previously subject to a temporary *waqf* shall in all cases revert to the founder or to his heirs when the *waqf* terminates.

The section of the Law bearing the heading 'Entitlement under a *waqf*' is of particular interest. Article 22, for example, provides that 'conditions imposed by the founder of a *waqf* on its beneficiaries shall be void if they restrict their freedom in regard to marriage, place of residence, or the raising of credit—unless, in the last case, the condition is genuinely to their benefit. Similarly, any condition the non-observance of which would occasion no loss of benefit to founder, *waqf* or beneficiaries shall be void'. But Article 27 lists certain exceptions to these new rules, and provides, for example, that a wife may always deprive her husband of any entitlement in a *waqf* she makes if he should divorce her or marry a co-wife while their marriage subsists. And here, again, Article 13 of the Lebanese Law largely follows suit.

[150] A few of the provisions of these laws were cited, as outstanding examples of *talfīq*, in Chapter II above. For a comparatively full discussion, reference may be made to my article 'Development in Sharī'a Law IX' (The Waqf System), in *The Muslim World* (Oct. 1952).

Still more significant are the provisions of Articles 23–30 of the Egyptian Law and Articles 36–9 of the Lebanese Law, which cover what may be termed 'obligatory entitlements'. Thus Article 23 in Egypt provides that a man 'may make a *waqf* of not more than one-third of his property in favour of whoever he wishes, be they heirs or non-heirs, or in favour of a charity, and the criterion shall be what constitutes one-third of the property of the founder at the time of his death . . . Subject to the provisions of Article 24, moreover, he may make a *waqf* of his whole property in favour of such of his descendants, parents, spouse or spouses, as are alive at the time of his death; while, if none of those specified in Article 24 are alive at his death, he may make a *waqf* of all his property in favour of whoever he pleases.' Article 24 then provides that 'subject to the terms of Article 29, such descendants, parents, spouse or spouses of the founder as are alive at his death must be given an entitlement, in any *waqf* that exceeds one-third of his property, equal to their rights of inheritance; and the entitlement of each will pass to his descendants after him . . . Such entitlement shall not, however, be due to any to whom the founder has given, by means of some other gratuitous disposition, the equivalent of their entitlement; while, where he has given them less than this, they shall have a right to an entitlement equal to the difference only.' Article 25, moreover, provides that none of these persons may be deprived of all or part of their obligatory entitlement except as provided in the following articles (e.g. if one of them has caused the death of the founder in any way that would debar him from inheriting his property, or where the founder has some good reason for so depriving him, etc.). Again, Articles 28 and 29 permit, but do not oblige, the founder of a *waqf* to provide that the entitlement of a spouse or parent shall be for life only, and shall pass to the founder's own descendants rather than theirs after their death, and also to grant to the offspring of any of his children who has died during his lifetime an entitlement in his *waqf* equal to the obligatory entitlement which would have been due to the deceased child had he been alive at the founder's death. Finally, Article 30 prescribes what shall be done if the founder deprives any of those with an obligatory entitlement of all or part of such entitlement, or if any such person should fail, without valid excuse, to bring an action to claim his right within two solar years of the founder's death, or has consented to the *waqf* in writing after his death. And again Articles 36–9 in the Lebanese Law are broadly similar.

The purpose of these provisions is crystal clear. Among the many criticisms of the *waqf* system as it had developed down the centuries was that it could so readily be used as a means of evading the exceedingly precise and rigid prescriptions of the Islamic law of testate and intestate succession—even, indeed, to the extent that a man might create a *waqf* in which he devoted the whole of his property to some charitable purpose (after, perhaps, reserving an income for himself, if he were a Ḥanafī, for the rest of his life, or making some suitable provision for his own livelihood by one or another of the devices sanctioned by the other schools), and might thus deprive his family of any share whatever in his property. Alternatively, he could name some of his relatives as beneficiaries to the total exclusion of others. So these provisions were devised to prevent any such action, with the result that the rules governing the disposition of property by means of a *waqf* have been brought much more closely into line with the principles which govern testamentary dispositions, on the one hand, and with the rights to intestate succession enjoyed by members of the nuclear family, on the other—although they also include a number of most interesting innovations. The juristic basis for these bold reforms must be sought in those Traditions which enjoin charity to one's own family before anyone else; in the opinion of certain leading 'Followers' of the Prophet that a man may not dispose of more than a third of his property in extraneous charity even during his lifetime; in the dictum of Ibn Ḥazm that any gift which does not leave enough for the donor's own needs and those of his family should be regarded as invalid; in Traditions enjoining impartiality of treatment between children; in the view of some Mālikī and Shāfiʿī jurists that a *waqf* in favour of sons to the exclusion of daughters is void; and in the opinion of Ibn Ḥazm that a *waqf* which favours one child compared with others is valid *per se*, but the benefit therein should be distributed equally between them all.

A primary emphasis is placed by the reformers on the evils, to which the former unfettered freedom had all too often given rise, inherent in favouritism and the hatred this engenders, in disinheritance as a result of malice or sudden anger, and in an utter disregard of the laws of testate and intestate succession. So in Egypt the Explanatory Memorandum states: 'Thus, in order to eliminate such tragedies and to follow the guidance of the Prophet; in order to act in conformity with the unequivocal spirit of the Sharīʿa and in accordance with the public welfare in an age in which the religious impulse has become weak and heterogeneous influences have obtained the ascendency; and in order to attain consistency and a mutual relationship between the rules of testamentary bequests and those of *awqāf*, it was decided to restrict the freedom of founders and to lay down the following rules...' As for the fact that these entitlements are limited to the immediate family, this is said to be justified by the consideration that such, normally, are the only persons who share in the founder's property and income during his life; while the right of a wife to exclude a husband who marries a co-wife or divorces her is expressly stated to represent a salutary check, in the interests of society as well as the individual concerned, on a husband's arbitrary exercise of his legal rights in these respects.

Another major reform in this Law which demands comment is the attempt which has been made to ensure the wise and energetic management of *waqf* property by equating it, as far as possible, with the private property of the beneficiaries. This result is achieved by providing for the compulsory and final separation of any beneficiary's share in a *waqf*, wherever this is feasible, from the rest of the *waqf* property; by enacting that he should himself be appointed its administrator, whenever he is suitable for such appointment; and by ensuring that each beneficiary's share in the *waqf* income should always go straight to his own descendants and that such distribution should never be upset unnecessarily. Where, moreover, the above provisions are inapplicable, the administrator must be chosen, where possible, from among the number of the beneficiaries and largely at the discretion of those with the major entitlements; shall be held responsible to the beneficiaries for negligence or wrongdoing; and is liable to criminal sanctions if he fails to present his accounts, together with supporting receipts, whenever the court shall so demand. The relevant provisions are set out in detail in Articles 32–49 of the Egyptian Law and Articles 40–3, 17 and 31, etc., in the Lebanese Law.[151]

In Lebanon, this Law is still in force as a whole; but in Egypt the more drastic step of completely abolishing private or family *waqfs*, which had been under consideration and debate for a number of years, was finally taken in 1952—so it is now only those sections of the Law of 1946 which concern public *waqfs* which are still applicable. Family *waqfs* have also been totally abolished in Syria and Tunisia. Curiously enough, moreover, there are scarcely any *waqfs*, other than mosques, throughout West Africa.

Reference has already been made to the problems caused in the Indian subcontinent, and subsequently in Aden, Kenya and Zanzibar, by a misunderstanding, on the part of judges trained in the English tradition, of the Muslim view of the essentially charitable nature of family *waqfs*—culminating in two most regrettable judgments by the Judicial Committee of the Privy Council in 1894 and 1952, respectively.[152] A not altogether successful attempt to get back to the true Islamic doctrine in this matter was made in India in 1913 by the Mussulman Wakf Validating Act (which was made retroactive in 1930), in Aden in 1939 by the Mohammedan Wakf Ordinance, in Zanzibar in 1946 by the Wakf Validating Decree and in Kenya in 1951 by the Wakf Commissioners Ordnance. But this last enactment itself made a clear-cut distinction

[151] For a very summary discussion, reference may again be made to my article in *The Muslim World* noted above. For the next few pages I have substituted *waqfs* for the more correct *awqāf*, for the sake of the reader who does not know Arabic.

[152] *Abul Fata* v. *Russomoy* [1894] I A 76; and *Fatuma* v. *Mohamed bin Salim* [1952] A.C.I.

between *waqfs* which are 'charitable' (*khayrī*), on the one hand, and 'family' (*ahlī*), on the other, in a way which is essentially alien to the traditional doctrine, but which corresponds fairly closely to the distinction made in Egypt and the Lebanon, for example, between public and private *waqfs*. So this change of attitude among modern Muslims might well be quoted in support of the decisions of the Privy Council to which adverse reference has just been made, were it not for the fact that these decisions were not reached on broad grounds of public policy, but on a process of reasoning, and an interpretation of some of the Islamic texts, which were manifestly mistaken.[153]

Little need be said about the law of gifts. In those countries in which the Sharīʿa has traditionally governed the lives of Muslims in the field of family relations, in the widest connotation of that term, it was natural that the Islamic law should also prevail in regard to gifts, since these are, in practice, largely confined to members of the family or to charitable donations (*ṣadaqāt*). Reforms in the relevant law duly appeared, therefore, in Judicial Circular No. 13 of 1913 in the Sudan, where the complicated Ḥanafī rules with regard to the gift of property held in common between two or more co-owners (or of property which is occupied by, or which occupies, some other property of which the would-be donor retains ownership)[154] were abandoned in favour of the considerably simpler doctrine of the other Sunnī schools. Again, in Circular No. 41 of 1935, the Mālikī law with regard to the passing of ownership in a thing given, and the circumstances in which the donee is entitled to take possession of it, were adopted in the place of the Ḥanafī rules which were previously in force. But in Egypt the law governing gifts was transferred from the Sharīʿa Courts to the National Courts some years before the former were abolished, and

[153] For a concise discussion of these two cases, cf. my article 'Waqfs in East Africa', in *Journal of African Law*, Vol. III, No. 3 (Autumn 1959), pp. 152 ff.; and for a reasonably full discussion of both the legislation and case-law up till 1952, reference may be made to my book *Islamic Law in Africa*, pp. 34 f., 63 ff., 93 ff., and 340 ff. My article 'The Religious Element in Waqf Endowments', in the *Journal of the Royal Central Asian Society* (July 1951), is also relevant.

[154] E.g. a gift of a field without the trees which are growing in it, or *vice versa*.

the relevant law was codified in Articles 486–504 of the Civil Code of 1948 (which correspond to Articles 454–72 of the Syrian Civil Code); and here the Explanatory Memorandum which accompanied the Egyptian Code, after pointing out how much more complete the new provisions were than those of the previous codes (which scarcely concerned themselves with anything other than matters of form), states that 'The draft derived the provisions regarding the relevant substantive law from the Sharīʿa, and particularly from Qadrī Pasha's codification of the law of personal status. The provisions regarding the form of gifts, on the other hand, represent a retention of the existing legislation, with minor amendments.' Much the same could be said of the law which governs pre-emption (*shufʿa*), death-sickness (*maraḍ al-mawt*), lesion (*ghubn*) and a number of other concepts taken over from the Sharīʿa, which are commonly included, today, in Civil Codes rather than in codifications of the Sharīʿa law as such.[155] In India and Pakistan, on the other hand, the law of gift (*hiba*) has never been codified and is still applied, for the most part, according to Ḥanafī principles—with the exception that a peculiarly Indian form of *hiba bi'l-ʿiwaḍ*,[156] or so-called 'gratuitous' transfer of property for a consideration, has been evolved by the courts. And the same thing is largely true of the law of pre-emption, although this is, in general, applied to Muslims in the sub-continent only under the umbrella of 'justice, equity and good conscience'—with the strange consequence that it is not applied at all in the State of Madras; that it has been enforced by legislation, but in a radically unorthodox form, in certain other areas; that it has been adopted by Hindus in some localities as part of their customary law; and that there is considerable confusion between the different courts as to whether it is properly applicable where the claimant and original vendor are Muslims, but the vendee is not.

In the Muslim world as a whole, however, the tendency today is for every part of the law to be codified, from whatever source

[155] Cf. pp. 92–4 above.

[156] Cf., in this context, *Mulla's Principles of Mahomedan Law* (16th edn., by M. Hidayatullah, 1968), pp. 168 ff.

it may have been derived, and for the distinct and separate jurisdiction of Sharīʿa courts to give way to that of unified, national courts of comprehensive competence. But this phenomenon must be reserved for consideration in the next, and final, chapter.

CHAPTER IV

Problems and Prospects

I. INTRODUCTION

In the previous chapters of this book we have been concerned with the background and pressures for law reform in the Muslim world in the last century or so, with the philosophy and methods which have characterized the recent reform movement, and with what has already been achieved by the reformers and the law which prevails today in most of the countries concerned. It now remains, therefore, to outline the pressures which still exist for changes in the law in many predominantly Muslim countries (or, indeed, those in which there is a significant Muslim minority); the debates to which these pressures give rise and the problems which confront present, or future, reformers; and the way in which these problems might conceivably be resolved. This is no easy assignment, and one which is inevitably exposed to the winds of informed, and legitimate, controversy; but it represents a task which falls properly within the theoretical competence of a lawyer. Finally, it would savour of cowardice, I think, not to indulge in some predictions, or at least speculations, about the way things are likely to go and the developments which may, perhaps, be expected; but this will inevitably involve exchanging the robes of an academic lawyer (which sit comparatively comfortably, if inadequately, on my shoulders) for the wholly unaccustomed mantle of the prophet.

The pressures for changes in the law which still exist in the Muslim world may be classified, broadly speaking, under three main categories. First, there are pressures for a return to the Sharīʿa, whether in whole or in part, in some of those countries in which the movement for reform has ushered in a system of law which is today largely secular. The most typical example of this phenomenon may be found in Pakistan; but tendencies in this direction also exist in a number of other countries, such as Libya. Next, and at the diametrically opposite pole, there are the pressures for certain relaxations in the scope of the Sharīʿa, or the way in which it is interpreted and applied, in those countries in which it is still comprehensive in its sway and rigid in its application. Here the typical example is provided by Saʿūdī Arabia; but a somewhat similar problem exists in countries where the population is basically Muslim but the government strongly influenced by communism or extreme socialism. Then again, there are pressures in many other Muslim countries for a more radical approach to the Sharīʿa as a whole, so that the disparate elements in the law which currently prevails—some of it recognizably Islamic, and some of it manifestly alien in origin and inspiration—may be integrated into a cohesive system which could be regarded as at once Islamic and reformed or, at least, consonant both with the basic principles of Islam and the fundamental requirements of modern life. Examples of this attitude can be found in one Muslim country after another. Somewhat the same could be said, in so far as matters of personal law are concerned, of what can most conveniently be discussed as a rather different problem: namely, the pressures brought to bear on the Muslim community, in certain countries which are not predominantly Muslim, either to abandon their personal law in favour of a uniform code, or at least so to reform their own law as to bring it into substantial conformity with that of their non-Muslim fellow citizens. Here the outstanding example is India; but Kenya, Tanzania and Ghana could also be cited by way of illustration. Interestingly enough, moreover, experience shows that, however widely the pressures and approach may differ in one category of country and another, some of the basic problems which are involved remain essentially the same.

2. PRESSURES FOR A RETURN TO MUSLIM ORTHODOXY

The reason why Pakistan represents the outstanding example of a country in which these pressures can be analysed today is not far to seek. Under the Moguls, as we have seen, Islamic law occupied a predominant, although by no means exclusive, place in the Indian sub-continent; but this was steadily eroded under the British Raj, so that the Sharīʿa may be said, in general terms, to have survived only in so far as the personal law of Muslims was concerned (and, even there, in a distinctly attenuated form). When the peoples of India began seriously to prepare themselves for independence, therefore, the Muslim community was confronted by the problem of the nature of the new State in which they were to live. Was this to be essentially secular, or even dominated by the concept and way of life of the Hindu majority; or were they to campaign for a State in which they themselves would constitute the majority and in which they could practice their own religion as they pleased—not only in private and family life, but also, perhaps, in the very organization of society and its institutions? It was their eventual insistence on this which led to Partition and the establishment of Pakistan ('the Land of the Pure')—made up of those parts of the sub-continent in which Muslims were in a clear majority—even though this involved the emergence of a State made up of two wings which were separated from each other by more than a thousand miles, and in which the people differed widely from each other in their linguistic, cultural and political background. There can be no manner of doubt, therefore, that Islam was the very *raison d'être* of Pakistan, for there was little else, except a certain Indian identity, which held the new and highly artificial State together; and this basic Indian identity might be said to unite the peoples of the Punjab and Bengal more closely than those who made up West Pakistan and East Pakistan, respectively, in everything other than religion.

Even so, there is scope for considerable debate as to how truly Islamic Muhammad ʿAli Jinnah intended that the new State should be. On one occasion he declared that 'The Muslims demand

Pakistan, where they could rule according to their own code of life and according to their own cultural growth, traditions and Islamic laws'; and on another that the Muslim League 'stood for carving out states in India where Muslims were in numerical majority to rule there under Islamic law'.[1] But on more numerous and more public occasions he emphasized that Pakistan would be a modern, democratic State, with sovereignty residing in the people, and with all the members of the new nation having equal rights of citizenship—regardless of their religion, caste or origin. He was himself, of course, essentially a politician who suited his speeches to his audience, and whose own vision was of a State which was distinctively Islamic, but in no narrow, rigid or orthodox sense of that term. But, however that may be, there can be no room for doubt that two ambitions—the one to be an Islamic State, and the other to be a modern, democratic State—are united, in manifest tension, in the aspirations of the people.

This was, indeed, vividly expressed in the Preamble to the Constitution of 1956—which was very largely retained in that of 1962, as amended by the Constitution (First Amendment) Act, 1963. In its revised form, this reads:

Whereas sovereignty over the entire Universe belongs to Allah Almighty alone, and the authority to be exercised by the people of Pakistan within the limits prescribed by Him is a sacred trust;

Whereas the Founder of Pakistan, Qa'id-i-A'zam, Muhammad 'Ali Jinnah, expressing the will of the people, declared that Pakistan should be a democratic State based on Islamic principles of social justice;

And whereas it is the will of the people of Pakistan that

(*a*) the State should exercise its powers and authority through representatives chosen by the people;

(*b*) the principles of democracy, freedom, equality, tolerance and social justice, as enunciated by Islam, should be fully observed in Pakistan;

(*c*) the Muslims of Pakistan should be enabled, individually and collectively, to order their lives in accordance with the teachings and requirements of Islam as set out in the Holy Quran and Sunnah . . . ;

[1] Cf. Khurshid Ahmad, *An Analysis of the Munir Report*, pp. 132 and 133, respectively.

(*d*) the legitimate interests of the minorities in Pakistan (including their religious and cultural interests) should be adequately safeguarded;

(*e*) the fundamental human rights (including the rights of equality before the law, of freedom of thought, expression, belief, faith and association, and of social, economic and political justice) should, consistently with the security of the State, public interest and the requirements of morality, be preserved, and

(*f*) the independence of the judicature should be ensured.

It is also noteworthy that the First Amendment Act reinserted in the Constitution the word 'Islamic' (which had been omitted in the Constitution of 1962) before 'Republic of Pakistan'. And under the 'Principles of Policy', in their amended form, a number of strongly Muslim clauses, such as 'No law shall be repugnant to the teachings and requirements of Islam, as set out in the Holy Quran and Sunnah, and all existing laws shall be brought into conformity with the Holy Quran and Sunnah', and 'Riba (usury) should be eliminated', are combined with others which proclaim the equality of all citizens before the law, their freedom of speech, and their freedom to profess, practise and propagate their own religion.

Much more recently, moreover, the 'basic norm' of the Constitution of Pakistan has assumed a major importance in the courts. This started in 1958 when, in *State* v. *Dosso*,[2] the Pakistan Supreme Court invoked Hans Kelsen's *Grundnorm* thesis to uphold the validity of a coup headed by Iskandar Mirza, who was President under Pakistan's first Constitution[3]—for Kelsen, in his General Theory of Law and State, had argued that a successful *coup d'état* or revolution, which effectively nullified the old 'basic norm', must be regarded as a law-creating fact which gives validity to a 'new legal order'. But in 1972, in *Isma Jilani* v. *Government of Punjab*,[4] a different bench of the Pakistan Supreme Court held that Kelsen's thesis about a successful revolution creating a new *Grundnorm*

[2] P.L.D. 1958 S.C. 533.

[3] Cf. T. K. K. Iyer, 'Constitutional Law in Pakistan: Kelsen in the Courts', in *The American Journal of Comparative Law*, Vol. XXI, No. 4 (1973).

[4] P.L.D. 1972 S.C. 139.

cannot properly be invoked in Pakistan. In the words of Hamoodur Rahman, C.J.:

In any event, if a *Grund Norm* is necessary for us I do not have to look to the Western legal theorists to discover one. Our own *Grund Norm* is enshrined in our own doctrine that the legal sovereignty over the entire universe belongs to Almighty Allah alone, and the authority exerciseable by the people within the limits prescribed by Him is a sacred trust. This is an immutable and unalterable norm which was clearly accepted in the Objectives Resolution passed by the Constituent Assembly of Pakistan on the 7th of March 1949. This Resolution has been described by Mr Brohi as the 'cornerstone of Pakistan's legal edifice' and recognised even by the learned Attorney-General himself as 'the bond which binds the nation' and as a document from which the Constitution of Pakistan 'must draw its inspiration'. This has not been abrogated by anyone so far, nor has this been departed or deviated from by any regime, military or Civil. Indeed, it cannot be . . .

It is noteworthy, however, that in the still more recent case of *State* v. *Zia-ur-Rahman*[5] he first quoted these words *verbatim* and then proceeded to insist:

It will be observed that this does not say that the Objectives Resolution is the *Grund Norm*, but that the *Grund Norm* is the doctrine of legal sovereignty accepted by the people of Pakistan and the consequences which flow from it. I did not describe the Objectives Resolution as 'the cornerstone of Pakistan's legal edifice' but merely pointed out that one of the learned counsel appearing in the case had described it as such. It is not correct, therefore, to say that I held it . . . 'to be a transcendental part of the Constitution' or 'a *supra*-Constitutional Instrument which is unalterable and immutable'.

But what, precisely, does the phrase 'conformity with the Holy Quran and Sunnah' really mean? It must be noted that this phrase falls far short of the classical doctrine of the sources (*uṣūl*) of Islamic law, for these comprise not only the Qur'ān and *sunna*, but also the *ijmā*', or consensus of jurists (as yet another authoritative indication of the divine will) and *qiyās*, or analogical deductions drawn

[5] P.L.D. 1973 S.C. 71.

from these primary sources. Traditionally, indeed, it is the consensus which determines what the Qur'ān means, what the *sunna* is, and how they are both to be interpreted and applied. In point of fact, moreover, the vastly greater part of the Sharī'a, as this has been developed by the jurists, is based on analogy and consensus; but the Constitution of Pakistan significantly confines itself to 'the Quran and Sunnah' alone. Even so, many problems remain as to what, precisely, this means in practice. In regard to the Qur'ān itself, for example, there is room for endless debate about whether some verses have been abrogated by others, as most Muslims believe; and, if so, which verses were abrogated by which? Again, what is the precise implication and application of the Qur'anic provisions? What, for example, does the prohibition of *ribā'* or 'usury' really mean? Yet again, are all the verses in the Qur'ān of equally universal and permanent application, as a rigid rule from which no exceptions whatever can be tolerated by the loyal Muslim, or are some of more basic authority than others? All these questions are, moreover, equally applicable to the *sunna* or practice of the Prophet of Islam; but in this case they are enormously complicated by the problem of the authenticity, or otherwise, of the exceedingly variant Traditions by which the *sunna* is established. And over all these theoretical and theological questions there broods the practical problem of who it is who should be empowered to give a decisive ruling on all these points, in terms of the law which is to be promulgated and applied in Pakistan?

In the proposals of the Draft Constitution of 1952, this was to be the duty of a Board of Five 'Ulamā' or experts in Islamic law. If any one of them were to object to legislation as contrary to the principles of Islam, then the legislation concerned—whether it had already been passed by the Assembly or not—was to be referred to the whole Board. If, moreover, the Board were to disagree with the Assembly, then the dispute was to be resolved by the Head of State or of the Unit concerned—while in some cases, a decision of the Board could be overruled only by a majority of the Muslim members, present and voting, in the relevant Assembly. But this suggestion was soon abandoned, and the proposal was made that the Supreme Court should be given the responsibility of striking down a law as contrary to the Constitution if it considered it to be contrary to the 'Quran or Sunnah'.

In the event, however, yet another solution to this problem was adopted. First, an 'Advisory Council of Islamic Ideology' was set up, the members of which were appointed by the President on the basis of their 'understanding and appreciation of Islam and of the economic, political, legal and administrative problems of Pakistan' —a dual qualification which is itself significant. This Council was 'to make recommendations to the Central Government and the Provincial Governments as to means of enabling and encouraging the Muslims of Pakistan to order their lives in all respects in accordance with the principles and concepts of Islam, and to examine all laws in force ... with a veiw to bringing them into conformity with the teachings and requirements of Islam as set out in the Holy Quran and Sunnah'. It was also 'to advise the National Assembly, a Provincial Assembly, the President or a Governor', in any question referred to it, on whether a proposed law was, or was not, 'repugnant to the teachings and requirements of Islam as set out in the Holy Quran and Sunnah'. Secondly, an Islamic Research Institute was established, the function of which was to 'undertake Islamic research and instruction in Islam for the purpose of assisting in the reconstruction of Muslim society on a truly Islamic basis'. But it is noteworthy that it was explicitly provided that 'The responsibility of deciding whether any action of an organ or authority of the State, or of a person performing functions on behalf of an organ or authority of the State, is in accordance with the principles of policy, is that of the organ or authority of the State, or of the person, concerned'; and that 'The validity of an action or of a law shall not be called in question on the ground that it is not in accordance with the principles of policy, and no action shall lie against the State, any organ or authority of the State, or any person on such a ground'. Even where proposed legislation had been referred to the Council for an opinion or advice, moreover, it might none the less be promulgated before any such advice was given if the Assembly, the President or the Governor concerned considered that, in the public interest, the making of the proposed law 'should not be postponed'. So it is evident that the advice of the Council, however persuasive, was not intended to be binding. And it is equally obvious that this represents a compromise, which the divided state of opinion in Pakistan no doubt demanded, between enshrining the 'principles of Islam' as the criterion by which future legislation should be judged, and to which existing legislation should eventually be made to conform, and ensuring that the will of the executive or the legislature, as the case might be, would in practice always prevail.

It is impossible accurately to assess the relative influence of all the different strands of opinion which exist in Pakistan and Bangladesh today. When I visited Pakistan some years ago, the situation in what was then the Eastern Province was very different from what must now prevail in the new State, so I will confine my remarks to what was then the Western Province.[6]

At one extreme there were the *ʿulama*, or traditional teachers, and that dynamic Islamic fundamentalist, Mawlānā Mawdūdī, who were united in their passionate belief that Pakistan must be an Islamic State in the traditional sense of that term; but, whereas to the *ʿulama* this meant something along the lines of the classical Caliphate, with virtually no deviation, to Mawdūdī it meant a combination of what he regarded as authoritative Islamic norms with such concessions to democratic principles and contemporary circumstances as seemed to him legitimate. But he, like the *ʿulama*, maintains that the Sharīʿa must be reinstated in its entirety, including the prescribed penalties for theft and adultery, etc.; and his only concession in this matter would be in regard to questions of priority and timing. The first essential, he insists, must be to ensure that the whole structure of life in Pakistan is brought into genuine conformity with the principles of Islam, for in a modern, capitalist State men and women are virtually encouraged, as he sees it, to indulge in dishonesty or illicit sex; but, when once a State

[6] Except to observe that the Constitution of Bangladesh makes virtually no reference to Islam, but that 'Muslim Personal Law' is still administered largely as before.

which was truly Islamic had been set up, all this would be changed, and anyone who was then so depraved as to commit such offences must suffer the prescribed punishments. And while he is sufficiently realistic to perceive that to create the sort of Islamic State he has in mind would entail a complete transformation of the educational system, with new training not only for children but also for their teachers, he is naive enough to remark that this process of reformation might well take from 'ten to twenty years'.

Non-Muslims, moreover, must not—in his view—be in a position to influence policy in such a State, so they must not hold any key office; they must be subject to much the same civil and criminal law[7] as their Muslim fellow-citizens, although they might retain their own personal law; and they should even be at liberty to propagate their own religion, although no Muslim would be permitted to respond. The *'ulama'*, for their part, are almost unanimously of the opinion that in an Islamic State the death penalty for 'apostasy' must be mandatory for any Muslim who abandons his religion; and it is clear from the Munir Report that their definitions of who is a true Muslim are so diverse, and their denunciation as an 'unbeliever' of anyone who differs from themselves so uninhibited, that complete chaos would soon prevail in any country run according to their principles. And Mawdūdī himself takes much the same view, although I think he would regard the death penalty as the maximum, rather than the mandatory, penalty for apostasy. But he believes that the judiciary should be completely independent of the executive (which is, of course, quite contrary to the classical pattern) and that suitably qualified women should have the right to vote, or even be elected to, a separate legislature to deal with such subjects as female education, hospitals and welfare—but that women must never sit with men in any National Assembly.

At the other extreme, I found a group of leading Pakistanis whose real desire was for a secular State, but one in which Islam was in somewhat the same position as the Church of England in this country. In other words, just as the Queen must, under the British

[7] I.e. with certain minor differences, as in the classical pattern of early Islam.

Constitution, be a Protestant, the President of Pakistan would have to be an orthodox Muslim, and just as it is customary in Britain to make some public acknowledgement of God on certain official occasions through the services of the established church, so too would be the position in Pakistan. If one were to ask Muslims of this persuasion the question 'Then why Pakistan?', I think they would reply that a secular State in which Muslims are in the overwhelming majority is a very different thing from a secular State in which Muslims would be in a manifest minority, for in the former, as distinct from the latter, they can be confident that any legislation will be such as they can generally approve. Nor is this attitude necessarily irreligious; for there can be no doubt that some Muslims conscientiously approve what is, in fact, the official position in Turkey today: namely, that Islam should primarily be regarded as a personal bond between individual Muslims and their Maker, and as a guide to their private lives, rather than a complex of commands and prohibitions, addressed to society as a whole, which must be enforced by the law-making and law-enforcement agencies of the State.

In between these two extremes stand a large number of educated Pakistanis who want their country to be an Islamic State in some real sense, but who would utterly repudiate what they regard as the medieval and obscurantist concept of that term advocated by Mawdūdī or the *'ulama'*. They have no wish whatever to go back to the prescribed penalties of stoning, hand-cutting and flogging, in spite of the fact that a former Chief Justice of Pakistan (himself a Roman Catholic) went so far, at a comparatively recent Commonwealth Law Conference, as to advocate the reintroduction of the practice of amputating the hands of those convicted of theft. Nor do they desire the prohibition of life insurance or fixed rates of interest,[8] the sale or consumption of alcohol or the display of films from the Western world. By and large, moreover, I think they are content with the legal system they have inherited from the days of

[8] Although some of the politicians have given a good deal of thought to how the requirements of insurance, banking, etc., could be reconciled with the relevant Islamic injunctions, as they understand them.

British rule, although all except the lawyers would welcome a reduction in legal costs. The demand of the former Chief Justice, to whom reference has already been made, for the substitution of a 'common law of Islam' (whatever that may mean) in place of an 'alien law', largely falls on deaf ears. And even in the interpretation of the Islamic law as such, the way in which the ground was prepared for the Muslim Family Laws Ordinance, 1961, and the reforms which were, in fact, included in its terms, themselves indicate an approach which is far more 'popular' than technical or expert.

Thus far the position is tolerably clear. What is rather more obscure is which way the majority of the people would go if their views could really be ascertained. There can be no doubt that the '*ulama*' could drum up very considerable support, or that the followers of Mawlānā Mawdūdī would also represent a significant number—since the declamations of religious demagogues would inevitably have a considerable impact on the common people. But whether the bulk of the population would really appreciate the sort of State these preachers wish to set up, if the facts could be adequately represented to them, is much more questionable. What is clear is that the moderates would find it considerably more difficult to present a convincing case; and it is for this very reason, among others, that it seems to me intrinsically unlikely that those now in the political ascendancy will ever allow a free, popular vote on such an issue.

Another country faced by a somewhat similar problem is Libya, although in this case, by contrast with Pakistan, it is the Revolutionary Government—and in particular, it seems, Colonel al-Qadhdhāfī himself—who favours a return (in part at least) to Islamic orthodoxy. A good deal of publicity has recently been given to the fact that amputation of the hand is to be reintroduced as the penalty for theft—although I have not yet heard of any instance of this punishment having actually been imposed. As we have seen, moreover, it is only properly applicable where two eligible witnesses can testify to having seen the very act of stealing some article from 'safe-custody'; and this must be exceedingly rare. But long before the present regime came to power the criminal law of Libya provided for criminal sanctions[9] to be imposed for the sale of alcohol to Muslims alone—although it was open to question whether this might not be successfully challenged under Articles 11 and 12 of the Libyan Constitution, which preclude any discrimination between citizens on grounds of religion, until the Supreme Court decided otherwise in 1957.[10]

3. PRESSURES FOR CERTAIN RELAXATIONS IN THE SHARĪʿA

At the opposite extreme from countries in which there are pressures for a return to Muslim norms stand those countries (of which Saʿūdī Arabia today represents the outstanding example) in which the pressure is in the precisely opposite direction: namely, for a certain relaxation of an all-embracing orthodoxy.

In Saʿūdī Arabia the Sharīʿa law, according to its Ḥanbalī interpretation, still reigns virtually supreme. Thus Article 6 of the Fundamental Law of the Hijāz, 1926, declares that 'The laws in the Kingdom of the Hijāz shall always conform to the Book of God, the practice of His Prophet and the conduct of the Companions of the Prophet and of their pious Followers'. A year later King Ibn Saʿūd, under the influence of the Wahhābī tenets which his family has so ardently embraced, proposed that a code of Islamic law should be drawn up which was based not only on the doctrine of the Ḥanbalī school but that of whichever school seemed closest to the Qur'ān and *sunna* on the particular point concerned—as advocated by Ibn Taymiyya and Ibn al-Qayyim.[11] But the Ḥanbalī *ʿulama'* soon persuaded him to abandon this project, and regulations issued in 1928 and 1930 make it obligatory on the *qāḍī* to follow the recognized Ḥanbalī texts.[12] In the Najd, moreover, the law is enforced by governors (*umarā'*) as well as by *qāḍīs*; and under the sway of the late Ibn Jalawī, for example, discretionary punishments

[9] The Intoxicating Liquors Control Law of Cyrenaica, Article 4.

[10] In *Faraj Ali Sharif Dinali* v. *The Public Prosecution of Libya*.

[11] Ḥanbalī jurists of distinctly independent views, who have exercised a lot of influence on the Wahhābī movement.

[12] Primarily, the *Sharḥ al-Muntahā* and the *Sharḥ al-Iqnāʿ*.

of very questionable orthodoxy—and sometimes of extreme severity—were not infrequently imposed.

Up to date only comparatively minor concessions have been made to the exigencies of modern life, although it is true that, alongside the Sharīʿa, there now stand an ever increasing number of administrative regulations promulgated by the government. These certainly have the force of law; but they are normally termed either *niẓām* (regulation) or *marsūm* (royal decree) rather than *qānūn* (the technical term ordinarily used for legislation). In 1931, moreover, a Regulation on Commerce was promulgated and commercial courts were set up in Jeddah, Yanbuʿ and Dammām; but these were subsequently abolished and their functions taken over by a Ministry of Commerce, which was established in 1954. Today the Regulation on Commerce (which is based on the Ottoman Commercial Code of 1850, but with all references to interest expunged) is administered by 'Chambers of Commerce'; and banks are now allowed to charge a 'commission' on loans, in place of 'interest'. This is a matter of considerable importance, since those in urgent need of loans were previously charged a ruinous rate of interest by private persons—even, I was reliably informed, by eminent religious figures who would officially condemn the whole transaction as illicit. Until recently, moreover, insurance contracts were allowed only in regard to maritime commerce; but this concession has now been extended to other forms of property insurance, although not to life insurance. Yet again, it is noteworthy that such regulations as those concerned with Labour and Workmen, Motor Vehicles, etc., have considerable repercussions on the Islamic criminal law; for, under the first, claims for compensation for accidents at work are decided by a special Commission composed of three members who are knowledgeable in legal matters (with the Chairman, at least, holding a degree in Islamic law); and, under the second, it is the police who investigate accidents and determine questions of guilt, leaving only the allocation of blood-money to the *qāḍī*. Numerous other regulations provide not only for social welfare, pensions and the discipline of civil servants, but also for the imposition of fines and terms of imprisonment—which may, on occasion, be combined with penalties prescribed in the Sharīʿa. Finally, provision has been made for appeals from a single *qāḍī* to High Courts composed of three or four judges;[13] and in 1954 a Court of Complaints (*dīwān al-maẓālim*) was also established.[14] A further point of considerable importance is that it was not until 1936 that the importation of slaves was largely prohibited in Saʿūdī Arabia, and not until 1962 that the status of slavery was itself abolished. And this, in its turn, has two main corollaries—the one of practical and the other of theoretical importance. In the field of practical law it almost certainly means (as in Northern Nigeria, where the same thing happened at a rather earlier date[15]) that there are still many women in Saʿūdī Arabia (and, in all probability, elsewhere in the peninsula) whose status, from the point of view of the religious law, is still that of 'slaves' with whom their 'owners' have the right of legal concubinage—and whose offspring, through any such union, would have legitimate status—even though the women now have the right to walk out and claim their freedom should they so wish. But the theoretical implications of the abolition of slavery are of very much greater significance, for Saʿūdī Arabia has in this case demonstrated conclusively that it is both able, and at times willing, to abrogate by statute law what many would regard as a basic right under the Sharīʿa—and to do this, almost certainly, in deference to political pressure and the weight of contemporary world opinion.

Particular interest, again, attaches to Royal Decree No. 1135, by which the late King Ibn Saʿūd ratified the oil concession first granted to the Standard Oil Company of California and subsequently inherited by the Arabian American Oil Company ('Aramco'), since it is from the exploitation of her vast reserves of oil that the phenomenal wealth enjoyed by Saʿūdi Arabia today almost exclusively stems. Naturally enough, this concession—conforming, as it does, to what has become a comparatively standard

[13] And these courts also try serious cases in first instance.

[14] Cf. in this context J. Schacht, *An Introduction to Islamic Law* (O.U.P., 1964); but there have been many developments since this was written.

[15] Cf. p. 114 above.

form of agreement in such cases—is *sui generis* in terms of the Sharīʿa, which goes into minute detail in specifying the conditions which regulate a series of named contracts, rather than enunciating those broad principles essential to any general law of contract. As a consequence, different parts of the concession would normally be classified under the Sharīʿa as *iḥyāʾ al-mawāt* (cultivation of undeveloped land), *iqṭāʿ* (land concession), *ijāra* (lease) and a form of *sharika* (partnership); but it includes specific provisions which might well be held, strictly speaking, to invalidate each of these contracts or dispositions in their classical form. Yet this concession (Article 31 in which states that any difference or dispute between the contracting parties shall be finally resolved by an Arbitration Tribunal) was certainly regarded as valid and binding by the King; and the Arbitration Agreement of 1955 expressly states that both the Government and the Company 'respect all the obligations which they have undertaken' and 'have never entertained the thought that they would not be bound by the agreements they have made and now make with one another'. There is, moreover, excellent authority in both the Qurʾān and those Traditions which are generally accepted by Muslims as authentic for the proposition that Muslims are bound by their contractual stipulations[16]—a principle which is reinforced by Ibn al-Qayyim's emphasis on the place of *maṣlaḥa* (what is 'beneficial') in the Sharīʿa, and which is clearly wide enough to cover any contract which the exigencies of modern life, or the circumstances of the contracting parties, may require. It would need to be qualified only by a specification of such contracts or stipulations as would be disallowed as contrary to public policy. But it must be recognized that this comprehensive and highly flexible principle is far removed from the rigid regulations which govern the named contracts which are discussed in detail in the classical texts of all the recognized schools of Islamic law.

[16] Cf. 'The Moslem Ruler and Contractual Obligations', by J. N. D. Anderson and N. J. Coulson, in *New York University Law Review*, Vol. 33, No. 7 (1958), pp. 917–33, together with my Opinion, and that of Professors Abū Zahra and Joseph Schacht, in Aramco's First Memorial in the *Arbitration between the Government of Saʿūdī Arabia and the Arabian American Oil Company*.

The only countries which may be thought in any way to approximate to Saʿūdī Arabia in strict adherence to the Sharīʿa as the fundamental law of the State, and in permitting only what seem to be necessary concessions to contemporary conditions, are the Yemen (now often termed North Yemen), Oman, certain other areas in the Arabia peninsula, Afghanistan and Somalia. In North Yemen, Imām Yaḥa did, indeed, make an attempt to enforce the pure Islamic law (according to the doctrine which prevails among Shīʿīs of the Zaydī persuasion), although this was, naturally enough, highly distasteful to the large number of Shāfiʿīs in that country. But in point of fact it is only the influence of Wahhābī teaching in Saʿūdī Arabia and a few of the neighbouring Sheikhdoms which has succeeded in superseding the customary law which still largely prevails in the peninsula—and particularly in the south. This represents a survival of the pre-Islamic customary law which has regulated the internal and external relationships of Arab tribesmen all down the centuries, and which is recognized—not only by those who profess to be strictly orthodox Muslims, but by all and sundry—as distinct from, and even in some points contrary to, the Sharīʿa.

Much the same is also true of Afghanistan, where the Sharīʿa, customary law and an ever-increasing volume of governmental regulations all jostle each other today in an uneasy, and locally variable, juxtaposition. As long ago as the time of ʿAbdur Rahman, who was Amir of Kabul from 1880 until 1912, a general assembly was formed from leading members of the ruling tribe, local chiefs (Khans) and religious leaders (Mullas); and it was the successor of this assembly, the *Loya Jirgah* of 1928, which rejected a radical programme of reform, proposed by King Amanulla, which would have had profound repercussions on the position of both Islamic and customary law and also on that of the traditional local leaders. ʿAbdur Rahman, moreover, confiscated the public *waqfs*, which had previously provided an independent source of income for religious purposes equal to about one-third of the total revenue of the State. He also established a King's Court, to which any case could be brought either on first instance or on appeal from a *qāḍī's* court; and this soon developed into a two-tier appellate system, with the consequence that the supremacy of State law over the Sharīʿa was effectively, if tacitly, established, and control over cases of crime or the transfer of property have remained, in practice, in the hands of the executive. In the provinces, too, many cases were heard, whether directly or on appeal, by the Governor or his officers as representatives of the King's Court—and this practice continued in some areas even after the Constitution of 1964. ʿAbdur Rahman's early attempts to organize the *qāḍīs*, moreover, developed in due course into a Ministry of Justice which became the focal point of the Muslim legal establishment; and under the Constitution of 1964 the judicial functions of this Ministry were separated from its executive functions by the creation of an independent judiciary administered by a Supreme Court (which was made up of progressive *qāḍīs*, secular lawyers and non-lawyers, with the balance of power on the secular side). Under ʿAbdur Rahman, again, several specialized courts were set up alongside the *qāḍīs'* courts—such as commercial courts manned by merchants in the principal towns, a revenue court, and a summary police court for political crimes; and while the commercial courts have now been handed over to the judiciary, a number of other 'statutory' courts have also been established under a single statutory court of appeal. The fact remains, however, that the limited jurisdiction of all these statutory courts leaves a wide field of residual jurisdiction to the *qāḍīs* (including cases of family law, succession, non-commercial transactions and common crimes, although it is some years since any of the 'prescribed' penalties were imposed). A short compilation in Persian codifying the law of crime, called *Amania* (after King Amanalla, who ordered its preparation), is still highly valued; but it is used only informally, and is now out of print. In the reign of Habibulla, moreover, a committee of legal scholars tried to fill the gap caused in Afghanistan by the general ignorance of Arabic—and thus of the standard Ḥanafī texts—by a massive seven volume work entitled *Sirāj al-Aḥkām*; but this fell out of favour after 1929.

The present position, therefore, is that the Constitution of 1964—which was only partially changed in 1973 when Sardar Mohammad Daoud Khan ousted his cousin, King Zahir Shah, and set up a Republic—is that the Ḥanafī law is to be regarded as applicable only where no statute law prevails. Under Amanulla a prodigious amount of legislation had been enacted, largely inspired by the social revolution effected in Turkey by Mustapha Kemal and the Young Turks; and many of these laws were re-enacted, in a modified form, after his downfall. Now, moreover, an Official Gazette has been started for the promulgation of statutory legislation, some of which has been drafted largely by foreigners (largely Egyptians); but it is only the Commercial Code which represents a simple translation from the Ottoman Code of the same name.

The outstanding examples of countries in which the population is basically Muslim but the Government strongly influenced by communism or extreme socialism are the People's Democratic Republic of (South) Yemen—i.e. the former Colony and Protectorates of Aden—and Somalia. Numerous references to the Family Law promulgated in South Yemen in 1974 have been made in previous chapters, but it is significant that the preamble to that Law unequivocally declares:

Whereas the Government appreciates the role of the family in building up society and providing its sons with a sound education which will make its young people an element in society which cares for the homeland and will sacrifice their lives in its defence and in building the united democratic edifice of the Yemen in a way which gives expression to the hopes of the working masses;

And whereas the State has regard for the need to organise family relationships in a way which is in conformity with the principles and objectives of the programme of the National Democratic Revolution and which precludes for ever all the old relationships which used to govern the ties of the Yemenī family and prevent it from playing a positive role in the building up of society;

And whereas the ties of the family, in all their forms, were not subject to any unified structure except those feudal relationships which made the noblest of human ties a matter of bargaining and put the fate of the Yemenī woman in pledge to the one who would pay the highest price;

And whereas the working classes among our people have given expression to their discontent and disapproval that family ties should remain in this evil state, it is incumbent on the revolutionary authority of the National Democratic Yemen to support the struggle of the Yemenī masses by this law, the Family Law, which regulates Yemenī family relationships for the first time in a way that opens wide horizons for creative activity and equal revolutionary relationships which will result in increased production, development and inventiveness.

It is also significant that the Law itself follows the general sequence and form of recent legislation in other Muslim countries in regard to such subjects as betrothal, marriage and divorce, and the paternity and custody of children, yet introduces a series of radical changes—for some of which no authority whatever can be found in the Islamic texts—designed to put wives on a substantial equality with their husbands in respect both to rights and duties. Thus marriage contracts must be registered and signed by both parties; dower must not exceed 100 dinars; polygamy is allowed only in very special circumstances; no divorce is permitted except by decree of court based on a genuine breakdown of marriage on certain specified grounds which are common to both parties; and the expenses of the wedding, matrimonial home, married life and the support of children are to be shared by the parties according to their means.

In Somalia, too, the revolutionary regime includes some who acknowledge extreme Marxist convictions: but the Chairman of the Supreme Revolutionary Council, General Maxamed Siyaad Barre (or Mohamed Siad Barreh) insists that the official policy of the Government is based on the principles of 'scientific socialism'. Being scientific, this is not, he insists, a doctrinaire socialism, but a socialism suited to local conditions and, in its Somali form, allegedly compatible with the teachings of Islam. As recently as 11 January, 1975, moreover, a Family Law of considerable proportions was promulgated.[17] The date itself is significant, for it was the anniversary of the death of the Somali heroine Xaawa Taako;[18] and the declared purpose of the Law, which was promulgated by the supreme Revolutionary Council and the Council of Secretaries (i.e. Ministers) in joint session, was to enhance the status and position of women. As in South Yemen, therefore, marriages may be contracted only by the consent and in the presence of both parties; polygamy has been severely restricted; the expenses of the matrimonial home and the support of children are to be shared; divorce is allowed only by decree of court and where the marriage has broken down or there is some legally recognized reason; and—unlike the South Yemen, where the Family Law did not venture to deal with questions of succession—females have been given a right to inherit on a par with males. But this last point, in particular, seems to have triggered off such a spate of denunciation from some of the religious pundits that the Government felt it necessary to take the drastic step of imposing the death penalty on several leading agitators—which provides an up-to-date warning of the opposition to which a sudden and authoritarian departure from some basic principle of the Sharīʿa may give rise in a country which is almost exclusively Muslim in its religious allegiance—even if, as in Somalia, there has been an age-old tradition of indigenous customary law co-existing with the Sharīʿa. This serves as a reminder of the considerable, although less violent, resistance in Iraq to the total—if temporary—abandonment of the Islamic law of inheritance in 1959.[19] But it must be observed that Somali customary law commonly denies women any right of inheritance whatever (which is, of course, equally contrary to the Sharīʿa), so it is not altogether clear whether the agitation against the recent decree was based exclusively on Islamic orthodoxy or on a combination of this with a fanatical adherence to traditional ways.

[17] No text of this Law is available at the time of writing, but a friend has been kind enough to supply me with the following information culled from comments in the Somali press.

[18] Who died in 1948 in the course of political demonstrations against the return of Italian rule in Somalia.

[19] Cf. pp. 55f., 70f., 150f. above.

Indeed, General Siad's speech on the day when the Family Law was promulgated attacked the previous law in a way which not only made no clear distinction between Somali customs and the Sharīʿa but appeared to suggest that the customary exclusion of women from inheritance was previously the official law of the land.

4. PRESSURES IN BOTH DIRECTIONS AT ONCE

Under this heading two quite different situations call for description and discussion. Of the first, Egypt, Iraq and Tunisia provide convenient illustrations, while of the second, Kenya, Tanzania, Ghana, Uganda and in particular India represent the most obvious examples.

In all these countries, without exception, Muslims are, in general, governed by the Sharīʿa, in varying degrees of orthodoxy, in matters of family law and succession, but in all else by codes of law which are largely of Western inspiration. But here the resemblance ends. Egypt, Iraq and Tunisia are all predominantly Muslim countries in which the pressure exerted by the more rigidly—and vocally—orthodox elements in the population is in the direction of a more wholehearted dependence on the Sharīʿa as the basic source of their 'general' law, while the pressure of more progressive thought is, on the contrary, for a further liberalization of the family law, which remains distinctively Islamic. In Kenya, Uganda,[20] Tanzania, Ghana and India, on the other hand, Muslims represent a minority in the population (even though, in Tanzania, this amounts to a very substantial minority, and in India to at least sixty millions); and here the pressures are confined to the field of family law, with the State pressing, in varying degrees of urgency, for the adoption of a personal law common to all its citizens, and Muslim opinion putting up an equally variable, but in some cases exceedingly strong, resistance.

In the first group of countries the pressure for a greater reliance on the Sharīʿa as the source of the general law was—at least at the

[20] For the law of succession in Uganda, cf. my note 'The Law of Succession in Uganda: an unreported case', in *Journal of African Law*, Vol. 7, No. 3 (1963), pp. 201 ff.

time when the Civil Code of 1948 was under debate—strongest in Egypt.[21] In Iraq the Majalla was at that time still in force; and even in the Civil Code of 1953 much of the ethos and many of the provisions of this Ottoman Law were retained. In Tunisia, again, the Code of Obligations and Contracts is, generally speaking, considerably more imbued with Islamic principles than is the Egyptian Civil Code, while the trend of opinion which prevails in the population at large is, almost certainly, even more secular than in Egypt. In these countries it is in Egypt, therefore, that this pressure can most easily be analysed; for there, at least, it derives partly from a natural reaction against codes of law which are of predominantly alien inspiration in favour of their own cultural heritage; partly from an aspiration to take the lead in evolving a distinctively Arab code of law which would forge a further link in the unification of 'the Arab Nation'; and partly from a genuine desire, among some elements in the population, that their way of life should become more distinctively and uncompromisingly Islamic—although it would seem that the last two motives are not quite so prominent today as they were a few years ago.

But it is precisely at this point that the problems which arise in such widely different countries as Pakistan, on the one hand, and Saʿūdī Arabia, on the other, inevitably occupy the attention of more conservative Muslims in Egypt, too: namely, the way in which they are to regard (and apply) the Qur'anic prohibitions of fixed rates of interest, contracts of a speculative nature, insurance, and the like. Was the prohibition of *ribā'*,[22] for example, intended to be confined to the exploitation of a brother Muslim's time of need, as many would argue, rather than the payment and receipt of modest rates of fixed interest on industrial ventures or on loans from, or deposits in, a bank? Again, could not many of these payments justly be regarded as no more than a commission or payment for services rendered? And while the conflict of conscience on such matters has, of late, been largely dissipated, for most

[21] Cf. pp. 82ff. above.

[22] Which, as we have seen, is commonly translated 'usury', but basically means any fixed rate of interest.

Muslims, by *fatāwā*, or religious opinions, issued by such leaders of orthodox opinion as the Sheikh of the Azhar or the Mufti of Egypt, the promulgation of laws of socialist inspiration (particularly under Nāṣir in Egypt, and under the rival Baʿthist regimes in Syria and Iraq) must have raised somewhat similar problems.

When we turn to the pressure from the opposite direction in these countries—namely, for a further liberalization of the family law—the basic problem is how far the current practice of promulgating progressive reforms on the basis of the juristic expedients which have hitherto proved so beneficial can be extended.[23] In Iran, South Yemen and Somalia, for example, it might well be argued that an adequate answer has been found—and actually promulgated—to the problem of divorce; and precisely the same could be said of the question of polygamy in Tunisia. But the basic rationale of these reforms is that a change in social circumstances provides an adequate justification for a change in law—a postulate which, however reasonable, has hitherto found only an exceedingly limited acceptance in Muslim jurisprudence. And it is precisely here that the recent prohibition of slavery, even in Saʿūdī Arabia, may be called in aid; for although most Muslims attempt to make a sharp distinction between the prohibition of slavery and the prohibition of polygamy (or, indeed, of unfettered unilateral repudiation of a wife by her husband), the contrary argument—that slavery, polygamy and unilateral repudiation are all permitted in the Sharīʿa but certainly not enjoined—can be maintained with at least equal logic.

A further problem which confronts orthodox Muslim opinion in these countries—even though it has, at the present time, little or no relevance in practice—lies in the realm of international law. Here, as we have seen, the classical view, which is still held in theory by the vast majority of orthodox Muslim teachers, is that the world is divided into those areas in which Muslim rule has been established (that, is the 'Abode of Islam') and all other countries (which constitute 'The Abode of War', and should be progressively subdued by means of the *jihād*, or holy war). It is true that an

[23] Cf. pp. 43–82 above.

imperative duty to resume that war is normally regarded as dependent on a summons from the Caliph, who does not at present exist, and also on a reasonable prospect of success for the Muslim armies, which is currently remote. But the problem remains whether the traditional teaching on this subject is basically valid; and this problem has become increasingly acute as more and more Muslim countries have joined the United Nations Organization. So the question is inevitably asked whether the traditional doctrine may not be mistaken, and whether the Qur'anic text about 'no compulsion in religion' does not, perhaps, constitute the fundamental teaching of Islam, from which the later injunctions about the *jihād* represent only a temporary, and particular, exception. Precisely the same reasoning, moreover, is sometimes used in regard to the so-called 'law of apostasy' in Islam; for might that not be regarded as providing a condign punishment for an act which could be equated with political treason when the very survival of the infant Muslim community was at stake, but as no longer applicable in days in which no such danger exists? And is not the principle of 'no compulsion in religion' equally applicable in this case, too? But to both these arguments the traditional answer relies on the doctrine of 'abrogation': namely, that the earlier and more tolerant verses in the Qur'ān were abrogated and replaced by the much more uncompromising 'revelations' of a later date.

Among those countries in which Muslims represent only a minority, however large, it is India which provides by far the most illuminating example. But Kenya, Tanzania, Ghana and Uganda fall into somewhat the same category, and the problems they face are, in their different ways, equally illuminating.[24] On the mainland

[24] Other examples can be found in Francophonic West Africa, where the former French administrations resorted to legislation in the sphere of family law far more freely than did the British. In several of these now independent territories, in most of which there is a Muslim minority, minimum ages for marriage (which must always be by consent of both parties) have been prescribed, polygamy has been forbidden or restricted, bride price has been abolished or controlled, and divorce allowed only by decree of court. But it is significant that no such legislation has been introduced in the Senegal, which is the most Muslim of the countries concerned. For details cf. Arthur Phillips and Henry F. Morris, *Marriage Laws in Africa*, pp. 37–9.

of Tanzania, for example, Islamic and customary law have for long lived side by side, and in some regions have interpenetrated each other. There are, of course, areas in which individual Muslims, at least, have adopted the Islamic personal law in a comparatively thorough-going manner; and there are many families in which some members are Muslims and some are Christians or pagans—and in such cases the Liwalis[25] usually, I think, try to persuade the parties to litigation to accept an equitable compromise. Again, there are tribes in which the Chief, or some other individuals, have embraced Islam, but in which customary law in practice prevails; and there are also legislative enactments which define in what circumstances the estate of a deceased person should be administered according to the Islamic or the customary law, respectively.[26] But the greater part of the population is made up of Christians or pagans (some of whom may profess a certain allegiance to Islam) divided into innumerable tribes, each of which has its own distinctive customary law—which has, of course, been somewhat modified in the case of practising Christians. This is the background against which recent attempts must be seen not only to record the customary law but to unify it, over broad areas of the country, by an authoritative statement of its basic provisions and a tacit suppression of local variants—in the form of 'Declarations of Local Customary Laws'[27] and 'Statements of Islamic Law'.[28] But the position was radically changed by the promulgation of the Law of Marriage Act, 1971, to which further reference will be made below.

In Kenya and Ghana the situation has in the past been somewhat different. First, the Muslim communities in these countries are distinctly smaller than those in Tanzania; and, secondly, the relevant proposals about a unified law of marriage, divorce and succession were, at first, much more national and comprehensive

[25] The local name for persons who combine certain administrative and judicial functions. It is a corruption of the Arabic *al-wālī*.

[26] See pp. 32, 157f. above for legislation covering both immigrant and indigenous Muslims.

[27] Cf. especially Government Notice No. 279 of 1963.

[28] Under the Islamic Law (Restatement) Act, 1964. E.g. especially Government Notice No. 222 of 1967.

in their scope—even extending to cover Christian, Civil or Muslim marriages under the relevant statute law. In Kenya these recommendations were set out, in the Reports of the Commission on the Law of Marriage and Divorce and the Commission on the Law of Succession respectively, in 1968—to both of which my friend and colleague, Dr Eugene Cotran, acted as Secretary; and the salient point of interest is that these two Commissions succeeded in recommending a law which is essentially unified, but characterized by a certain degree of internal flexibility, for all the inhabitants of Kenya—Christians, Muslims, Hindus and pagans, sophisticated and unsophisticated, urban and rural—within those spheres of life in which the present law provides for maximum divergence, and in which feelings, both religious and traditional, run exceedingly high. This, in itself, was a remarkable achievement; and if, as the Commission believed, the time has indeed come for the elimination of those divergencies in personal law which now exist in Kenya, then the broad lines of the proposed legislation certainly merit consideration in some detail.

Understandably enough, the major opposition to these proposals has come from the Muslim community, which argues that their law is part of their religion and is therefore protected from statutory interference by Articles 22 (i) and 179 of the Constitution. But this argument was rejected by the Commissions—as, indeed, it had to be, unless the Government was to abdicate all responsibility for legislative reforms in regard to whole areas of the law which touch the lives of ordinary men and women more closely than any others. The Commission on the Law of Marriage and Divorce accordingly set out its basic premises, clearly enough, in the following terms: 'We thought that there should be the minimum interference with religious and customary practices; in general, that no one should be required by law to do anything which is forbidden by his religion or tribal custom; but we considered that the law may properly restrict or prohibit the doings of acts which religion or custom may allow.' This seems to represent a very fair distinction, which has, indeed, been accepted in part by a number of Muslim countries which have introduced reforms in the field of family law in recent years. But the traditional Muslim attitude, of course, has always been that statute law must neither permit what God has forbidden nor forbid what He has permitted; and it is undeniable that the legislation proposed by the Commissions would not only restrict what the Sharīʿa allows but would permit a good deal which it explicitly prohibits. Nor can it really be argued that this means no more than that a pious Muslim must impose on his conduct, as a matter of conscience, somewhat stricter standards than those which the general law of the State may demand; for the fact remains that a husband or wife is inevitably affected by what the other party may decide to do, and this is also true of other members of the family circle.[29]

A detailed examination of the proposals, moreover, immediately reveals the scarcely surprising fact that, judged by strictly Muslim principles, they represent a distinctly mixed bag. Some of them run completely counter to the Sharīʿa, while others are fully consonant with its classical principles, or at least with those legislative reforms which have been introduced in recent years in so many Muslim countries. The Commission clearly believed, for example, that polygamy would tend to die out in Kenya; that the law should do all that was reasonably possible to discourage its practice; but that the time had not yet come when it should be actually prohibited. So Recommendation No. 10 proposed that the law should 'recognize two distinct types of marriages: the monogamous and the polygamous or potentially polygamous', and that the character of a marriage should no longer depend on its form or on the personality of the parties, but exclusively upon their express agreement at the time of the contract. Under Recommendation No. 12, moreover, this agreement would be binding on both the parties 'during their lifetime and whilst the marriage subsists', and could not be altered by the unilateral action of one of them or by a change of religion by either or both; but the conversion of a potentially polygamous marriage into a monogamous union, or of

[29] Cf. my 'Comments with reference to the Muslim community', in a special issue of the *East African Law Journal*, Vol. v, Nos. 1 and 2 (1969), devoted to these two Reports.

a monogamous marriage into a potentially polygamous one, 'by a joint declaration of husband and wife freely made in the presence of a registrar and recorded in writing', should be permitted. But while these proposals are contrary to the classical doctrine of the Ḥanafī, Mālikī and Shāfiʿī schools, according to which all Muslim marriages are potentially polygamous, they would be largely acceptable to Ḥanbalī opinion (except, that is, for the question of a change of religion, or the remedy available to a wife whose husband agrees that their marriage should be monogamous, but then proceeds to marry a second wife); for the Ḥanbalīs, as we have seen, insist that a Muslim is bound by his stipulations in matters, such as polygamy, which are allowed, but certainly not required, under the Sharīʿa. But the position is very different when we find that Recommendation No. 16 proposes that no statutory limit should be imposed 'restricting the number of wives a man may take under the polygamous system'; that Recommendation No. 14 provides that the law 'should not attempt to regulate polygamous households, as for example by requiring the husband to accord equality of treatment to his wives'; that Recommendations Nos. 55 and 56 provide that 'marital duties be not defined by law', but that the law should 'provide expressly that no-one has the right to inflict corporal punishment on his or her spouse'; and that under Recommendation No. 7 a Muslim would not be precluded from marrying a wife contrary to the bar of foster relationship or 'unlawful conjunction',[30] under the Sharīʿa.

In regard to divorce, Recommendation No. 110 states that this should be only by decree of a court of competent jurisdiction; Recommendations Nos. 106 and 114 propose that the basis for a decree of separation or divorce should 'not be specific matrimonial offences but the general ground that the marriage has broken down'; Recommendations Nos. 112 and 113 that no-one should be permitted to make a petition for divorce 'within three years of his or her marriage except by special leave of the court granted on the ground of exceptional hardship suffered by the petitioner' or, in any case, unless the matrimonial dispute 'has been referred to a

[30] Cf. pp. 105f. above.

conciliatory body and that body has failed to settle the dispute'; and Recommendation No. 115 that, without limiting the discretion of the court to act on any relevant evidence that a marriage has irreparably broken down, a whole series of specified circumstances may be considered to constitute evidence of such breakdown. It is noteworthy, moreover, that these circumstances include adultery, cruelty, wilful neglect, desertion, voluntary separation, incurable illness, change of religion and 'the pronouncement of three talakas by the husband, where the parties were married by an Islamic ceremony'. This means, of course, that *no* formula of repudiation pronounced by a Muslim husband, and no 'apostasy' from Islam, would, *per se*, effect a divorce, but only provide evidence that the marriage had broken down. But although this, and much else in these Recommendations, clearly runs counter to the classical doctrines of the Sharīʿa, the proposals as a whole are closely similar to those of the Family Protection Act in Iran, and have some points in common with the Muslim Family Laws Ordinance in Pakistan and the Law of Personal Status in Tunisia.[31] It is also noteworthy that Recommendations Nos. 130 and 133 would give the court the power to order a man to pay maintenance to his 'wife or former wife', or a woman to pay maintenance to 'her husband or former husband where she has the means to do so and where he lacks means and is incapacitated by mental or physical ill-health'; that Recommendation No. 134 provides that the amount of this maintenance should be 'left entirely to the discretion of the court, without any guiding formula, to be assessed basically on the means and needs of the parties but taking into account the degree of responsibility which the court apportions to each party for the breakdown of the marriage and . . . also the customs of the community to which they belong'; and that Recommendations Nos. 140 and 136 provide that such maintenance should 'cease automatically' on the remarriage of the person concerned, 'except where the parties have agreed otherwise', but that in all other circumstances it should 'subsist during the joint lives of husband and wife'. It is clear that these Recommendations not only run counter, in several respects,

[31] Cf. pp. 60–1, 126–30 above.

to the traditional provisions of the Sharīʿa, but also go considerably further than the reforms introduced in recent years in Syria, Tunisia or elsewhere.[32] And precisely the same is true of Recommendation No. 138, which proposes that the court should 'be given power in its discretion to order the division between husband and wife on divorce of any assets acquired during the marriage by their joint efforts', and adds that 'in dealing with any application for such division, the court should be required to have regard to the customs of the community to which the parties belong, to the contribution they have respectively made towards the acquisition of such assets', to the needs of the children of the marriage 'and, subject to the foregoing, should lean towards equality'. This power should, moreover, also extend to 'property owned before marriage which has substantially improved during marriage'. But this Recommendation, wholly admirable as it is on grounds of social justice, has no parallel in Islamic law.

The proposals put forward by the Commission on the Law of Succession are still more radical in their nature when viewed in terms of the Sharīʿa. This Commission took as a premise 'that the time had come to unify as far as possible the law applicable to all the inhabitants of Kenya, without regard for the religious or customary laws by which they had previously been bound, but that certain exceptions to this principle must, for the present, be permitted'. Any new law should, moreover, be as simple as possible, and such as the people could understand and accept; it must be compatible with the African way of life and cause as little offence as possible to African customs and beliefs; but it must also 'encourage national unity and economic advancement, and have as its primary concern the distribution of a dead person's estate "in such a way as to achieve fairness among his immediate family and, in particular, his dependants".' Naturally enough, the primary opposition to the work of the Commission again came from the Muslim community, which argued that the Islamic law of inheritance was divinely revealed and that any abrogation of it would encroach on their constitutional right to 'manifest, propa-

[32] Cf. pp. 59f., 123–5 above.

gate, teach, practise or observe' their religion. But the Commission insisted that 'the laws of succession, though intimately bound up with religion in the case of Muslims and others, are proper matters for State legislation', and 'failed to see how the enactment of a law of succession which differs from the Islamic law of succession would prevent Muslims from manifesting, practising or observing the Muslim religion, especially where there is freedom of testamentary disposition'. So—with the possible exception, for the present, of 'certain kinds of property situated in certain areas of Kenya'—the Commission proceeded to propose a system of intestate succession which was completely at variance with the Sharī'a, and a law of testamentary dispositions which included none of the restrictions imposed by the Sharī'a, but which would, nevertheless, afford Muslims the opportunity to provide by will that their estate should be distributed according to the dictates of their religion.

Space precludes any discussion of the detailed proposals of this Commission other than in broad outline. All persons in Kenya were to have the capacity to make a will at the age of eighteen,[33] and a testator was to have the right to bequeath the whole of his estate precisely as he might desire, except only that 'a court should have power, on the application of a dependant, to vary the will of any testator who had failed to make provision for that dependant'.[34] The term 'dependant' in this context was defined, moreover, as including a wife or child (even if the wife was separated from the testator, and 'whether or not such wife or child was maintained by the deceased immediately prior to his death');[35] and also a husband, parent, grandparent, grandchild, stepchild, brother, sister, or a child whom the deceased had taken into his family as his own ('provided that he or she was maintained by the deceased immediately prior to his death'),[36] while the word 'child' was to be taken to include an illegitimate child, a child still unborn at the death of the testator, and a legally adopted child.[37] Subject to the rights of any such dependant to make an application to the court (which

[33] Recommendation No. 3.
[34] Recommendation No. 21.
[35] Recommendation No. 22.
[36] Recommendation No. 24.
[37] Recommendation No. 23.

'should have a complete discretion to vary or refuse to vary'[38] the will concerned), a testator should be entitled to provide that his estate should be distributed according to any law of succession he might choose.[39] But a will would be regarded as automatically revoked by any subsequent marriage of the testator, except only that a will explicitly made in contemplation of marriage with a specified person should not be revoked by the contemplated marriage.[40]

These Recommendations clearly differ radically from the prescriptions of the Islamic law of bequests, although they certainly make it possible for a Muslim to ensure by will that his estate should be administered strictly according to the precepts of the Sharīʿa (except only for the right of a dependant to appeal to the court if he thinks that he has been unjustly deprived or excluded). Where, however, the deceased had not made any such testamentary provision, the Recommendations put forward by the Commission for the disposal of his intestate estate run counter to the Sharīʿa at almost every point. First, it was proposed that a sort of discretionary trust was to vest in a surviving spouse, while children, whether male or female, were to be accorded equal shares, with a 'rule of substitution for a grandchild for his or her parent where the parent dies before the intestate'. In default of spouse or children, moreover, the estate was to be inherited by the father or, if he were dead, by the mother; then, in default of either parent, by brothers and sisters in equal shares, with a rule of substitution; or, failing any brothers or sisters of the full blood, by those of the half blood in the same way. Finally, in default of all these, the estate was to go to 'the relatives who are in the nearest degree of kindred up to and including the sixth degree'; or, failing them, to the State. And further Recommendations covered such matters as the cessation of a widow's life interest if she remarried; what was to happen where a man was succeeded by more than one wife; and the precise rights of illegitimate or adoptive children.[41]

The Commissions appended to their reports two draft Bills

[38] Recommendation No. 25.
[39] Recommendation No. 26.
[40] Recommendation No. 15.
[41] Recommendations Nos. 31–45.

designed to give legislative effect to their recommendations. The Bill concerned with the law of succession was, in fact, duly debated in the Kenya National Assembly in November, 1970, but met with severe criticisms—partly, as might have been expected, on the ground that it was contrary to the teachings of Islam. So it was initially 'tabled' for six months, and it was not in fact until 1972 that it was enacted, with minor amendments,[42] as the Law of Succession Act—to be brought into effect 'by Notice' on an unspecified date. But it is significant that no such notice has yet been given, and that the draft 'Law of Matrimony Act' has up till now not even been introduced in the Assembly.

Curiously enough, however, the main proposals of the Commission on the Law of Marriage and Divorce were almost immediately adopted in Tanzania, where they were actually put into legal effect in 1971 by the Law of Marriage Act; for, although there are far more Muslims in Tanzania than in Kenya, the political stability which prevails on the mainland enables the Government to introduce such legislation without much overt opposition—and the Act does not officially extend to Zanzibar, since personal laws are not included in the 'Union list' of the Interim Constitution of Tanzania Act, 1965 (although I am informed that the Marriage Act is, in practice, partially followed there as well).

There are, however, a number of interesting differences between the Tanzanian Act and the Kenyan proposals, which may be summarized as follows:

(1) The Law of Marriage Act has adopted the proposal that there should be a dual system of monogamous and polygamous (or potentially polygamous) marriages,[43] and the provisions as to how

[42] The most significant of which seems to be that, in place of the provision in Recommendation No. 24 that the term 'child' was to include an illegitimate child, Section 3 (2) of the Act provides that it is to include 'any child expressly recognised or in fact accepted by the father as a child of his own, and any child for whom the father has in his lifetime voluntarily assumed responsibility'.

[43] Although the definitions provided in Sections 9 and 10 of the Act are both repetitive and somewhat confusing. Cf. J. S. Read, 'A Milestone in the Integration of Personal Laws: The New Law of Marriage & Divorce in Tanzania', in *Journal of African Law*, Vol. 16, No. 1 (1972), p. 24.

the one can be converted into the other,[44] except that in Tanzania it has been provided that 'No marriage between Christians which was celebrated in church in Christian form may, for so long as both parties continue to profess the Christian faith, be converted from monogamous to polygamous'.[45]

(2) There is nothing in the Act which corresponds to the explicit statement in Recommendation No. 16 that there should be no statutory limit 'restricting the number of wives a man may take under the polygamous system', but it may be inferred that this would also be true in Tanzania from the absence of any provision to the contrary. Similarly, while Section 57 in the Act follows Recommendation No. 13 in enacting that 'where a man has two or more wives they shall, as such, enjoy equal rights, be subject to equal liabilities and have equal status in law', it seems probable that the substance of Recommendation No. 14 (that the law 'should not attempt to regulate polygamous households, as for example by requiring the husband to accord equality of treatment to his wives') has also been tacitly accepted—although it might be open to a Muslim wife to argue that the phrase 'equal rights' should, in the absence of any provision to the contrary, be regarded as including that equality of treatment which Islamic law requires in such circumstances.

(3) When Section 17 of the Act provides that a girl who is under the age of eighteen, but not less than fifteen,[46] may be married only with the consent of father, mother or guardian (if alive), it explicitly adds that, where a marriage is contracted in Islamic form, it shall be lawful for the 'kadhi' to refuse to perform the ceremony if any requirement of the law of Islam 'which relates to the obtaining of any consent' by some other person has not been complied with.[47] But this right of refusal does not, it would seem, extend to any other point in regard to the proposed marriage, such as the

[44] Cf. Sections 10 and 11 of the Act, together with Recommendations 10 and 12 above. [45] Article 11 (5).

[46] Or fourteen in special circumstances, at the discretion of the appropriate court.

[47] Cf. Recommendation No. 21, which makes the age up to which a guardian's consent is required 21, but omits the clause about a *qāḍī*'s right of refusal.

Islamic prohibition of marriage between foster relatives or of a polygamous union with two sisters, etc., contrary to the prohibition of 'unlawful conjunction'.

(4) Both the Tanzanian Act and the Kenyan Recommendations would prohibit those *mut'a*, or specifically temporary, marriages in which Shī'is of the Ithnā 'Asharī persuasion still indulge, since marriage is defined in Section 9 of the Act as 'the voluntary union of a man and a woman intended to last for their joint lives',[48] and both provide for notice of objection to the husband's marriage with another wife to be given (and judicially considered) where, 'having regard to the husband's means, the taking of another wife is likely to result in hardship to his existing wife or wives or infant children, if any', or where 'the intended wife is of notoriously bad character or is suffering from an infectious or otherwise communicable disease or is likely to introduce grave discord into the household';[49] but the Act also prohibits a marriage with a widow or divorced woman, previously married in Islamic form, if contracted 'during the customary period of *iddat*'.[50]

(5) Sections 72–3 in the Act provide that either husband or wife 'may bring a suit for damages against any person with whom his or her spouse has committed adultery' (unless the aggrieved party has consented to or connived at the adultery) or who has 'enticed or induced his or her spouse to desert him or her', whereas Kenya Recommendations Nos. 75 and 76 would make both adultery and enticement criminal offences—but with the proviso that no prosecution should be instituted except on the complaint of the aggrieved spouse.

(6) Section 99 in the Act, like Recommendation No. 114, makes the breakdown of the marriage the sole ground for divorce, and Section 99 provides that 'no decree of divorce shall be granted unless the court is satisfied that the breakdown is irreparable'. But whereas, under Recommendation No. 115 (j), the pronunciation

[48] Cf. Recommendation No. 1, Section 38 (i) of the Act, moreover, expressly provides that a marriage is null and void 'if it is expressed to be of a temporary nature or for a limited period'.

[49] Section 20. Cf. Recommendation No. 15.

[50] Section 38 (j).

by a Muslim husband of three '*talakas*' was to be regarded as 'clear evidence that the marriage has broken down, though not, by itself, conclusive evidence that the breakdown is irreparable', Section 107 (3) of the Act provides that where a Board has failed to reconcile the parties to a marriage in Islamic form and, subsequently, 'either of them has done any act or thing which would, but for the provisions of this Act, have dissolved the marriage in accordance with the Islamic law, the court shall make a finding that the marriage has irreparably broken down and proceed to grant a decree of divorce'. Under Section 112 (3), moreover, 'the marriage shall, unless the court otherwise directs, be deemed to have dissolved as from the date when the dissolution would, but for this Act, have taken effect under the Islamic law'.

(7) Section 115 (f) of the Act explicitly provides that, where the parties were married in Islamic form, the court may order a man to pay maintenance to his former wife 'for the customary period of *iddat* following the date on which the divorce takes, or is deemed to have taken, effect'. To this there is no parallel in the Kenyan Recommendations.

(8) Section 125(2) of the Act provides that 'In deciding in whose custody an infant should be placed the paramount consideration shall be the welfare of the infant' and, subject to this, the court shall have regard to the wishes of the parents of the infant, to the wishes of the infant (where he or she is of an age to express an independent opinion) and to the customs of the community to which the parties belong—but with a 'rebuttable presumption that it is for the good of an infant below the age of seven years to be with his or her mother'.

(9) It is noteworthy, moreover, that while it is expressly provided[51] that 'the rules of customary law and the rules of Islamic Law shall not apply in regard to any matter provided for in the Law of Marriage Act, 1971', no direct reference is made to the existing enactments which set out the Islamic law on matters *not* included in the Act—e.g. rules regarding dower in the Statements

[51] By a new subsection (3 A) inserted in the Judicature and Application of Laws Ordinance.

of Islamic Law. This presumably means that every provision in these Statements which is explicitly or implicitly covered by the Act is repealed, but that the Statements remain in force in regard to points to which the Act makes no reference whatever.

A somewhat similar attempt to unify the law was made in Ghana in 1961, in the form of a White Paper on Marriage, Divorce and Inheritance. This proposed that a man should be allowed to register one wife only, but that if he 'marries or has issue with another woman, this will not be an offence'—regardless of whether he had previously contracted a marriage under Christian, Islamic or customary law. But this met with widespread opposition. Leading Christians objected strongly to legislation which would fundamentally change the nature and implications of a specifically monogamous marriage (although it is very common, in West Africa, even for Church members to indulge in 'customary' marriages). Similarly, Muslims protested that there was no justification whatever in the Sharī'a for a second wife being accorded a position of manifest inferiority. Even among those Ghanaians who still follow their tribal religions, moreover, many could see little or no merit in these proposals. So, when a draft 'Marriage, Divorce and Inheritance Bill' was published a year later, it is noteworthy that this made provision for the registration of only one 'marriage' rather than only one 'wife'; that the phrase 'any other woman with whom a man has children' had been substituted for any reference to other 'wives'; and that no explicit mention was made of the fact that relations with other women would no longer 'constitute an offence'—although this would, no doubt, have been the case. The opposition persisted, however, and the draft Bill (even in a third version, put forward in 1963) duly disappeared from sight—unmourned, it would seem, by more than a small minority. But a draft Intestate Succession Decree is currently under discussion in Ghana which is designed to take the place of Section 48 of the Marriage Ordinance, Section 10 of the Marriage of Muhammedans Ordinance and customary rules relating to intestate succession, and thus introduce a uniform law for all Ghanaians. This proposes that, where the intestate is survived by a spouse, a parent and a child or children, all household chattels should be divided equally between the spouse and children, and then one-eighth of the residue should go to the surviving parent, one-eighth to the 'family', one-fourth to the spouse and one-half to the child or children. Where, again, the intestate is survived only by a spouse and parent, the spouse shall be entitled to one-half of the residue and the parent and 'family' to one-fourth each. Further details seem unnecessary in this context, except to observe that no distinction whatever is envisaged between males and females.

In Uganda, again, a Commission was appointed in 1964 to 'consider the laws and customs regulating marriage, divorce, and the status of women in Uganda, bearing in mind the need to ensure that those laws and customs while preserving existing tradition and practices, as far as possible, shall be consistent with justice and morality and appropriate to the position of Uganda as an independent nation'. In 1965, moreover, this Commission duly submitted its recommendations, which were partly based on the Ghana Bill. Thus: (1) Except for those who already had more than one wife (who might register all their existing marriages), no person was to be allowed to register more than one marriage, under penal sanction, unless the earlier marriage had been dissolved. (2) Where a man and woman had been 'living together or otherwise for a period of not less than twelve months as man and wife', it should not be lawful for either party to deny the subsistence of a marriage between them. (3) The mother of a child was to have the right to sue the putative father for adequate maintenance for both herself and the child. (4) The father of a child born out of wedlock was to be given the opportunity at any time to legitimize the child by an affidavit supported by a further affidavit sworn by the mother. (5) Divorce was to be only by decree of court, after an attempt had been made to reconcile the parties. (6) Where a man or woman died intestate, the surviving spouse, if the marriage had been registered, was to take a life interest in one-third of the self-acquired property of the deceased; but this interest was to terminate on remarriage. The remaining two-thirds of the self-acquired property was to go to the children, whether born of a registered marriage or not, as tenants in common; but a surviving parent of the deceased would also get a share in this two-thirds, with a life interest only. (7) Any person who was of age was to be entitled to make a will virtually without restriction—except that, if he had not made reasonable provision for his children, then the High Court could, on application, direct that such provision should be made out of the estate.[52]

But the country in which pressure for the abandonment of 'Muslim Personal Law' in favour of a 'Uniform Civil Code' arouses the greatest controversy today is unquestionably India, although no draft of the sort of provisions which would in fact be included in a uniform code has yet seen the light of day. The concept of such a code arises directly from Article 44 in the 'Directive Principles' of the Indian Constitution, which requires the State to 'endeavour to secure' for its citizens 'a uniform code throughout the territory of India'. But Article 37 makes it clear that these Principles, while 'fundamental in the governance of the country', are not enforceable as such; and the impatience shown by some leading Hindus in this matter seems to me mistaken. Far from encouraging the Muslims to introduce those reforms in their personal law which have long been overdue—and which have, in fact, recently been introduced in a considerable number of predominantly Muslim countries—this impatience has had the precisely contrary effect and given rise to a feeling of insecurity in the Muslim community which is damaging to the interests of the country as a whole. But it is important, in this context, to understand the point of view commonly held by both Hindus and Muslims in this matter.

The Hindu majority base their case not only on the fact that India, as a secular, democratic State, should in principle have a uniform law for all its citizens, irrespective of their religious allegiance—as envisaged in the Directive Principles—but on the further contention that they have themselves radically reformed their personal law by the promulgation of the Hindu Marriage Act, 1955. This Act, which prohibits polygamy and provides for

52 Cf. Henry F. Morris, op. cit., pp. 41 f.

judicial divorce on a basis of strict equality between husbands and wives, was in fact forced through in the face of considerable opposition from Hindus of a more conservative and traditional persuasion. It is only natural, therefore, that the question should be asked why, in the Muslim minority alone, a man should be permitted to enjoy the 'privilege'—or at least the concession—of being allowed to marry as many as four wives, to divorce his wife at his unilateral discretion, and to take a share in the estate of his parents (and certain other relatives) which is double that allotted to corresponding females—or, indeed, why Muslim women alone should suffer such inequitable treatment. The fact that polygamy is, in practice, very rare in India—and, indeed, that it does not appear to be any more common among Muslims than it is in reality, whatever the law may prescribe, among Hindus—is not regarded as of any great relevance compared with the point of principle involved.

Among the Muslims, on the other hand, there is a small body of individuals, of what might be described as *avant garde* views, who would welcome a uniform code, but an overwhelming majority which is fanatically opposed to the very idea. This opposition stems from two distinct, if inter-related, considerations—the first theological, and the second socio-political. The theological objection is, of course, that Islamic law is based on divine revelation, represents an essential part of their religion, and is authoritatively incumbent upon them. But the socio-political objection is, I think, at least equally strong: namely, that any abandonment of their personal law would lead to a loss of their identity—already, as they would argue, undermined by the displacement of the Urdu language and certain Muslim educational institutions from their pristine position—and that the distinctive character of the community would be lost. It is, of course, precisely this last point that the more convinced 'secularists' most desire: an India in which communal and religious loyalties are completely submerged in a common citizenship and religious differences are confined to matters of faith and worship.

All this is understandable enough. But the result, in cold fact, is that the Muslim community as a whole resists even the most obvious and socially desirable reforms in its personal law, on the ground that any change in it whatever would represent the first step down a slippery slope which would inevitably end in the introduction of the dreaded uniform code. What they fail to realise, as I see it, is that a house which is in good repair is much better able to resist wind and tide than is a building with shaky foundations and structural weaknesses. So the introduction of reforms in regard to those points in their law which give rise to the most pertinent criticisms from their Hindu fellow-countrymen—and which have already, for the most part, been remedied in a number of leading Muslim countries without any sacrifice of what they consider to be the essential principles of their religion—would not necessarily, by any means, represent a step towards the suppression of their law, but might, on the contrary, help to save it from the threat of abolition. In any case, would it not be infinitely preferable for reforms in Muslim personal law to be proposed by the Muslims themselves, rather than imposed on them against their will by the majority community? Should the Indian Government eventually decide to force through a uniform civil code, moreover, would it not still be in the interests of the Muslim community to have defined what they believe to be the essential elements in their law, in contradistinction to the vagaries and abuses which at present discredit it; for it must be presumed that a uniform code for all the inhabitants of India would be one in the preparation of which all the different communities had co-operated on a principle of give and take, rather than a code formulated exclusively by the Hindu majority and then enforced on everyone else, irrespective of their traditions or religion.

The fact remains, however, that when I paid a visit to India in January, 1972, at the invitation of the President of the Indian Law Institute (that is, the Chief Justice of India), to give a series of lectures, to take part in a special seminar on 'Islamic Personal Law in Modern India' and to give any advice I could on the future of 'Muslim Personal Law' in that country, I found the vastly greater part of the Muslim minority, for all its numbers, more on the defensive than any other Muslim community I had ever visited.

And I had got precisely the same impression on two previous visits, the second of which—also at the invitation of the Indian Government—was to take part in a Symposium on 'Changes in Muslim Personal Law' which was arranged to coincide with the International Congress of Orientalists in New Delhi in 1964.[53] So it was a distinct encouragement when the Seminar of 1972, in spite of its comparatively representative character and the wide differences in approach manifest among its members, eventually agreed unanimously that 'Muslim Personal Law', as currently applied by the courts in India, did indeed stand in urgent need of reform, and that a Working Party should be set up (under the joint aegis of the Indian Law Institute and the Faculty of Law of the Aligarh Muslim University) to study, in cooperation with Muslim scholars with a more traditional approach to Islamic law and theology, how the necessary reforms could most appropriately be effected.

The papers I presented to that Seminar pin-pointed the major issues which, it seemed to me, called for consideration, the problems to which these issues gave rise, and the way in which the necessary action could, perhaps, most easily be taken. Thus in my first paper I briefly discussed a number of problems, such as polygamy, divorce, succession and the custody of children; and in the second, in rather more detail, the Islamic law of testate and intestate succession, and the administration of a deceased person's assets after death.[54] But all these points have been discussed already in this book, and it seems unnecessary to reproduce here the specific suggestions I made about their application in the context of the circumstances which prevail in India today.

[53] Cf. *Proceedings of the Twenty-Sixth International Congress of Orientalists*, 1966 (Vol. 1), pp. 79 ff.

[54] Cf., for all the papers presented to the Seminar, *Islamic Law in India* (The Indian Law Institute, 1972, ed. by Tahir Mahmood).

WHAT OF THE FUTURE?

All that now remains is to indulge in what may well prove to be the folly of hazarding a few tentative predictions of what is likely to happen in the future, and the way in which the various pressures and tendencies which are already apparent in different parts of the Islamic world may be expected to work themselves out. Was Justice Hegde right, for example, when he confidently asserted, in his Address of Welcome to the Seminar in India to which reference has already been made, that 'Religion-oriented personal laws were a concept of medieval times. That concept is alien to modern societies which are secular as well as cosmopolitan. Under our Constitution we have decided to build a secular society. We have decided to separate religion from our secular activities. Personal laws deal with our secular activities. So long as our laws are religion-oriented we can hardly build up a homogeneous nation. A society which is compartmentalized by its laws can hardly become a homogeneous unit. It can never become secular. In such a society it is scarcely possible to separate religion from politics. In the Constituent Assembly, vested interests—Hindu as well as Muslim—had bitterly opposed the enactment of Article 44.[55] But the founding fathers of the Constitution, in the national interest, refused to bow to their pressure. There is no justification to adopt a different attitude now. I have not been able to find any justifiable reason for not implementing Article 44 of the Constitution'.

Yet the reason (whether 'justifiable' or not) why no such action has been taken is clear enough. While the overwhelming majority of some sixty million Muslims is strongly opposed to such action, it would be hazardous for a Government which is dependent on the ballot-box to risk the loss of so many votes. There is, moreover, a very real sense in which it is more difficult for a non-Muslim Government to legislate for a substantial minority of Muslims in matters which they regard as essentially part of their religion than it is for a 'Muslim' Government to legislate in such matters for its

[55] Cf. pp. 211–13 above.

co-religionists. It was for this reason that the British were so hesitant to legislate in regard to the religious practices of either Hindus or Muslims in what was then 'British India'. And it is for this reason that it was distinctly easier for the Government of Pakistan to introduce the Muslim Family Laws Ordinance of 1961 than it would be for the 'secular', but Hindu-dominated, Government of India to take any similar action. It is probable, indeed, that the more often and emphatically people like Justice Hegde make the sort of statements I have quoted, the more resistant the Muslim community will become; and it seems to me unlikely that an essentially pragmatic Government will risk alienating very substantial support by forcing through legislation on a matter which is of comparatively little political or economic importance.

What, then, of the more distant future? It is distinctly possible that the Muslims of India will eventually agree among themselves to sponsor legislation which would introduce some of the reforms which have already been effected elsewhere. I am, indeed, informed that the main reason why the 'Working Party', which was to have been set up as the result of the Seminar of 1972, was never in fact formed, was not because of opposition from intransigent Muslims of traditional views, but rather the objections raised by those who, like Justice Hegde, believed that 'Each change in the law creates its own vested interests. If we effect merely changes in the Islamic law, those changes, in their turn, are bound to create new vested interests. Those changes, instead of becoming stepping-stones towards the enactment of a common civil code, may become road-blocks'.

But if the Muslim community continues to drag its feet, it seems most unlikely that the present situation can persist indefinitely. If nothing is done, some crisis will, in all probability, eventually occur in which the Government of India feels compelled—and strong enough—to take decisive action. But it seems to me rather more likely that the more controversial differences in the law which now governs the personal lives of Hindus and Muslims, respectively, will gradually be lessened or even eliminated, whether by legislation which commands substantial support from both communities or by judicial decisions which are quietly accepted.[56] And this might well pave the way for an acceptable symbiosis of the two communities in a legal structure which made specific provision for certain minor differences, or which took the form of a law of marriage and divorce which was uniform and basically secular, and a law of succession which was equally secular but included the right to vary its intestate provisions by testamentary dispositions. A partial advance towards some such goal might, indeed, be made by an enactment under which any Muslim who wished was given the right to opt out of the jurisdiction of his or her personal law, in much the same way as is currently open to those who marry under the Special Marriages Act.

It is clearly much easier to introduce a uniform personal law in countries such as Kenya, Ghana and Uganda, where the Muslim community is much smaller and less strongly imbued with Islamic orthodoxy—or, again, in countries in which Islamic and customary law interpenetrate each other as widely as they do in Indonesia or the mainland of Tanzania—than it is in India, with its history of factional strife. And the same is also true, although for very different reasons, in countries ruled by a dictatorial regime such as that of Ataturk in Turkey, post-war Albania, the U.S.S.R., or even Somalia (or possibly Zanzibar) today. There can, indeed, be no doubt that it was, in part, the complete political ascendancy of the Neo-Dustūr party in Tunisia which silenced orthodox opposition to certain secularist tendencies in the Law of Personal Status in that country.

Next, what of countries such as Saʿūdī Arabia, Oman, North Yemen, Morocco and even Algeria? Here one thing at least seems obvious, namely, that the rigid Islamic puritanism of Saʿūdī Arabia, which has already begun to weaken in some points, cannot long withstand the increasing pressure of her vast wealth—and the increasing industrialization and imports, Western life-style and foreign experts, which this wealth is already bringing in its train. This means that, if the present regime remains in power, we are likely to see a steady trend towards the sort of legal system—partly

[56] Cf. pp. 77–82 above.

Islamic and partly Western in character—which currently prevails in the more advanced and Westernized Arab countries. But it would be pure speculation to attempt to predict what might happen if the present form of government were to be overthrown—although this, obviously enough, must represent a distinct possibility. It would then be anyone's guess what would take its place, for there are clearly a number of different possibilities. There might, conceivably, be a puritanical revival or reaction, such as is currently manifest in some measure under the present regime in Libya; but it seems unlikely that any such impetus would survive very long in the face of the inroads which the political, social and economic influences of the outside world will almost certainly continue to make. Again, there might be a left-wing revolution, leading initially to a sort of fusion between Islamic and 'socialist' law (as in Algeria, South Yemen and Somalia today),[57] and perhaps to an eventual triumph of Marxist secularism. And yet another possibility would be the emergence of an allegedly 'democratic' regime—after a period, perhaps, of military rule—which would, in all probability, greatly accelerate the present trend towards a legal system broadly similar to that of Egypt, Iraq, Syria or Iran.[58]

As for Oman, North Yemen, Morocco and Afghanistan, it seems probable that what has been said about Saʿūdī Arabia applies, *mutatis mutandis*, to them also. Pakistan, on the other hand, represents a somewhat different problem, since it has already (as part of what was once 'British India') progressed much further along the road of Westernization, but has recently been thrown into considerable controversy and uncertainty in regard to what it means to be an 'Islamic State'—and, indeed, whether this is what its people really desire. If totally free elections had been held a few years ago, with no restrictions on the activities of the religious leaders, it seems uncertain which way the pendulum would have

[57] It must be remembered, however, that Algeria was previously incorporated in metropolitan France, and that it was only in matters of personal status that French law did not prevail; while in South Yemen and Somalia there is a heritage of English and Italian law.

[58] Although none of these countries can be regarded as particularly democratic today.

swung; but I very much doubt if the issue is so evenly balanced today. To begin with, it was Islam alone, generally speaking, which held together the two widely separated and very heterogeneous Provinces which made up that somewhat artificial State; but the Eastern Province has now become independent Bangladesh, and its political future is shrouded in complete uncertainty. It may remain as it is today: a predominantly Muslim and allegedly socialist country, somewhat like Algeria. Again, the present regime might well collapse under the weight of poverty, calamity and increasing anarchy; and almost anything might then take its place. And it even seems possible that Bengal as a whole might draw together, on the basis of its common language, culture and history, and form a secular State in which Hindus and Muslims live together much as they did before Partition—whether as a wholly independent national State or in some form of federation with India. As for Pakistan as it now is, it seems exceedingly unlikely that either the political leaders or the Army will ever allow the *'ulama'*, or even Mawlānā Mawdūdī, to take over.[59] If I had to venture a conjecture, I would guess that it will probably tend to develop in much the same way as the more moderate and progressive countries in the Middle East, now that the ideological link with Bangladesh has been severed—although it is distinctly possible that this development will be characterized by a process of 'stop–go' rather than steady and unbroken progress.

Finally, what of those countries, to which reference has already been made, like Egypt, Syria, Iran, Iraq and Jordan? Here the most likely development, it seems to me, is along the lines of a prediction I made as long ago as 1956, when (after summarizing the reforms which had already been introduced in most of these countries) I wrote:[60]

It seems obvious, then, that reforms of this sort have come to stay, and probably to multiply. Not only so, but the general pattern of development is becoming increasingly clear. Originally (as has been seen) the

[59] Cf. pp. 180–3 above.

[60] Cf. 'Law Reform in the Middle East', in *International Affairs*, Vol. 35, No. 1 (1956), p. 51.

Sharīʿa, in theory at least, reigned supreme. Then a sharp distinction was made between Sharīʿa courts which were to continue to apply the pure Sharīʿa, and Civil courts which were to apply codes which were largely Western in origin. Later, again, the pressure for reforms within the sphere of the Sharīʿa itself could no longer be resisted; and this has resulted not only in certain fascinating innovations—which throw into bold relief both the progress of social development and the triumph of modernism over theological and juristic conservatism in the countries concerned—but also in an increasing tendency to codify the principles of the Sharīʿa. Parallel to these developments, of more recent years, has emerged a tendency to introduce new civil codes, characterized by an attempt both to expand their direct debt to the Sharīʿa and to evolve a certain synthesis between Western and Islamic concepts. Thus the barriers seem to be slowly crumbling both between the two systems of law and between the courts which apply them; for it is obvious that a codified personal law could be applied as effectively by a judge trained in a modern Law Faculty as by a *qāḍī* steeped in the learning of the classical texts. This coincides, moreover, with an increasing demand, in some quarters, for the suppression of the multiple courts of the various religious communities. It would seem likely, then, that the future will witness the disappearance of both Sharīʿa and community courts and the application, by unified national courts, of a body of codified law which represents, throughout, a certain synthesis between Western and Islamic concepts, the former paramount in civil, commercial, and penal law and the latter in the field of personal and family law (together, in the latter, with certain special provisions peculiar to the Christian and other non-Muslim communities).

This prediction found a partial fulfilment almost as soon as it was written, for an announcement was made in Egypt, even before my article was published, that both the Sharīʿa courts and those of the various Christian and Jewish communities were to be abolished, and all jursidiction was to be concentrated in the National Courts; and this reform was almost immediately put into effect. Islamic law still, of course, governs the family relationships of Muslim litigants, and questions of succession for all Egyptians regardless of their religion; but all such litigation is now handled by a special division of the National Courts—although this was, at first, largely staffed by *qāḍīs* recruited from the former Sharīʿa Courts. I originally thought that judges trained in modern law schools would soon assume full control, but the piecemeal reforms long since promulgated in Egypt in regard to marriage and divorce, together with the comparatively complete codifications of the law of inheritance, bequests and *awqāf*, have not yet been incorporated in a single, comprehensive code of personal law—although several drafts of such a code have been successively prepared and discussed. It is largely for this reason, I think, that some of the judges who serve in this division of the National Courts are still, it seems, being recruited from those who have had a largely traditional training, for many points still come before them for decision which have not yet been covered by any legislative enactment and in regard to which recourse must still be had to the classical texts. This is a matter of considerable importance for the way in which the law is to be interpreted and applied, for a study of case-law in Iraq, for example, has clearly shown that the intervention of *qāḍīs* imbued with traditional ideas and prejudices can largely rob statutory reforms of the effect which the legislature intended[61]—particularly, of course, when the legislation concerned has not been drafted with sufficient precision. So the question arises why successive Egyptian Governments have postponed the enactment of any of the codes which a series of expert committees have prepared. And to this the probable answer is that any Egyptian Government might well hesitate, on the one hand, to promulgate a code of personal law which could be regarded (at least from the feminist standpoint) as more rigidly conservative and traditional than that of Tunisia or even Syria—seeing that Egypt was for many years in the vanguard of the movement for reform, that it aspired (under Nāṣir, at least) to play the leading role in the revolutionary renewal of the 'Arab Nation', and that it is still the most advanced Arab country in commerce, technology and learning—but might equally hesitate, on the other, to alienate an influential body of orthodox Muslim opinion in a matter which it may well regard

[61] Cf. a LL.M. thesis for the University of London in 1967 by Nemat al-Naqeb (Niʿmat al-Naqīb) on 'Problems of Matrimonial Law in Contemporary Iraq'.

as of little practical importance. But, however that may be, the promulgation of a comprehensive code of some sort is, I think, in the long term virtually inevitable.

What form, then, is a code likely to take? It is, of course, impossible to predict future political developments in Egypt; and on these almost everything depends. But if there is no major political upheaval it seems likely that legal developments will in fact take the course I predicted in 1955, although these may well come in successive stages. Thus it seems to me certain that the whole of the law will be codified, and probable that the code or codes concerned will be largely, but not completely, homogeneous. In the sphere of personal law I would expect the relevant provisions to take a recognizably Islamic form, but with radical concessions to contemporary opinion in such matters as the prohibition of polygamy or of any divorce other than judicial, while in criminal law, commercial law and the law of 'obligations' I would expect the structure to remain essentially Western in origin and inspiration, together with the retention of certain concepts and detailed provisions drawn from the cultural heritage of Islam (but with an unequivocal acceptance, as at present, of fixed rates of interest, insurance contracts, and the like). Much the same could be said, *mutatis mutandis*, of countries such as Iran, Tunisia, Syria and the Lebanon, with Iraq, Jordan and the Gulf Sheikhdoms following rather more slowly in the same path. I would also expect a certain softening of the law which at present prevails in regard to 'apostasy' from Islam or the marriage of a Muslim woman to a non-Muslim husband[62]—which might at first take the form of legislation somewhat along the lines of the Indian Special Marriages Act.

But there are, of course, a number of possible alternatives. On the one hand, there is always the possibility of a revival of Islamic orthodoxy and fervour, although I should doubt whether this would prove more than a temporary phase, at least in so far as the law is concerned. On the other, there might well be a rapid swing to a secularist attitude, with religion largely confined to matters of

[62] It is, perhaps, of some significance that the Tunisian Law of Personal Status includes no provision whatever on this subject.

worship, belief and personal behaviour rather than courts of law. This is the path that Turkey took under Ataturk—largely because he lost patience with the hagglings, disputes and delays which characterized an initial attempt to quarry from the Islamic sources a personal law which was suited to the needs of contemporary life; so he decided to abandon the Sharīʿa and adopt the Swiss Code almost *verbatim*, in order that text-books, judicial decisions and educational material would all be readily available. A somewhat similar upsurge of secular radicalism seems, moreover, to have precipitated the recent Family Law of South Yemen and Somalia, respectively; and future developments along this same line might well, of course, take an increasingly Marxist form—for, although Islam has often been regarded as a powerful bulwark against atheistic Communism, the fact remains that, if Muslims become disillusioned with their monolithic religion and its distinctive ideology, it is comparatively easy for them to switch over to another monolithic ideology which seems to pay more tangible dividends. But ʿAbd al-Rāziq and many others have shown that the secularist position, vis-à-vis the law, can equally well be embraced on very different, and even on theological, criteria.[63]

[63] Cf. pp. 181–2 above.

INDEX